Gin and Tonics Across Worcester

by

David Macpherson

Introduction

From May 5th, 2014 to September 28th, 2015 I wrote a blog called Gin and Tonics Across Worcester. The idea was simple. I was to go to every bar in the City of Worcester, Massachusetts and have a gin and tonic. I then had to find my way home and write about it.

I had simple rules for the tour, as I called it. I was to pay in cash. I was to have only one gin and tonic and leave. I would always tip. I would ask for the basic gin and tonic. I didn't want the fancy stuff. Just the cheapest one they made. Most of the gin was well booze. I was to be anonymous. To that end, I called myself Dante of Worcester, and I was taking a tour of hell (I mean all the bars in town). I had a stupid idea of calling all my companions and friends my Virgils. (I think that died down as the blog continued.)

There was to be no food or other drink on the tour. I also broke most of these rules, but I mention those instances in the blog when they happened.

Other rules developed as I went on. I was not to go to chain restaurant/bars. I was trying to find out why people loved the bars they went to. I didn't want to discover why anyone might love TGIFridays. I was going to skip most social clubs as well. And I would not pay a cover charge to go into a place. Also, no strip bars. If I was trying to discover why people go to certain bars, I already had the answer to those. So why go?

I didn't plan anything. I just went where I thought it would be fun to go. I didn't make lists of places to go to until much later in the project. I had no idea that I would get to 144 bars. I did not get to every bar. Not even close. But 144 was much more that I even thought possible.

The blog was never a huge hit, but it had its readers. I was lucky that it was discovered by Victor Infante of the Worcester Telegram and Gazette. When he wrote about it, the readership went up exponentially. Some of the commenters praised the project. Some thought I was being a pretentious prick. They were not wrong. I accepted every comment submitted to the blog and thanked everyone, whether they thought I was great or an idiot.

One person commented that I was a wimp. I should have gone to every bar in a week. Hey, if he wants to try that, more power to him.

The question of course is, why the hell would I want to have a drink at every bar in the city? There is no satisfactory answer.

My friend, Tony Brown, was starting a weekly performance art venue in 2013 and I thought I would go to each bar in the city and write a haiku about each place. This was a stupid idea (even for performance art) and I never did anything with it.

But it got me thinking about going to every bar in Worcester. Why do we need so many bars? Why do people go to THIS bar and not THAT bar? I decided that it might be interesting to explore that. I realized that there needed to be a common factor and that would be having a gin and tonic. Every bar should be able to make a gin and tonic. Some might be able to make Negronis. Others could make Mojitos. But not all bars cold make all cocktails. But a gin and tonic? Every bar can make a gin and tonic. (turns out one bar could not make it)

The entries will explain my thinking and my experience a lot better than any introduction. But let me just say that this was a wonderful experience. I got to know the City of Worcester really well. I feel like I learned so much from going to places I never would have gone otherwise.

In many instances, I would go to a bar for a gin and tonic and then head to my bar, NIck's. There I would talk to the bartenders and the regulars about what I saw and what I was thinking from my experience. Their opinions wound up in my writing. It was an open secret around Nick's that the Gin and Tonic blogger was a regular.

The book is organized in the order I went to the bars. I didn't post them that way. I sometimes wrote out of order. I did only a brief proofread when I first put this out. For this book, I did make an effort to correct errors and typos, but let's be honest, there are a shitload of typos and mistakes I missed.

The difficult part of writing these was how local and inside jokey I should be. I knew my audience was mostly Worcester folk, so they didn't have to have jokes about Kelly Square explained to them. However, I didn't want this only to be a Worcester read. I was attempting something more universal. I don't think I succeeded, but, hey baby, I tried.

There were things that went on that I didn't bother to explain too much. We had a terrible winter that year, about a hundred inches of snow. This slowed down the tour. I couldn't find parking in a lot of Worcester. The Red Sox had two seasons during the writing of this book. They sucked both years. This was the time of DeflateGate. That was an incident where the Patriots were accused of deflating footballs. It was ridiculous to write about it then. It is ridiculous to be writing about it now.

Five years on and many of the bars are gone. I have added updates to fill you in.

I never intended to write bar reviews. I was just taking a tour of a landscape. I hope you enjoy coming along on the tour. I hope you have a fine cocktail while reading. May I suggest that you have a gin and tonic?

Stop #1 - The Diamond Inn

The Bar: The Diamond Inn

    The Address: 271 Grafton St

    The price: 5 bucks

    Did they ask me if I wanted a lime: She did ask. "You want a lime?" I said of course.

    What was the type of gin: She asked what I wanted and I shook my head and said whatever she has. That is one of the rules of this exercise. I will not ask for a particular gin. It was just some well gin, pretty harsh.

    What was the gin and tonic like:It was in a pint glass with a good amount of ice, but the over abundance of gin took care of that. It was a splash of tonic to anoint the gin only. It was cheap end gin in a glass. I was pretty loose when I left. This is when I realized that I couldn't sample more than one or two bars a night doing this Gin and Tonic survey.

    The Joint: It had so many beer and liquor signs around the place I was feeling like I had vertigo. There was space in the place, but the bar area felt cramped. It was dark and didn't feel all too clean. They had the prerequisite dart area, but no one was playing. There was pool, there were tables strewn about.

    General Impressions: When I came in, not too many people in at this time of day, a large guy was entering screaming the lyrics to some song. The people behind the bar shook their heads and smiled and started chatting with him. It was pretty empty but they had two bartenders working. One came over to me and then shouted to the other to take care of me. What? Was I too hot potato for one bartender? It was not a friendly place, not to newcomers ordering gin and tonics at least.

    Will I come back: After ten minutes, I headed to the door for my escape. I had to slide past the young woman who was eight months pregnant as she hobbled into the bar. Now, it doesn't mean she was going to drink, but it was just the perfect thing for me to see as I was leaving, thinking, get me the hell out of here. Does that answer the question? It's no. I'm good, but I don't need to come back.

2019 Update This was not the first bar I went to for this project. Earlier that same night, I went to a different first bar. I had seen this bar for many years. I went in and had a gin and tonic and had many adventures and I thought I was off and running. Only to discover that the first bar was actually in Millbury. It was not in Worcester at all. Off to an auspicious start.

Stop #2 - Cafe Neo

The Bar: Cafe Neo

The Address: 97 Millbury St

The price: Six bucks

Did they ask me if I wanted a lime: No, they just put it in and much to my pleasure, the bartender cut the wedge right from a lime. I thought, that's a classy move in a joint like this, this drink is going to be good. Oh, silly Dante, silly silly Dante.

What was the type of gin: He asked me if I had a preference and I said no. I got some no name bottle brand. No name brand stands for quality after all.

What was the gin and tonic like: For such a flourish as cutting the lime right in front of me, this was a dud. It had a lot of flatish tonic and ice that melted immediately, or so it seemed. This is my clever way to say that the drink was weak and watery. It didn't have a lot of taste.

The Joint: This is a dive where those who like it go. The bar area is to the right when you get in and its kind of cramped. There are tables to the left. The back of the bar was large and cluttered, like the design was inspired by a yard sale. A fixer upper kind of joint. The thing I noticed in my ten minutes of servitude there was how weird the front windows seemed. They were big and large and allowed us to see the outside, Millbury Street. But that is reversed. We are in the fishbowl, being looked at. I think a bar should have small windows. More a concept or theory of window than an actual one. If I am drinking in a dive, or worse, singing Celine Dion on the Karaoke at a dive, do I want the outside world to gawk at me? No. If I am at a joint to drink and get down with my bad self, then I want little chance from the outside to see me. I wonder what this was before it was a bar to have windows like this? A shoe store? A beauty parlor?

Which stands to reason, because the people here now have shoes and are filled with untapped beauty,

General Impressions: It was the day before St. Patrick's Day and they were going all out. If when you I say all out, you know I mean Karaoke. I walked in and someone was wailing away at a David Bowie song. He was generally in key and could follow the words on the screen, in Karaoke at a dive bar parlance, that means he did an award winning performance. When I set myself at the bar, they told me to help myself to the free St. Patrick's Day food spread. They were in warming pans, there was cabbage, there was a corned meat. I passed. .For a Sunday afternoon, there was a good amount of folk, about 15 or so people. People were talking in their groups. They wore a lot of green. These were not my people, but they liked being around each other. Drinking their beers. Readjusting their St. Patrick's Day hats on their heads. Pushing the unappetizing food around the plates. Good times.

A couple went up next on Karaoke and did the Kid Rock -Sheryl Crow duet, Picture. Here's what I can say in good conscience, the woman was slightly more equipped to do the song. She could stand without leaning on to a table and she could read the words. She couldn't hold a note, but she could stand and read and that was adequate. The guy was in hell. He couldn't see those wordy things flashing on the screen at breakneck speed. He couldn't navigate the theory of gravity. This version of the song felt like it went on for twenty five minutes. It was epic. I was already done with my watery drink, but I had to stay to the end. How could I miss such theater? The guy was helped back to his chair by the woman and I was out of there.

Will I come back: If I ever get a hankering to drunkenly sing Nights in White Satin to the melody of House of the Rising Sun while forgetting every fourth word, then this might be a place to go. Otherwise, I will pass.

2019 Update *- A commenter on the blog said that the bar used to be a donut shop. See, mystery solved.*

Stop #3 - Suney's

The Bar: Suney's

    The Address: 216 Chandler Street

    The price: 5 bucks

    Did they ask me if I wanted a lime: No. I just got one.

    What was the type of gin: He asked what I wanted and I said it didn't matter. I received a well gin, nothing remarkable.

    What was the gin and tonic like The drink came in a pint glass with a lot of ice. It was a serviceable drink, nothing more, but not terrible..

    The Joint: A few years back they redid the storefront and it is a good looking facade. But facade is all it is. You walk in and you get a dingy dark saloon, the kind that Jack London used to pass out in. There is a bar in the back left. There are a few tables. Dart board. It all looked like it needed a fine washing. There were duct works above me. Painted black. Beautiful old tin ceiling, painted black. (I see a red door and I want it painted black.....Mick Jagger would have done well here). This color choice makes the joint feel small and dim.

Behind the bar area is a fair sized dining area. I went in the afternoon and no one was eating. It looked like an old school cafeteria. This too felt like it needed a good washing if not a complete overhaul. My thought was that I would never eat here, but I heard from one of my Virgils, Bartender Brian, that Suney's food is great. That the chicken they have on the weekend is worth the trip. I asked him if it was worth walking through the dingy gauntlet of the bar area and he said yes, so there you go. When getting a bite to eat, close your eyes and walk thirty feet until you smell good vittles.

    General Impressions: There were four or five at the bar. The bartender responded to me quickly and professionally. The type who sit at a bar on a nice Saturday at the end of March, the first nice weekend all year, is the kind that take their bar sitting and beer drinking serious. I ordered the gin and tonic and the bartender said, "Better weather must be coming, people ordering gin and tonics all of a sudden." -"I didn't know Gin and Tonics were seasonal," I said. The bartender nodded like one of those old sages, "People want to drink gin and tonics when the weather's good. I like them in the summer. Just the thing." I didn't know I was going to learn important lessons here so I just replied, "I was just in the mood for one."

So now we all know kids, there are certain sure fire signs of spring: the groundhog not seeing his shadow, flower buds appearing on red maple trees, the song of the titmouse and now we have the increased ordering of gin and tonics.

I drank my drink and left. I was there for ten minutes.

Will I come back: Probably not. The decor just killed me. Nothing wrong with a run down joint, but this didn't have much appeal to me. If Bartender Brian wants to take me for dinner in the restaurant area, I could be convinced, but I will walk through the bar quick like.

Stop #4 - The Blackstone Tap

The **Bar**: Blackstone Tap

The Address 81 Water Street

The price Six dollars

Did they ask me if I wanted a lime Yes, and I got one.

What was the type of gin: It was a well gin.

What was the gin and tonic like It was a pint glass with a hell of a lot of ice jammed in. It tasted okay, nothing memorable either way. This is from a visit I had two months ago, and I just can't seem to remember all that much.

The Joint: Let it be known, I have a thing for places that have exposed brick for walls. This place made me happy in that regard. They had all the cool bar things, like special drink machines and neon signs. It is a big place with games in the back. A bunch of young men were playing darts in the back, being louder than their numbers would suggest.

General Impressions: I suppose the fact that it took me two months to write this up is indication that the place to compell good or ill. It was a good middle of the road place. Nothing spectacular, a little dull in the way that it feels like a lot of sports bars. I had a drink at a bar, and that pretty much is it.

The bartender was animated. Excited about the Red Sox opening day in Boston. He loudly told the guy who was near him (so near he didn't have to shout, but this is Sox opening day and one must be boisterous) that he was going, he didn't have a ticket, just to go and drink and be part of the scene. He was the only bit of excitement there.

Will I come back: Maybe yes, it is such a neutral place that I don't mind if someone suggest we go there. If someone suggests another place, and not this, I would be cool with that too. What can

I say, in the Land of Zero to Ten Rating Scales, you have just entered the Number Five.

2019 Update - This was closed a few years back as part of a drug bust. The owner was doing something the Feds didn't agree with. It has been re-opened as the Rock Bar. There is rock present.

Stop #5 - The Greyhound Pub

The Bar: The Greyhound Pub

The Address 139 Water Street

The price Six bucks

Did they ask me if I wanted a lime: No, he just put it in

What was the type of gin: Well gin

What was the gin and tonic like: It was alright, not too memorable, but fine all the same.

The Joint It's a big old box, with a ton of Football (and I think Rugby) pennants and posters. There is a dart board. Not a bad place for an Irish joint. It was a Sunday and only a few guys were at the bar.

General Impressions Sorry folks, this one will be short and devoid of humor I think. I didn't have much humor there or even now when I think of being there I ain't feeling funny typing this.

I was not welcome there. I wasn't tarred and feathered or called a stinking interloper. The bartender sure showed with his gaze, and his body posture, that he wished I wasn't there. He and his people talked about business, making a few derogatory comments about certain nationalities. I was not asked if I wanted another drink. I was not asked to leave, but sometimes you don't have to be told out loud to know what is wanted. I was happy to leave. I am sure the feeling was mutual.

Will I come back: No

2019 Update - This closed within that year. I was happy to hear it. I really hated my short time at the bar. It was reopened as Rocky's, which I review later in this book. Rocky's closed and now it is Boardroom.

Stop #6 - Marty's

The Bar: Marty's. Formerly the space for Magoo's.

The Address: 225 Canterbury St

The Price: 5 bucks

Did they ask me if I wanted a lime: Yes.

What was the type of gin: He asked me what kind of gin I wanted, I told him I didn't care. He looked at his bottles and poured Tanqueray into the glass. It was a twelve-ounce glass, that reminded me of old Coca-Cola glasses.

What was the gin and tonic like: I tasted the gin, I tasted the tonic. There was not too much ice. It was a decent drink. I got a slight buzz, but I wasn't floored. The Tanqueray certainly helped.

The Joint: I was driving around and just saw this bar. This was not a planned visit. I figured it was fine to go and try it. Was I a little scared that it was going to be sketchy? You bet. But I am still early on in this project and I don't know what to expect when going into a strange bar on a street I don't often drive down. If this could be the result, all of these visits will be very pleasant indeed

.

I walked in on a Sunday at 5 pm and I was shocked to see a brightly lit bar with a few set areas and about 15 or 20 people sitting and talking. There was a set area for darts and three people were playing. Groups were talking and cross pollinating. People were friendly. One guy was going on and on about a video he had on his phone where an eighty year old woman was in a dancing contest. He kept on saying that that was how he would like to be when he was old. He was showing it to a lot of the folk present, even talked to me about it. The place was clean. You could see the bar and everyone was smiling and it was pretty loud.

General Impressions: It felt like I was the only one who didn't know anyone. But I didn't feel excluded. I was just drinking my high ball and watching the show. So this is a neighborhood bar. Now is this how it is on a Saturday night. I wouldn't know, but for a Sunday afternoon, this was a lively group. I felt comfortable there. It was the first time that I started this where I wanted another drink and to stay for a spell. I was watching the folk play darts. I was listening to conversation. There was a large span of ages at the bar and everyone was chatty with each other. I could have just picked the happy moment at an unpleasant place, but I don't think that was the case.

Will I come back: This is the first one of this exercise where the answer is a strong yes. It will not be my once a week joint, but it will be a place I can imagine going with someone if we are nearby. I was there for nearly thirty minutes, my longest time, and I had to make myself go to another bar. I was happy where I was.

2019 Update - I am not exaggerating when I say this, but if I didn't go into Marty's when I did, I would probably have ended this project. The first bars I went into were depressing and I was questioning if this was worth my time. I hadn't started writing the blog, I was just taking notes and prepping the style. This was the sixth bar, and it was a happy place that reminded me that going to bars can be and should be fun. This also got me through the next stretch of lousy bars.

Stop #7 - Mickey O'Neill's

The Bar: Mickey O'Neill's formerly Nuff Ced. Now it is this authentic named bar, as every bar in merry old Ireland is called. I had to look up the name of this one a few times, even after I went. It just won't stick in my head, like it's not a real name. Bartender Brian called a bar named like this Paddy McDrinky. But hey, you know it's an Irish bar. Actually I think it would be much cooler if a bar named this was actually a Kosher Deli. Now that's a place name you'll never forget. Come to Mickey O'Neill's for the Matza Ball Soup. With a name like Mickey O'Neill's you know this place is a Mitzva!!!

The Address: 377 Park Ave

Price: Six dollars

Did he ask if I wanted a lime: No. He just put it in.

What was the type of Gin: This place had a nice selection of gins: I saw Boodles and Bulldog and other non-alliterative choices. After looking at the bottles, the bartender picked up the Tanqueray and poured me a good one.

How was the Gin and Tonic: It was good. I thought it was a decent cocktail.

The Joint: This used to be a different bar, Nuff Ced. But the bartender told me a few months back they redid it as a traditional Irish bar. What is a traditional Irish bar really? If you said the kind you would see in Hollywood movies, like Darby O'Gill and the Little People, than this is a traditional Irish bar. The place was crazy clean. The floor was hard wood. The bar was spacious. There was a communal table in the middle of the space. There were fake signs you might pick up in Home Goods that seem to be the kind of signs a bar would have. The liquor selection was excellent. There were single malt scotches and good Irish whiskeys and other fine spirits.

But I just couldn't get over how this felt more like a set for an Irish Bar than an actual one. It was just me, the bartender and a couple guys setting up instruments to play later in the evening, so it did feel unreal, like we have the barn dressed up for the play, but no actors.

General Impression: When I'm the only paying customer in a joint, it's hard to really judge a place, but I just couldn't get over the set design feel. You want to film a movie at an Irish bar, this might be a fine place, but you want to sit and have a drink, I think there might be other more comfortable places. The bartender was friendly enough. He told me he has enjoyed the shift from Meat Market joint, when it was Nuff Ced to this more laid back joint now that it was this faux Irish Bar. Told me it was the same owners, they just wanted a different feel.

Will I Come Back: I don't think so. It did have a great liquor selection, the best I have come across in this tour so far, so if I wanted a nice drink I might think of coming here. But I have a feeling I will find other places in Worcester that have a good selection of spirits that are more comfortable.

2019 Update - This didn't last too long. It was fallow for a bit and then became Whiskey Tango. That was gone fast, as well. It is now a coffee shop.

Stop #8 - Gallagher's

The Bar: Gallagher's

The Address 97 West Boylston St

The price: 3:75 (cheapest so far, you pay for what you get, but still it was under four bucks for a 12 ounce gin and tonic, you got a problem with that?)

Did they ask me if I wanted a lime: No. Because he didn't have any to offer. The friendly guy behind the bar said, "Now I can't give you a lime, because we don't have any. There is a lime shortage. Can't afford it. It's in the paper, the T and G had a thing about it. It's like three dollars for two limes. The weather was terrible in Florida, they have no limes. All the bars around are going to be hurting for limes." This I didn't know about, but boy how he told me. He spoke with speed and conviction, I was going to believe him that there are no limes in Worcester, damn you global warming!!!!

What was the type of gin: The bartender asked me if I wanted Tanqueray or well and I said well would do.

What was the gin and tonic like: It had a lot of ice and I don't know if the well gin was flavorless or that what I like about gin and tonics is the lime, but man it was flavorless. Had a kick. It just had nothing that made me pleased in the mouth when I drank. It was 3.75 and that means it don't need to taste like nothing but a buzz. It did that fine.

The Joint: This is a small place. Smaller than my living room. There is a bar with 10 or so stools and three tables. That's it. Don't have to worry about that evil bar kitchen infecting the gestalt of the place, there's no room. It has two Bud neon signs in the place. One is a Bud Man neon sign, and that means hip cred. There are two flat screens giving Keno and another bar gambling game. There is sports on, the Sox were playing. It is brightly lit, though that might be because it was a slow Wednesday night, and it is nice to be at a bar where there is the local paper, and wonder of wonders, you have enough light to read it.

General Impressions: While you read this, sing to yourself the Joe Walsh song, "Life's been good to me so far," because that's one of the songs I heard there and that is how I felt about being there. The bar's been good to me so far. There were three other people there on the eight o'clock Wednesday night, but it didn't feel empty. There was a guy with a beer and a whiskey and a couple, who knew the bartender's name (or as we call them, regulars). They seemed to be having a swell time.

The music was loud and classic. Classic Rock! You have to write Classic Rock in capitals, because it is its own State of Mind. I walked in and there was Neil Young's Rockin the Free World (the g missing in the word Rocking for a sense of irony) and I felt warm and comforted. By the time I had my drink well in hand, the song was now the epic "Life's Been Good to Me So Far." The guy in the couple went up to the jukebox machine The woman of the couple spent the time he was away silently singing along to the song. I didn't know I was a lip reader, but I am sure she was silently saying, "My Maserati goes 185, I lost my license, and now I don't drive." During the momentous guitar break, she was keeping the beat with her hand and duck walking her head back and forth. It's a hell of a song. The guy came back and she stopped this personal performance, and I was upset, she should have kept on going, the hell with the man. Just sing along and have a great time whether the old man is around or not. Love your Classic Rock.

When what I heard next from the jukebox machine was Kid Rock, I knew the getting out was rapidly approaching. I have done eight stops in this tour of every Worcester bar and now I have come across Kid Rock's dulcet tones twice, is this a harbinger of future doom? I hope not.

Will I come back: Yeah, not a strong affirmative, but I liked it here. It was pleasant, it was comfortable. When I left, the bartender thanked me for coming. How odd is that? I could see myself going here when I was single. This was a place to kill time in. This would be a great place to sit by myself and be sad and morose. I could be happily lonely in this joint. It is small enough to feel safe. And let's be fair. under four bucks for a cocktail. Sign me up.

Stop #9 - McGuire's

The Bar: McGuire's

    The Address 5 Saugus Place (off of Cambridge Street)

    The price: 5.50

    Did they ask me if I wanted a lime. He did and put it in with no extra charge.

    What was the type of gin: Tanqueray. This was the standard gin for the order. The bartender said that that's one of the reasons that makes McGuire's the hidden jewel of the Worcester Bar Scene, the five fifty tanqueray and tonics (more on that further down the review, how can I leave that comment alone?)

    What was the gin and tonic like: In a pint glass with a lot of gin. It was a good strong drink. It was a little too much gin, but it was refreshing. Can I just say I finished the whole glass? Such a good boy I am.

    The Joint: I'm not sure if this is a hidden jewel but it is kind of hidden. Off of Cambridge Street, across a parking lot. There doesn't seem to be a main entrance, just a bunch of side doors you can slink into. The place is a pretty nice sized box. A nice size bar. A pool table. Darts for the darty. It has a dive feel. Kind of run down, not pristine clean. Not a bad place for a beer. And it felt very roomy.

    General Impressions: It felt very roomy because I was the only one there. When I walked in I didn't even see the bartender, thinking me alone, in a strange lost scene from a Twilight Zone episode. This was Wednesday around nine of an evening. The bartender was very friendly and made me a fine drink. I noticed they were having 50/50 raffle and I asked about it. The bartender told me it was for another bartender who had gotten in a bad car accident and it was for medical expenses. I bought two tickets.

This got us into other conversations. I asked if it was always this slow on Wednesdays. He said not always. Their dart team was playing a bout at Marty's down the street and they no doubt would show up later. I mentioned that I liked that place and he said it was good but they had kooky hours. Not opened on Monday, things like that. The bartender told me he sold antiques, that he went to estate sales and storage unit auctions and we talked about that for a while. It is always a pleasure to find out how other people live and how other people value the things around them. These are the benefits to chatting at bars.

We talked some more and he spoke of this joint with pride. Said where else can you find a Tanqueray and Tonic for five fifty. I couldn't deny this, so took a long sip from my drink as if that was agreement enough. Then he said the joint was the Hidden Jewel of Worcester. I can get snarkier than I already have been, but hell, how often do you see such pride in a run down gin mill? This should be something praised and not mocked, but I might mock just a tad more.

A woman walked in and the spell of a bar all to myself was broken, besides, my drink was done, and I really wanted to head home, so I did.

Will I come back; How can I say no to the Hidden Jewel of Worcester? In all seriousness, I had a nice half hour drinking my drink and talking to the bartender. Nothing wrong with a conversation with booze in the mix. I might check it out again. Which is the first time I say this in this tour. I just can't tell what the place is about with just me in there. I liked it, but who knows what the regulars are like. So, yes, maybe.

2019 Update: I did go in one more time. It was not as welcoming. The last I saw, the bar was now a Pot Club. That's where you can bring your own pot and smoke it there. You have to purchase a membership. They changed their name to be more potty. I don't know if that is still happening.

Stop # 10 - Brook's

The Bar: Brook's

The Address 245 Lincoln Street

The Day and the Time Sunday at five, this was Mother's Day

The price I can't remember and can't find my notes, but I think it was five bucks.

Did they ask me if I wanted a lime Yes

What was the type of gin It was bar gin.

What was the gin and tonic like I must say, up until "The Incident" everything about the place was good and enjoyable. The drink was a pint glass number and it was good, it was not going to get mentioned in the gin section of the Wine Spectator, but it was nice company

The Joint They had stools by the front door outside so people can smoke while seated. Its a kind flourish I am sure. Going in, the carpet was dingy and the place still smelled of every cigarette ever smoked in the place. It was ingrained in the very wood. There was a long bar on one side where everyone was. The bar was pretty well crowded, which is nice to see. There was a low wall that divided the joint, the other side was where one played pool and darts, though no one was there. They were all drinking and talking. This was neighborhood bar all over. Everyone knew everyone else. Some were talking loud and joshing with the bartender. A couple guys would go over from time to time to the darts area to talk private like.

General Impressions Before "The Incident" I was composing in my head a pretty positive dispatch for this stop on the tour. I was composing in my head how every neighborhood needed a place to feel like you are part of the crowd. Early on a Sunday and everyone was just doing their thing. It was nice.

And then......

The guy, who was talking to a lot of folk, came up to where I was standing by myself, minding my own business. He walked up to me full, so I couldn't miss him. "Hi," he said his name and put out his hand. I told him my name (I didn't say Dante, for those who are interested) and took his hand. He didn't shake it as much as imitated a pneumatic press. He smiled at me, but the smile didn't get up to his eyes, ya know. "First time here." I said it was. "What brings you here." Now there are a lot of things I could have said, like "I'm a narc on duty" or "I go to bar to bar in town and have a gin and tonic and write about it" which are great ways to shorten my life span. Instead I said, "I was just driving by and saw the place and figured to have a drink." The guy never stopped staring at me, he nodded with that smile and said "Yeah, this is a good place for that." Its amazing all the things he told me that were not included in his words. Like, I don't know you and I don't like that and I got me a strong grip if you didn't notice before. What are you going to do about it.

He walked away from me, giving me the illusion of choice in the matter. I got the hell out of there. I didn't leave, I retreated.

Now I could be wrong, he could have just been friendly. But, I'm not wrong. Since then I have been more careful on where my eyes are while I have my gin and tonic, but man, what a welcome. Sometimes a neighborhood bar is for whom the bar considers to be neighbors, so be careful how you look and present yourself.

Amount of Time in the Joint 10 minutes

Will I come back No thanks. I don't know who my welcome wagon friend was, if he is there all the time, but I don't need the apparent risk. I was more welcome at Pleasant Cafe than here.

This was hard to write, and that sense of threat almost made me end this little project right there, but I am glad I continued.

Stop #11 - Art's Diner

The Bar: Art's Diner

The Address 541 West Boylston St

The price: He asked me if I wanted a small or large and I didn't know what to do. What was the goal here? To sample or to get the most out of the experience? I am sure I had one of those weird twisted faces of indecision on my face. I finally realized I had had a gin and tonic earlier and do I really want a super sized burden. I got the small and it was 4.35. Haven't seen that price range before, but it was under five bucks, so that's a good thing in this tour.

Did they ask me if I wanted a lime: Yes. He put a wedge in thank goodness for that.

What was the type of gin: I told him no preference and I got a well bottle.

What was the gin and tonic like: Flavorless. It had no character. It had a lot of alcohol, but it didn't taste of much, which is why I was happy for the lime garnish. It was a twelve ounce glass.

The Joint: This place has character. A good sized bar, tables for diners behind and a good section for pool table and dart board. It has a run down though clean look. The floors have a great black and white tile design, like the hallway from my grandmother's apartment building in Brooklyn(now there's an odd aside). It has down home local bar cred but it also has a nice hipster feel to it,

General Impressions: There were a few women who were joking with the bartender. The bartender was kissing and being affectionate with one of women. There was a lot of volume going on for so few people. The guy sitting next to me at the bar was gone, real gone, tongue out, not being able to form sentences to the bartender. I don't know if it was because of a long life of drink or some other reason. The bartender kidded him, not in a bad way, but as in a friendly, we take all kinds here, sort of way.

I didn't have much to pay attention to so I found myself watching the TV next to the bar. It had on the Ang Lee Hulk movie that my friends told me was awful. It certainly looked like a train wreck. I watched a big green cartoonish Hulk jumping around the desert being chased by helicopters. If I was at home, drinking a beer, I would have turned the channel. But I was at a bar. My choices were not my own. I chose to be here, I chose the drink I was having, but the TV was what was on, and I enjoyed being tortured by a lousy movie. I didn't have a say in it. The movie was on, and the lack of decisions was a pleasure. This always happens to me at bars. I will love whatever is on the TV, even if it is the Snooker Competition on ESPN Two. Candlepin Bowling on TV? If it is on the bar TV, you bet. A pleasure.

Will I come back: Maybe. It was quiet when I was there and I can imagine it being pretty packed. But the laid back attitude was pretty appealing. The bartender with his pride and joy, the classic car in the parking lot, was fun and full of energy. If I'm in the area, why not?

2019 Update: This closed for a bit and now it is back and thriving. Their Facebook page does show that they call themselves Art's now, and not Art's Diner. It's a fast paced world, who has time for two words?

Stop #12 - Galway Bay Pub

The Bar: Galway Bay Pub

    The Address 186 Stafford Street

    The price $5.25

    Did they ask me if I wanted a lime She did.

    What was the type of gin It was a well type.

    What was the gin and tonic like It was in a pint glass, with a good deal of gin, but it wasn't too alcoholic. It had pretty good flavor. Was it the tonic? Was it the gin? Was it because I downed it quickly and I didn't give the ice enough time to melt and dilute it? Who knows? Not me. I ain't a drink critic. I'm a tourist here.

    The Joint: I had a Dr. Who Tardis moment when I walked in. It looked like a small little joint and when I walked in it was a good sized place with booths, a big U shaped bar and place for bands to play. If a Dalek came out of the bathroom, I wouldn't have been surprised.

    This is an Irish Bar, the kind you want. Dark, heavy wood, a lot of bottles at the bar. When I wrote about Mickey O'Neil's I said that place felt like a fake Irish pub, this was more what it should be. Comfortable.

    General Impressions It was a Thursday afternoon and only a few people were there. The bartender was talking to the other guy at the bar and she kept on talking. They were into a lively conversation and she got to me and my order after a minute. She talked to the guy some more and asked me if I wanted a lime. She talked to him for a bit longer and then she made my drink. I gave her my money and she held on to it for two minutes before she got around to making change, she was conversating for god sakes. This is a bone of annoyance to me. I know its slow, I know you like talking to people, but I would like my drink. I really think a bartender should tend bar, and conversations can be put on hold. Maybe coming to a bar on an off time is how you tell how the place really is. Here I found that the conversation she was having was more important than attending to customers.

I didn't stay long, about five minutes. I had a call and had to go, but I don't think I would have stayed for too much longer.

Will I come back No, and it wasn't because of the bartender, the coolness of the joint far out weighed my pique. No, the parking there is awful. It is on a busy intersection and one of the roads is one way and it was nerve wracking to leave the place. I'm still looking for the ultimate Irish bar in Worcester. This was closer, but I just want one that's easier to get in and then escape from.

Stop #13 - Fat Tony's Pub

The Bar: Fat Tony's Pub

The Address 1051 Main Street (This used to be down the street and when I started this tour, I was sad to see it was gone, because this was a place I was always curious about but too wary (read scared) to go in. But with the tour, I have to go to every bar, so there you are.

The price: 5.50

Did they ask me if I wanted a lime. Yes, and he squeezed it and then put it in

What was the type of gin He asked if I wanted Tanqueray or House. I liked how he said house instead of well. House gin makes me think of a sweet subtle little house red the Italian restaurant's owner makes in a vat in the back parking lot. It was a wonderful thought, but of course it was not meant to be.

What was the gin and tonic like: It had flavor. Boy howdy it had flavor. It didn't taste exactly right. It coated my mouth like syrup. After I left, I went to the place Bartender Brian was working and had a B and B to get the taste out of mouth.

The Joint: It was a clean, open place with a bar that gave the bartender plenty of room. It had a sign saying they had jello shots for a dollar. The drinks came in fake mason jars that had an ad on it for Bud Light Lime Ritas. There was a group of women in the corner and I was surprised because this didn't feel like such a girls night out joint. I found out later there was about ten men, probably their men, in another room. This separation of men and women was surprising, like I was at an Orthodox Bar Mitzva.

General Impressions: This is a bar for tough people, though they drank differently than that. A woman at the bar had a green drink, and the designated incessant talker at the bar asked what it was, it came back that it was a Tipsy Turtle which had Medori. The bar talker than went rhapsodic about how he used to drink

Midori all the time. He loved Midori Martinis. Oh how he loved Midori Martinis. He asked the bartender if he knew how to make Midori Martinis. "Yeah, you put Medori in a martini glass." The bar talker focused on me when I ordered my gin and tonic. "Gin. Wow. Someone's ordering gin. Who orders gin anymore. I used to drink gin." Of course he did. This was odd, I didn't know I was drinking one of those forgotten cocktails from pre-prohibition times. Yes the forgotten drinks of yore, the Corpse Reviver and the Gin and Tonic.

I couldn't get the taste of the drink out of my mouth so decide my time was almost up. I was surprised that the place only had about 10 or so folk in it on a Saturday night, but as I got up to leave I noticed there was a whole other room. A games room. Filled with darts, pool table, video games and men. 12 or so very hard men. Some met my gaze wondering why I was there. Just leaving friends, just leaving.

Will I come back: No.

2019 Update: The bar is gone. It is now a furniture store.

Stop #14 - Herbie's

The Bar: Herbie's

The Address: 1030 Southbridge St

The price: 2.50. Wow. I mean wow. She told me the price, and the place was crowded so I didn't quite hear her so I asked for the price again and she said, "Two Fifty." This was so unprecedented. But that seems to be the name of the game at Herbie's. I looked at the menu they had, which was handwritten and then Xeroxed: all of the food was between 6 and 10 dollars. This is a heavenly place for budgeters!!!

Did they ask me if I wanted a lime: She did.

What was the type of gin: Well gin. Was I expecting a hand made gin from London for two fifty? I did not.

What was the gin and tonic like: It was about 10 or 12 ounces and it was fine. Had some punch, had some flavor, it wasn't bad. But baby! It was two hundred and fifty pennies! For that price, are you looking for some transcendent drinking experience?

The Joint: It is a big block of a building. Filled with tables. They obviously expanded because there is a clear difference between the two rooms and the bar snaked haphazardly between the two rooms. It has a run down, though not dirty feel. You are not there for décor, you want cheap Chicken Parm and a two fifty pint glass of Bud Light. You come don't come here to feel like you are immersed in art. For that, go to Worcester Art Museum. The parking was insane, I had to park on a side street. But I didn't have a Safari like trek, it was all manageable.

General Impressions: This is why this tour is so fascinating to me. Everyone should tour their city, find a reason to go to places you didn't know existed. I was just driving by, after doing an errand and saw Herbie's. I had to figure out it was a bar and then said, hell with it, I will go in and check. And here was a packed place, filled with drinkers and eaters and a large swath of people having a good time. Now I know a place for cheap, hearty food (don't know if its any good, because on this tour I have a strict rule, one gin and tonic and nothing else. And then I move on, like Shane)

The bar was packed and I had to stand. The bartender got to me quickly and everyone was in conversations or stuffing their faces or watching the Keno. All good bar practices. The restaurant tables were also all filled, mostly with an older crowd. And this was a Wednesday at 6. Crazy busy. I lasted the length of my drink, ten minutes.

Will I come back: I think yes, but not for the bar, I want to try the food. When I have an urge for fried carbs and protein I want to try this place. The food had a comfort vibe going and no one was unhappy poking at their plates. As a bar, I don't know. I like bars that are not waystations for food. I want bars to have their own personality. Also, I like to comfortably sit at a bar, call me kooky. I might have a drink there if I am heading to Auburn, and have time to kill, but I know I will come back to try the food. Say hello to a new food joint and goodbye to any intentions to diet.

Update 2019: This is the funny thing about the "Will I come back" section of the reviews. They were never accurate. I said I would try a place again and never did. For Herbie's, I did go back, but not for the food. For the bar. And I liked the bar. All I can say is, don't trust that Dante, he never tells the truth.

Stop #15 - Patsie Dugan's

The Bar: Patsie Dugan's. This was Emerald Isle. When it closed they hastily put up a new sign with the new name, but there is still Emerald Isle signage visible. Nothing changed from what I hear.

The Address 49 Millbury Street

The price Six dollars

Did they ask me if I wanted a lime She did

What was the type of gin It was well gin.

What was the gin and tonic like It was strong. Oh friends, it was strong. The bartender made up the drink like it was a dare. She took out the pint glass, Put in ice. Poured in an inch or two of gin. Looked at it, poured some more gin in. Looked one more time and put more gin in. There was enough space in the glass for a tiny baptismal amount of tonic to be anointed upon it. I just stared at it, like I was given the lady or the tiger to chose between. I mean I do like a stiff drink, but I also like being to walk and breathe and function. My choice was to ignore the drink and let the ice melt. I was not going to stand afterwards if I didn't. So I just sat there waiting for ice to melt. After about ten minutes the bartender came over to me with a concerned face. "Is the drink okay?" That was sweet, it was nice for her to notice I wasn't going near the thing. I lied and said, "Oh its fine, I'm just a slow drinker." I eventually drank it, and it was a lot of poor gin mocking me. I drank it and hobbled over to another bar where I had a diet coke.

The Joint I don't know if this is the way it is every day, but it struck me as sad. The place is large, with a bar area that is slightly tight, and a dance area and then a large dining area. The only place people sat was the bar area. The dining area didn't just seem slow, but unused, like it was a prop to a restaurant scene in a play. People were drinking this Wednesday night, but not too many. They talked to each other, but mostly they looked at their phones. Tapping away, smiling at what they scrolled upon. No one was eating, just drinking, it didn't seem like anyone was working the kitchen, if there was a working kitchen. And all of that space not used mocked the present at what this place once was but isn't anymore.

General Impressions I drank my drink slowly and watched a dull scene. I am sure that there are times when this is a lively joint, but it wasn't this day. It was a way station, the bar you were at when you were waiting for your mates to come and then go to some place better. I thought the bartender was nice for noticing me not touching my drink, but that's it for me liking it. Not much of a vibe or a personality, just a place that used to be filled with people, and now a place where you can get a powerful glass of booze.

Will I come back No.

Stop #16 - The Perfect Game

The Bar: The Perfect Game

The Address 64 Water Street

The price 7 dollars. This was my mistake, because I got boondoggled a wee bit. She asked me what kind of gin I wanted, do I want Tanqueray? And I said, whatever, it doesn't matter. That was not the right answer. I should have said, no, not that effete over wrought spirit, I will have what is kept in the Purgatory of the Well. But I got Tanqueray, and a very pricey drink..

Did they ask me if I wanted a lime: Miracle of miracles, I just got one without her asking.

What was the type of gin: It was Tanqueray. Like I said. Tanqueray, despite myself.

What was the gin and tonic like: It was fine. Flavor, not too much ice, right amount of tonic. But, as I will say later, I drank faster than I should have. Drink faster, Dante, drink faster.

The Joint: This is a sports bar, with a capital bahhhhh. It has brick walls, a big bar, tvs all over the joint. There is a second room for diners, but everyone, about ten or so, were at the bar, which is a U shaped model. I have a thing for brick wall, former factory sites, and I skew favorable to places like this more than I should, but there you go.

General Impressions: I was here for seven minutes, only because I could not drink fast enough. The first couple of minutes. these were that honeymoon period, that blessed moment.

It was a nice night, six o'clock on a June Sunday. There were a few tables outside on the sidewalk, getting that Worcester elan vibe. The tables were empty except for one old guy with a wine glass that he was slowly working at. After a few minutes he got up and slowly, slowly, almost painfully, got to his feet and navigated the task of reaching out his hand and grasping his wine glass. He then slowly

slowly turned and slouched shuffle stepped to the bar area. We were all watching the progress. A youngish guy at the bar smiled teeth and said "Hey, you finish the marathon the other day?" He laughed hard at what he said. The old man just kept shuffling to an open stool. "You finish the marathon?" the youngish guy asked again and brayed laughter. The old guy sat next to an old woman eating a sandwich and fries. "He doesn't know what you're saying," she said quietly. The youngish guy said, "Hey, you finish the marathon?" The old guy looked confused. Not drunk confused, but suffering through years of dementia confused. He said, "I won it." This got the youngish guy and others to laugh hard.

I found myself in the middle of a long story. I am not a regular, so I am in the sixth or seventh chapter in a long tale that I have not read. I don't know what I am watching, but the laughter being emitted was not a kind type. The youngish guy repeated how great it was that he finished the race and laughed and laughed. The old woman said, "He doesn't remember the story he told. He doesn't remember." The youngish guy laughed at this as well. The bartender nodded and said in a slightly uncomfortable fashion, "It was a funny story."

I don't know what the story the old man with dementia said, and the thing I could tell, is that he didn't know the story either. There was more laughter, more comments on the guy who didn't know he was being laughed at. He sat blankly sipping at his wine.

I drank my gin and tonic like I was desperate for it, I needed to leave. It is amazing to think that I saw this happy mocking of the old man in just three minutes of me sitting there. Was I just lucky to see this, or is that how the bar at Perfect Game is? I don't know. I don't care. I was gone before I could even consider the question.

Will I come back: No. The fries looked good, but no. No.

2019 Update: The Perfect Game is no longer in business. I weep for it not. In it's place is Maddi's Cookery & Taphouse.

Stop #17 - The Arcadia Club of Worcester, also called the White Eagle

Bar: Arcadia Club of Worcester - The White Eagle.

The Address: 120 Green Street.

The price: Four Dollars

Did they ask me if I wanted a lime- No, hell i was lucky I got a drink, let's not quibble over bar fruit, shall we?

I should explain. When I came in on a Sunday at 8, there were two people working, but the woman bartender was out front smoking a cigarette so the honor of waiting on me was given to a young man with welcoming look (I'm sure that won't last long) I asked him for a gin and tonic and I swear there was a look of panic on his face. He went over to the bottles behind the bar and stared. And stared. And stared again. He took out a pint glass and looked at the bottles again and hoped something would come to him like inspiration. He leaned into the ear of the now returned female bartender and asked her something. She shrugged and pointed and he made me a drink. He put it in front of me and said, "Sorry, I've only been here for three weeks." I smiled graciously.

But let me just say, what the hell? Is the Gin and Tonic such a strange exotic concoction that after three weeks he didn't come across such a thing? As I go on this tour I am seeing that the gin and tonic can be perceived as a foreign invader into this land of Bud Lights and straight whiskeys. Poor gin and tonic, you need a support group and a public awareness campaign. Buck up little gin and tonic, we still love you.

What was the type of gin - Whatever the confused young bartender found and poured, I think it was gin, yeah, I'm sure it was gin. Let's call it gin.

What was the gin and tonic like: It was fine. I had already had a few drinks at another place, which is not fair for me tasting the drink here, but there you go.

The Joint: I was there only briefly, just to have my drink and go. The place was large. Big and boxy. More spacious than it needed to be. It had the feel of a waiting room. Waiting for what, that is truly up to you. There were several rooms moving back. The ceilings were high, the place had a strange cold lighting. This felt like a set for a low budget movie where the seedy main character would come in to meet someone, have a drink, start a bar fight, move to the next set.

General Impressions: This was one where I didn't even know it was a bar. For years, when I was driving on Green Street, I would see the cool old school sign for the Arcadia- White Eagle, I had no idea what the hell it was, I thought it was a welfare hotel with nifty signage. But I was talking to Short Order Steve and he told me about it, how he would pass it to go to one of his favorite places, The Banner, and he never had the nerve to go in. I had a few, so I didn't care. I went in and went out. Kind of like the kid who was dared to go into Old Lady McGuillicudy's Haunted House - no one has ever come out alive. Well I went in, the place was fine and I left.

Will I come back: Maybe if I was younger, and wanted to be cool and authentic, but I don't need that. It was alright, and then we move on.

Stop #18 - Madigan's Again

The **Bar**: Madigan's Again

> **The Address** 545 Southwest Cutoff

> **The price** Four Dollars for a twelve ounce glass

> **Did they ask me if I wanted a lime** Not only did he not ask if I wanted one, I didn't get one.

> **What was the type of gi**n: This must be said that Madigan's is not a place for mixed drinks. They only had 30 liquor bottles total behind the bar. This is a beer place. The bartender sheepishly said, "We only have Tanqueray, that alright?" Sure, sure.

> **What was the gin and tonic like** I like lime in my Gin and Tonics. But it was pretty alright. He didn't kill it with too many ice cubes. A nice drink to finish off a tough work week.

> **The Joint:** This is a tiny tiny place that caters to their people. There are darts and that seems to be what the place is about. I was the only person there when I came in. The bartender was friendly, we spoke about golf for a bit (yeah, me such a golfer, feh). The place is pretty run down and it feels that that is the way they like it. A clean pristine veneer would feel weird. This is an old bar for older folk, got a problem with that?

> **General Impressions:** This was such a little box. The guy tending bar was playing some bar video game when I came in, but was happy to serve me. Then an older couple came in, they got their drinks without asking. They both had plastic holders to keep their keno cards. They played their cards, they waited to win. They kept on talking to the bartender. Another guy came and he gave the couple hugs and they talked about friends and what they were all doing. He got his drink without asking as well.

> Right before I left, watching everyone laughing and hugging and being happy and belonging, I suddenly became melancholy, which is what caused the next paragraph.

The thing about bars is that the first time you go in, you are the stranger. You are the other. You are the person that no one knows. When THEY come in, THEY are greeted like old friends, slapped on the back, given their preferred beer without even asking, allowed to place themselves on their appointed seats like royalty. You have to ask for a drink, and don't forget to be polite. Don't forget to not look at anyone too long. Don't forget that you are a guest here. You are paying for your seat, but that doesn't give you rights to the stool you are sitting. This is a rental. You are a rental, you are the face in the back of the crowd. You will finish your drink and leave, this is not your home, this is not your place. Every time you go into a new bar is a lesson in loneliness. You are the only one not knowing anyone. Everything is new and unfamiliar: The stool, the set up, the way the bar feels on your resting arm. The only thing vaguely familiar is the gin and tonic in front of you. Enjoy your drink, leave a tip as you move on to something or somewhere you can call your own.

Will I come back: No, it was a small little joint, not mine. For a place where people play darts and keno, this is a fine place to put down stakes, just not for me.

Stop #19 - Union Tavern

The Bar: Union Tavern - this is where Creegan's Pub used to be.

The Address 65 Green St.

The price Seven Dollars. This again was me making a mistake, the bartender upselled very smartly and I, who should know better, fell for it. He said, "Tanqueray alright?" and I said sure instead of saying "Just well drink please." I looked and well drinks are five fifty, so there you go.

Did they ask me if I wanted a lime He did.

What was the type of gin Tanqueray, dammit. I got to follow my own rules.

What was the gin and tonic like: It was good, it was in a pint glass, it tasted decent. Nothing to fight over or be put through a window for, but it was good.

The Joint A nice open place with a good sized bar. The place was clean and presentable with darts and pool in the back. The front is for drinking, fella. The crowd was mostly young, mostly town. They talked about cars, the demise of the Summer National, how a guy on the street was talking nonsense about how rare and powerful his car was. The bar had many many bottles of flavored vodka, (Though the bartender said to a regular, that he didn't care for flavored vodka seemed to be against the very idea of it. Which was a big plus for the guy and the joint, having a bartender have an opinion on the product. He made a drink for a woman with one of them and he tried to make it better, by suggesting that he can add other spirits to it to make it taste more palatable, though the woman was happy with what she got.)

General Impressions A bar for Worcester folk in their twenties and thirties, they felt happy being there and talking Wormtown to Wormtowners. In the last bar I went to, I was waxing sad that I was too young for the crowd, now I am too old for this place. When will I find a place made for a finicky middle aged person such as myself?

The big event discussed when I was there, was a bar fight in the place next door. A guy was put through a plate glass window. The bartender wasn't in the bar when I entered, he was at the other bar looking at the security footage that explained the whole event of the bar fight. He narrated it to his regulars, he even began to act it out. As if the back of the bar was center stage, he was performing the one man show - Kid through a Plate Glass Window. Who needs Spaulding Gray or Eric Bogosian, when we are blessed with the bartenders of Worcester? I was listening to the tale of bar tabs and retribution and broken windows, but then I realized, this is not why I come to bars. To hear of the misfortune of others. Well, not that much, at any right. I finished my drink and left the bartender in mid performance.

Will I come back: No, it was a fine place with a good selection, but this was not my crowd. The wonderful thing about having so many bars is that you can have choices of where you can melt into and where you can stand out for a little bit, and leave.

Stop #20 - The Banner Bar and Grill

The Bar The Banner Bar and Grill

The Address 112 Green Street (wow, this is the third bar in a row on Green Street, this is actually looking like a tour or at least a crawl, so I better find another street for the next one, just to spice things up)

The price: 5.50

Did they ask me if I wanted a lime: This is the first time that I didn't sit at the bar, and the first time I brought a Virgil with me, I had my friend Epicure Eric in tow. We sat at a table, for six on Sunday, it was the last open table, and I just did a fast order to the waitress, where I said well gin with a lime.

What was the type of gin It was well.

What was the gin and tonic like: I had a fun time at the joint with Eric and the gin tasted good, maybe it was the mood, maybe it was a good cocktail, probably a little bit of both.

The Joint: Short Order Steve said this is one of his favorite places, so when our first choice for food and a drink was packed, I suggested this place. I told Eric that I was going to do the tour and the rule of course is that I just get a gin and tonic and nothing else, no second drink, no food. Eric smiled at me, like I was such a silly boy.

This is a nice place. A restaurant bar. The seats were comfortable and there were a lot of flatscreens around with sports showing. I said to Eric that it was a sports bar. Eric said it felt like an Irish Bar. He then asked me what makes a sports bar and an irish bar, and I paused, I don't know. I really don't know. Can someone help me with this. I mean you can watch sports at an Irish bar, and I am sure there is more than one sports bar where a happy drunk would sing out a broken rendition of Black Velvet Band.

We got our drinks and I looked over at the bar and someone got the onion rings and they looked good. Eric said we can have some. I told him my rules. He ordered onion rings and when they came he took pleasure in watching me instantly tuck in. They were delicious. Eric liked how they didn't use bread crumbs and I liked how you can taste the onions. I guess if I was going to break a rule, I might as well do it with something delicious.

General Impressions There was a lot of people there, but it didn't feel packed. It was a well run joint, we got our food and drinks in a timely fashion. There was a couple odd things that happened. The big one was the dance of the competing waitresses. When we sat we got a red haired waitress and she got our drink orders. A minute later a brunette waitress came by and asked if she could get out drinks, we said we were already taken care of. Then the red head waitress took our food order and a minute later the brunette reappeared to see if we wanted any food. This happened two more times, first the red head and then soon after the brunette. Obviously there was a fight over tables, it was slightly strange.

The other thing was when we were walking into the bar the door man was staring at us, or at least it looked like he was looking at us, but then he said, "They're towing my car" and ran out into the street. When we saw him as we were leaving, we asked him about his car, and he said the tow truck wasn't taking his truck, but was just parking so he can go to the Banner for dinner. Isn't that sweet? But let me tell you, the look of anger on the door guy when we were coming in made me feel slightly off.

Will I come back Yes. I think this might be a place for beer and fries. It was a good welcoming place, despite the Waitress Roller Derby Throw Down.

Stop #21 - The Cosmopolitan Club

The Bar: The Cosmopolitan Club

The Address: 96 Hamilton Street

The price Five dollars

Did they ask me if I wanted a lime: He did and I got it, but he missed putting it in and it fell out and hit the bar. He gave me another, which added double the lime flavored goodness, score!!!

What was the type of gin: It was well.

What was the gin and tonic like: It was alright. Nothing spectacular, but it didn't coat my mouth with a film of despair, so there is that to recommend it.

The Joint: The is the unknown bar. Several people asked me what the latest bar I hit for this tour and I said, The Cosmopolitan Club, and not a one ever heard of it. One thought I made it up, or perhaps the gin and tonic was dosed and I hallucinated a mirage of a joint. That's the thing with this place, it seems like this is the prototypical neighborhood bar, it caters to those who can walk to it and pretty much no one else. There is a lot to say in praise of a bar that is for the local environ. It is long and thin and is dark. It is a bar. The place has a good liquor selection and the beers sound interesting, not just Buds and Coors here, which is nice. The bartender was welcoming. It felt like a lot of other neighborhood bars (once again, not a bad thing)

General Impressions: It was quiet on this Sunday night, with three people in the bar, they all knew one another by name. I focused on the Sox game, or so it seemed. The bartender was a bit of a talker. A raconteur, if you will. He was talking to a couple at the bar. First he said that people should know that he hates Christmas. Why do you have to pretend to like a present some one gave you, or they give you a present and you don't give them one. Yeah, Christmas sucks. His favorite holiday is Black Friday, that's his holiday because its a present that he wants, that he buys. The way it should be. Actually, he goes on Thanksgiving, because the Walmarts in Connecticut are open Thanksgiving day. Last time, he was three sheets to the wind driving down to the store. It was Thanksgiving so he celebrated with Wild Turkey. He likes being an asshole at the stores during Black Friday, blocking people, walking slow, taking the last thing not because he wants it but that the lady behind him wants it. That's one of the best parts.

Soon, one of the guys at the bar said goodbye and walked home. Another went out to smoke a cigarette. It got quiet in there. I finished my drink and left.

Will I come back: There is something to be said about a little known place that caters to the people around it. I like that. But I don't live around it. The beer and liquor selection is tempting, but its a bar for the neighbors, and barring what the old Narragansett Commercials stated, I am not their neighbor, I am a tourist here. So I will say no.

Stop #22 - The Press Box

The Bar: The Press Box. This is a cool name for a bar, in my humble touristy opinion. You have two of my favorite aspects of bardom, obvious sports references and a hint of the literate. It isn't just a sports bar, we are referencing writers here folks. I guess the only way to make the name of the bar even better is to rechristen it, the Press Box for Women Writers with Loose Morals (yeah, a little too verbose, but it is a work in progress)

The Address 536 Lincoln Street

The price: 5.75.

Did they ask me if I wanted a lime: He did.

What was the type of gin: I got well, because I asked for it by name. Not that well is a name, it is more of a location.

What was the gin and tonic like: It was a pint glass with a hell of a lot of ice. Not too much flavor, but it was alright.

The Joint: This is an old school bar. It is on the second floor of a building. You have to come in from the back, which probably suits some customers just fine. The place is a comfortable size. It has a section with a good amount of tables. There are newspapers and books around to peruse. It is brightly lit and the bartender was quite friendly. The place was this side of grungy, but it was presentable enough and had a comfortable feeling.

General Impressions: I don't know this answer, I am just asking, but are there bars that never are busy? This is the first bar in my tour (22 bars so far) where I have been in before. The first time was a Wednesday at seven and it was practically empty. And now it was a Friday a little before eleven at night and it was practically empty. Are there places that can survive without a rush? Can a slow trickle make a place viable?

There were three guys at the bar pleasantly annoyed at the Sox for losing another. There was a foursome at a table playing cards,

I don't know but I think they were playing Bridge. This is cool, I haven't seen anyone at a bar playing cards yet on my tour, this is a perfect thing to do at a low key bar, I think. The bartender talked to his regulars, got me to add my two cents on the Sox's miserable year (I don't follow sports but since I've been on this gin and tonic kick, I have learned a few key phrases of disgust toward our local team that keeps me in good stead.) I like how it was bright in there, you could read a book. I like that there seemed to be no attitude, no pretensions. A good solid bar where you can hang out with friends at a table or be by yourself and drink your drink and read the paper.

Will I come back Yeah. I think so. If I am in the area. If I want to chat with a friend or just read a book. It is not convenient for me with where I live, but the place was comfy.

Stop #23 - Moynihan's

The Bar: Moynihan's

    The Address 897 Main Street

    The price 5.00

    Did they ask me if I wanted a lime He did, though in a way that he seemed annoyed about all of this lime discussion. As if he is up to here with people asking for citrus with their booze.

    What was the type of gin: I have learned my lesson so I said "well" right away and he looked at me, looked at the bottles and then said, "You know there's no difference between well gin and Tanqueray, they're both five dollars." So I told him that I will have a Tanqueray.

    Let me just say here, that's weird. Why would the well gin and tonic be the same as Tanqueray. Tanqueray costs a little bit of money, while the well gin is usually a dollar ninety five a case. Why wouldn't there be a difference in price. I ain't no bar whisperer, I just thought it odd. Nice to have a Tanqueray and tonic for five bucks though.

    What was the gin and tonic like: It was nice. Small, but nice. He didn't kill it with ice and there was a good amount of liquor. It was not a knock your socks drink, but on this tour, I'm not looking for that.

    The Joint: This place is old school authentic. It was large, with booths, tables, a double bar. Large mirrors with beer and booze logos on them on all the walls. One of the Mirrors stated that they have been serving Budweiser here since 1935. There is a video game by the door. It feels like the joints they wrote about in Joseph Mitchell essays. This place rocks. It's also kind of shabby. I texted Bartender Brian when I was there and he told me that this was the first place he ever had a drink and I should try the pickled eggs and then texted maniacal laughter.

General Impressions It was 12:30 in the afternoon on a Tuesday when I sidled in. Only a few people were there. They talked about sports, about who the Celtics should recruit. They talked about how things in Worcester used to be, they talked about people they all knew. Some guys left to get back to work, others came in. It had a sad feel, but a nice sad feel. One weird thing happened. A young man came in heading towards the back. He was shirtless. The bartender said, "Hey, you have to wear a shirt in here." The young man said, "Oh yeah, I forgot." He kept on walking to the back while putting on his shirt. He went to the men's room. He was there for a couple minutes. Then he came out and walked out of the bar. I don't know what that was about.

I feel like I was in time warp. I spent 30 minutes in there and had no idea where it went. The people at the bar talked slow, drank slow and suddenly time was fleeting. I played a game of Galaga before I left, feeling happy with the level I made it to. I left, expecting to emerge to find that I was in there for twenty years instead of a half hour.

Will I come back: I'm going to say no, but qualify it. It is a really cool looking place. This is like a bar of long ago, because it really is. On the other hand, its kind have gotten a run down bottom barrell feel as well. I think every person who digs bars should get themselves here once, hell, have a pickled egg (you brave soul) and then move on to another bar. This is in Main South, and I don't find myself there much, so I will say no, but check it out, do.

Stop #24 - Breen's Cafe

The Bar: Breen's Cafe

    The Address 16 Cambridge Street

    The price 5.50

    Did they ask me if I wanted a lime He did

    What was the type of gin: It was Tanqueray. I wasn't given a choice, he just walked over to the bottles, picked it up and poured. I guess this is their standard gin, which is okay by me. He filled up a pint glass with ice and then began to fill it with gin, and fill and fill. This was a heady drink.

    What was the gin and tonic like For one filled with liquor, it was surprisingly flavorful. I liked it, but of course, I liked being in this bar, so what is the ratio between taste of drink and comfort level in environment? Which makes the drink better - the ingredients or the place you are sitting?

    The Joint: A good sized bar with a grill attached to the back bar area. There were tables and a long shelf in the middle to lean on and to drink at. It has age, but it looked presentable, clean enough. The bartender was attentive and friendly enough. He noticed that I looked at the chalk board that had the menu written on it and he asked "You want some food?"

    I thought the bar food looked good, and it was being made right in front of us, which is always a bonus to me. I liked the fact they had a burger called the Friendly Burger. Friends, is there any kind of burger that isn't friendly? I don't know of a mean spirited burger.

    General Impressions: By the time I left at two pm on a Tuesday, there were over 25 people at Breens. This was not expected. Folks were eating burgers, talking in groups, looking at the World Cup coverage. One woman was at the bar reading a book, That is something I want to see more of, where someone can just plant themselat a bar with a book and feel happy and welcome. With

25 people, the place did not feel crowded at all, the bartender and the cook were working quickly and efficiently. There was a nice neighborhood feel to the joint, but not in an exclusionary way. I think the idea that so many different people were here in the middle of the day says something about Breen's. I lingered, I was happy to just sit and drink.

The parking is lousy, by the way. They have parking to the side and in the back, but its not great, I can see myself wanting to avoid going there on busy times.

Will I come back Yes. This is one of those I was wrong about. People mentioned Breen's to me, but it always looked like a dive. It did not bode well to me. Man was I wrong. I really liked it. You can meet friends, have a burger, read a book, drink in solitude. This place multi-tasks.

On looking at my notes, it seems that this neighborhood has the most bars I would come back to. In this little area on and off Cambridge Street, there are three places I liked: Breen's, McGuires, and Marty's. There a few other bars in the area the tour has not hit, but this is pleasant to see. A cluster of nice local bars.

Stop #25 - Varsity Bar and Grill

The Bar: Varsity Bar and Grill (I didn't see anything about food there, so maybe the grill is more

of an aphorism)

The Address 9 Kelly Square - this is where the Grey Hound Pub used to be, and then moved down the street.

The price 5.50

Did they ask me if I wanted a lime: No she just put it in. Howrah!!!

What was the type of gin I have no idea, she didn't ask and I didn't see what wild concoction she put into that pint glass cauldron.

What was the gin and tonic like: Not a bad drink. Nothing wrong about it, it was the absence of poor, it didn't distinguish itself, but it didn't trip in a ditch.

The Joint: This is my first music oriented club on the tour. I didn't know that when I walked in, but I was greeted with dark red walls, and a long padded bench on one side for sitting with some tables. There was a DJ booth and over the bar were five flat screen TVs all playing the same thing, which was MTV2 and what I think was the show Awkward. The music playing was modern Hip Hop. This was a place to dance and get close, with it not being a large place, you had no choice, the only thing you need is people, which there wasn't. It was empty when I walked in on Thursday at 9:30 and I was pretty surprised by this, down the street at the Grey Hound there was a growing crowd. Here was two bartenders and four other people.

General Impressions: The two bartenders wore skimpy clothes. They had a lot of tattoos and skin showing. They seemed distracted despite the light crowd. A guy came in who was an owner or manager and the bartenders told him they couldn't work the stereo system to pick music and they had no coca cola syrup for the bar taps. The guy set things up and music was playing. As I was there, a few more guys came in, parking their bikes, and sat at the bar. They seemed to know each other. They just sat waiting for something to happen, people to show, magic to happen.

I came too early for the fun madness. Maybe people will show at ten or eleven. Perhaps midnight is when it all starts. I hope they got people, though to be fair, I drank my drink and was pretty disengaged.

Maybe this is why people show up to parties late. They never want that awkward moment of seeing the place unfilled. You see the problems in the paint color scheme. The artistic failings of the bartender's tattoos. You see the seams and the ripped scrims. The coca cola not being available, The staff not knowing how to set up the stereo. The question is for those who like to arrive to their theater early, can you still enjoy yourself as you watch the paint on the sets dry?

Later, that night, I saw people gathering outside the bar, smoking cigarettes. Perhaps the party started. The fun officially began after my tour visit.

Will I come back No.

2019 Update: This did not last. It wagone in a year. It is now a bagel place.

Stop #26 - Rivalry Sports Bar

The Bar: Rivalry Sports Bar - this was the location for the old bar Jeff's. Maybe this is me but I think Rivalry is a pretty lame name for a bar. I mean, Rivalry to whom? Are we just against everyone in general? Is it a rivalry between sports bars and cocktail lounges? Which would be kind of cool to see. There used to be a bar in town called the Alibi Bar, and that was the top for bad bar names, so Rivalry will have to try harder next time.

The Address 274 Shrewsbury Street.

The price 6 bucks

Did they ask me if I wanted a lime She didn't ask me and I just got it, which was nice. I was going to take this category out of my review and then she went and gave me one without me making a peep

What was the type of gin It was a well gin.

What was the gin and tonic like It was fine, a little on the weak side, but it was alright, There is something to be said for low expectations, you are never totally disappointed.

The Joint It feels like someone saw a picture of a 1960s men's club interior and said, "That. I want my bar to look like that." There is wood paneling. There are black padded stools and chairs. There is a section where there are black leather couches. This is the place you can imagine the wannabe Gilded Age Industrialists to sit and drink their port and smoke their cigars, consulting their pocket watches, waiting for an important telegram.

General Impressions This was a Sunday at six in the afternoon. No one was there, but the bartender, the owner of the place and another guy. The other guy was waxing nostalgic about the times where cops wouldn't pull you over when you were half in the bag, as long as you were heading home. Now they pull you over, can you believe that?

The bartender was nice and responsive. She was friendly. The bar had on the Sox game, they lost (natch). The owner was telling the bartender to offer a kind a beer they can't seem to move for a discount, though it still wasn't moving, what's wrong with this beer?

I was talking to Bartender Bart about the bar and he told me it was kind of amazing to see on a weekend night. Sometimes the bar would be wall to wall packed and then in an hour, it would be empty. The tide of people just moving on to the next thing, looking for some new thrill, or at least the next one. Me too, I was gone in twenty minutes.

Will I come back No, nothing wrong, Just not for me. The place is clean though, pretty as a picture, just not a picture I want to cut out of magazine and pin on my chalkboard.

2019 Update: Rivalry folded. Then it was Frank's. Now it goes by the spooky moniker of Dark Rose Saloon. I know nothing about the place, but I picture a lot of middle aged goths drinking mead and listening to recordings of Black Tape for a Blue Girl.

Stop #27 - Cisero's

The Bar: Cisero's

    The Address 17 Suffolk Street

    The price 3.25

    Did they ask me if I wanted a lime No, and I didn't get one.

    What was the type of gin: It was a little known limited distillation made from the tears of the undeserving (you know, well gin)

    What was the gin and tonic like It was in a ten ounce plastic cup, with a few unhappy cubes of ice. It tasted like gin, I suppose. But it could have also tasted of Generic Hooch. On talking about this visit on the tour afterwards I was told people don't get cocktails at Cisero's. They get beer and shots. Look at me, I am an exotic anomaly.

    The Joint. This is a biker bar. People with bikes go here There is a lot of talk about what goes on there, and what the people who go there are like. On this Sunday that I went in, there were five or six guys in motorcycle leathers drinking and talking. There was a pool table. There was a sign saying that anyone selling drugs in the bathroom would be scratched. There was an odor. The place had a funk going on. There was a need for a good cleaning.

    General Impressions: I have to say, I was scared going in. I mean I am a middle aged hoity toity fellow who will order a Benedictine and Brandy on a whim (hell, I am the kind of a guy who uses the term "on a whim"). This is not my natural habitat. But I went in and ordered and kept my talk and my eyes to myself. The guys, only guys there, were willing to bring me into conversation. Simple things, there was a Walking Dead marathon on the TV and I was able to answer their questions about the show. Like I said, I am the guy who knows about Walking Dead, on a whim.

One guy at the bar, with a prosthetic metal leg and enough attitude to survive any type of apocalypse, looked at the screen with just a little bit of disdain and said, "I don't get it. Why do the zombies make noise when they're coming? Why do they make any noise? They're dead. They don't breathe." I looked at him, the biker sage, and said, "Yeah, you're right." Truth found in a biker bar.

Will I come back Are you kidding?

Stop #28 - The MB Lounge

The Bar: The MB Lounge (The Male Box, baby)

The Address 40 Grafton Street

The price 7.50 (I have left the cheap gin mills where a fiver can take care of a fella, welcome to the pricey part of the bar landscape) He did ask if I wanted a small or a big and I picked a large, which was in a pint glass.

Did they ask me if I wanted a lime He did. He was a very friendly bartender.

What was the type of gin I got well, which made the seven fifty a tad more surprising.

What was the gin and tonic like It was fine. Nothing fantastic, but it was alright. Sometimes you pay a cover to get into a joint. Sometimes you buy a drink and that's your ticket to the show.

The Joint The first thing you have to realize is how inconspicuous the bar is from the outside. I have gone by it countless times and didn't know there was a bar there. The windows are darkened and the MB Lounge sign is subtle. It looked like it was closed. I went in and I was assaulted by color. In a good way. This was 8:30 on a Wednesday and ten or fifteen were there. There were setting up for some kind of event because the disco ball was spinning and the colored lights were going about. The bar has tables and a good sized bar. The bar area was full and I had to take my drink to a side table, which is a decent place for me to watch what was going on. As I was leaving, more and more people were coming in, it looked like people were coming for the event, whatever it was, there was a microphone set up by the DJ.

General Impressions I don't know when the last time I was at a gay bar. I am not gay and its been years since a friend took me to one back in New York. I didn't know what to expect. I found a very nice attitude, with people talking and chatting. It was a nice place where people can be comfortable. The goofy lights just added to it. The bartender shouted out something about Ethel Merman and I felt relieved. If I stayed longer, would Ms Garland's name been mentioned? I hope so. This was the perfect place to go to after my stop at Cisero's, which was the bar I went to before this.

Time Spent in the bar: 20 minutes

Will I come back Yeah. I have friends who would like the place and the way you can be seen and still feel yourself. Its a hoot.

Stop #29 - The Dive Bar

The Bar: Dive Bar - you gotta love the name

The Address 34 Green St

The price Eight dollars (crikey)

Did they ask me if I wanted a lime He just put it in

What was the type of gin I don't know, they just made it

What was the gin and tonic like Okay, this is was not a bad drink....at first. As I was drinking and talking to Bartender Bart, I suddenly had a weird realization. There was a different flavor to the gin and tonic. I sipped. I sipped again. And yes, there was a black licorice flavor. Like sambuca or ouzo, or any of the other anise flavored drinks that I avoid with nimble ease. I looked at Bart and asked if there was any gin that had a anise flavor. He couldn't figure it out. So, the drink wasn't bad, but it didn't taste like gin. Weird.

I talked to Bartender Brian after the fact and the only thing he can guess is that some sambuca or something so flavored splashed on the ice container and that ice made it to my drink. I think that's as good an explanation as any, but let me also state, I paid eight bucks for a two ingredient cocktail (not counting the lime) please let it taste of those two things only.

The Joint This is a high end drinking hole, built in the bones of an old gin mill. I was here once fifteen years ago when it was a dive. Now it is snazzy and there was a bunch of people at the tables out back. Not too many in the bar area, which was fine because it was tight. Dark and cool looking, though this was an unpleasant humid night (Wednesday for point of fact) There were people sitting by themselves, which is a nice thing to be able to do at a bar. There was a young woman sitting near me gazing at her phone. She looked really sad and unhappy about something, I hope it was not me sitting near that put her in such a funk. This maudlin feel was odd in the setting, like they should have been playing old country songs about the dog running off with the truck or something.

General Impressions I went in and there was a dead night feel and I was about to leave and come back another day so that I could get a better sense of the place. People really like this joint and I wanted to get a good reporting of it for the tour. But as i was about to split and try again at another bar, I saw Bartender Bart who was out with a friend. I sat down and we chatted. I got my drink, and I stayed.

He knows about the tour and he and his friend went on about all the weird places I have to check out. There is a chinese restaurant lounge that sounds absolutely bonkers. He went on about an almost bar fight at Jak's Pub with a local drunk. There were many funny stories about bars that were not the one we were in. I had a great time chatting,, but it felt like it was in spite of the present location and not because.

The bartender was not very present and I got no vibe on the joint pro or con. It was a place where we talked about other places that I might like to be. It was a strange stop on the tour, but it felt more like a staging ground and not a place to be. Maybe it was the sad girl near by, maybe it was the star anise flavored gin and tonic, maybe it was my antsy mood brought on from the muggy bar, but I got nothing out of it.

Amount of Time in the Joint 20 minutes

Will I come back Nah. I can see myself following a friend who wants to go in for a fine beer, but I don't think I will initiate a trip there.

2019 Update Just last week, it was announced that the building's owner is going to focus on a family business at that location and so Dive Bar will be a memory in one month. This is going to happen more and more in Worcester. In the area, they are building Polar Park, the new Triple A Minor League Park for the Red Sox. Progress is coming in

Worcester, or so they inform us. Kelly Square will be redesigned. Rents are already going up. By the time I finish with these updates (a month or two, if I get my act together) more places might be closed for the potential gold mine that the future brings. More money. More progress.

DAVID MACPHERSON

Stop #30 - Beatniks

The Bar: Beatniks

The Address 433 Park Ave

The price 6.50 (man, I am beginning to feel nostalgic for the six dollar cocktail. The last two bars I went to were eight dollars and seven fifty. Welcome to high cost of well drinks)

Did they ask me if I wanted a lime Yes he did, in a nervous fashion, but more on that in a moment.

What was the type of gin He asked if I wanted Bombay, and I said no, just well, and he said Well, I can give you well. I hate to say this, but more on this behavior further in this tourist log.

What was the gin and tonic like He asked me was it good (never had anyone ask me this before) And I told him it was good. It was. A good amount of ice, not too much, but enough to keep it cold. It was a wee bit on the weak side, but a fine run of the mill highball.

The Joint I have been meaning to get in here. They do have cool events and the vibe is something I heard about it. But as I was entering I saw the sign saying there was going to be karaoke this night. My thought was "Crap. Run Dante, run away." But I am a professional anonymous blogger, and I have my pride (yeah, I keep it in my glove box) so I went in. It's a good sized place. There is two areas, one with bars and rat pack era booths. Then we have the dance/performance space. That space had lights flashing and music pumping, but no one singing to projected lyrics. This was a good moment. I like a well attended bar, but I love when no one shows up for karaoke even more. It's like sing-a-long Christmas to me. The place had a nice cool kid vibe and comfortable. There was art on the walls, as well as gig posters for events that happened at Beatniks. I heard that there is a new owner, but that things have not changed, and that's a good thing, because its a cool place.

General Impressions My impression? Well, let's slow this down, bring up the lights, so I can sit on my stool and talk to each and everyone of you.

For the first three months of this blog I had forty five views. That's it. But one of those was Victor Infante from the Telegram. He wrote a little piece about this blog and now two and a half weeks later, this blog now 2200 views. Thank you Victor. When he wrote this, I was excited, but I also was worried that I would be found out. That people at bars would be looking for me. But I went to 7 more bars and none of that happened. Until now.......

Let me just say that in the land of keeping things on the DL, I do a lousy job. I mean, I go into a bar, and ask for a gin and tonic, and I am specific that I want well gin and then I drink it, look intently at the other bar goers, like I am an odd stalker and then I leave. I am the worst secret agent ever. But that's the mission, that I chose to accept (Mr. Phelps)

Now let's go back to my time at Beatniks. There were only a few people there, which was alright because no one was singing Karaoke. I asked for my gin and tonic and the bartender asked for my ID. Now, I am a guy in his forties who looks like a guy who is in his forties. There is no chance I am a nineteen year old with bad skin trying to get a buzz on. I go on that he made my day thinking I was young, but it was weird and he looked nervous. He was nervous when I asked for well gin. Then he asked after my first sip if it was good. It was good, but what a strange question. He was nervous around me. Usually people would be nervous around me when I was single and I would ask them out on a date, not for someone to make me a cocktail.

The place was a comfortable joint, but then as I was leaving and I went to my car to write up my notes, it hit me, he got my real name, he seemed nervous about me getting a well gin and tonic. Now I could be wrong, but I talked to a bartender friend and he was kind of sure that he figured who I was and why I was there. So the question is, will he give out my name? Will he say he sussed me out? And then the real question, who cares? I could be wrong. He might not have been nervous with me, but yet....

Will I come back Despite his non cool reaction, the place is cool. I liked it. I hope to not come back when there is karaoke. That's always a rule for me. But I can see myself going back there.

2019 Update After talking to others and thinking about it, the guy didn't figure me out. He was just a nervous lamb. Man, how I come across as a self-important idiot in this post. But hey, I am not going to change the kind of idiot I am or was.

Stop #31 - McDonald's Tavern

The Bar: McDonald's Tavern

The Address 440 Grove Street

The Day and the TIme 8:30 on a Tuesday in the Summer. The baseball All-Star Game was on, if that gives you an idea of when it was.

The price I think it was six bucks, but it was a while ago and I can't find my notes.

Did they ask me if I wanted a lime Yes

What was the type of gin I don't recall

What was the gin and tonic like Fine

The Story: This should have been an easy one to write, but for some reason or other, I have found it near impossible to write about this little known pub. Its attached to the Worcester Fitness Club, inside it, and it's decorated all in dark, clunky wood and little light. The first time I went to the bar, I didn't order a drink, I just looked around and left. This was early in this tour, looked around and thought the bar too strange to do it at that day. Why did I think that. First, I have been to bars in athletic clubs before but this had a weird vibe. This was a Wednesday at nine or so and when I came in, the bar was full of older men, not a seat was available. All older. This was something I wasn't expecting. Now I didn't stay long, but my memory was that they were all at the bar and they could see the cardio area of the gym and the men were looking at the women on the bikes and treadmills. When I went back a month or so later, I realized I was wrong, there was no easy way for someone at the bar to look at the people in the gym. My mind played tricks on me. Maybe I was trying to explain why they were all there.

The second time I was there, I had my gin and tonic and listened to the few people talk to one another. It was not busy, but it did go to the older age side of things. They all seemed to know each other. This seemed like their place after work or whatever. But when I was there, I just felt sad. I don't know if its because I remembered aspects of the place incorrectly, or that the dark setting and the wood just hollowed me out. Maybe it was the old person's bar surrounded by all this exercise and activity, an oasis of blessed sloth. Exercise for an hour or two and negate the whole process by having a few cocktails. Maybe it was because the bar smelled of chlorine from the pool (which is reason enough to not return). I don't know.

As I went on with this blog and the months went by, it just got harder and harder to think of something to write about this place, and get my feelings straight on it. I even played with the notion of going back there again, a third time, have a gin and tonic and try to come up with something to say about it. But I have now gone to over 53 bars on this silly project and have about 60 or 70 more to go to, so I don't fancy the notion of going back and giving this bar proper reporting. So instead, you get this rambling missive of a review.

About this project, it's really not about the gin and tonics. It's about the act of going to a bar. It's me trying to figure out why we pick the places we like to go to. Why we socialize the way we do in these public spaces. What is expected of us when we are there and what do we expect in return. Maybe something about this bar, this space, cradled inside a large gym complex, made me think. In my forties, this is not the place I chose to be, to be a part of, but what about twenty years from now, will I be that guy at the bar in the blazer talking about my golf swing? Will I wonder where everyone is, because this place usually is filled and active? Will I begin to dream of a place where I can have a drink that mingles with the aroma of chlorine?

2019 Update This still stands as my most confounding piece to have written. I just didn't understand what I was seeing. Then, a few years after doing the tour, this showed up in the comments sections. Here is what Crissy wrote. It is everything I was hoping to find when going to a bar. Thank you so much Crissy,.

"I had to giggle when I read this post....My dad is one of the older gents you may have seen at the bar. And I had to take the chance to share another perspective about this bar.

My dad is 68 years old and visits the fitness center 6 out of 7 days a week (he golfs on the 7th day. Each day he looks forward to his 1.5hr workout and then his hour of socializing by having a beer with his buddies at this bar. The other hours of his day are filled with being the primary caretaker of my mom who has advanced Alzheimer's. A woman who really should most likely be in a care facility at this point but my dad just won't allow it....he says it will break his heart to have to leave her there. His time is extremely limited because of the amount of care mom needs and it's difficult for him to fit in anytime for himself.....so this situation really works for him. My main objective in mentioning all this is just to say how thankful I am for this tavern.....it's the only part of my dads day sometimes where he can find community and connection. -Crissy"

Stop #32 - Jak's Pub

The Bar: Jak's Pub (This used to be the Red Baron Bar for forever)

The Address 536 Main Street

The price 5 bucks

Did they ask me if I wanted a lime: Yes and he put it in.

What was the type of gin Just well.

What was the gin and tonic like: It hit me at first as way too strong and then it mellowed out, as if it was not mixed well. But I had a nice conversation with the bartender/owner, so it tasted just fine when I was done.

The Joint: I am predisposed to this place and not in a good way. Over a decade ago, I worked right next to the location when it was the Red Baron and it was a dive like you read about. I would be going into work at 8:30 am and if I got a chance to peek in, I would be blessed with a view of a half dozen or more willing citizens occupying the stools, drinking breakfast. As employees of the nearby business, we were told not to be found there. But it was bought by a guy in 2011 who made a go of it, but he had to close for a while this year, because he works in Boston and he is the only employee, so couldn't make it work. It has been up again now for three weeks. It only had two other people in the bar at the time. But the place is nice. Solid, clean bar. Bar in the back, you have to pass the pool table to get to it, but you won't feel too winded.

General Impressions There was not a lot going on, only two customers there at nine on a Friday. (I can't seem to find a busy bar it appears) The bartender asked if I was coming from the play. I guess the Hanover had a play going. I just said I was happy the place was open and wanted to try it. He started talking to me. He told me he was the owner Rob. He bought the place in 2011 and tried to make a go but he now works in Boston and he was trying to do it all by himself. He was closed for a while and opened again three weeks before. He talked about how this might be the time to start again. He talked about creating a safe place, a place people want to come back to. The key is sticking with it. Just being open and letting people know he is there. That it is not the Red Barron, it is a nice bar you can go to before or after a play or concert. He was earnest and I want him to do well. I mentioned that the pool table kind of breaks the flow of the bar and he smiled. He likes the pool table. He practices when he is at the bar by himself. He hasn't gotten better, but he he keeps on trying.

Rob said, he wasn't looking for everyone in Worcester to come to him, just the people in the nearby two blocks, that's all he wants. There is a lot of folk in that small stretch of real estate, but they just need to know he is there. I love that notion. He's looking for those close to know there is a safe haven to have a drink. To drink before a play, after a play. After class. Before class even, you rebel. Create a place for people who are around to go to. This location, with the Hanover and with the satellite for the Community College coming in, is a place where people can feel safe and comfortable. That's his hope. I like his concept of the local.

Amount of Time in the Joint: 20 minutes (pleasant conversation for most of it)

Will I come back Yes. Next time I go to the Hanover. Next time I am in downtown for downtime, I will go there. More than I liked being there (which I did) but because I want a place in that location to work. I want a good bar to go to after seeing some concert or some theater. I want to feel that Worcester has these options. I want this to work. I want to have choices to go to in downtown. This might be a more political motive than I usually have, but the hell with it, I love this town, I want it to work. And good places to have a drink are a part of its success.

2019 Update *It didn't work. It was closed soon after this posted. Then it was sold. It opened up as Muse the next year. It is nice to say that Muse is still in business. More on Muse later in the tour.*

Stop #33 - Moynagh's

The Bar: Moynagh

    The Address 25 Exchange Street

    The price 4 dollars

    Did they ask me if I wanted a lime: He asked me a lot of things about my drink, as it it was some unique novelty item, like the whoopy cushion or the joy buzzer. He asked me if I really wanted the house gin. Asked me twice. And then asked me if I wanted a lime. And then couldn't find a lime in the joint. I guess he either found one or he cut one fresh, but what a joy, there was a lime. I did say, after he made fun of the house gin, that of course I need a lime, it can't do anything but improve the taste (yeah, I'm sure I ingratiated myself to him at that moment).

    What was the type of gin House baby. He even identified that benighted brand as if it was something that needed to be scorned.

    What was the gin and tonic like Mediocre, but it's what the bartender said it would be. Four dollars for an okay drink, Okay

    The Joint The bar is one of the oldest in Worcester. It's an old school Irish bar, where there is a very long bar and a dart board. The bartender was loud and talkative. That's nice. He made it a friendly experience. There was a light crowd for this Friday night. All men. One guy was reading a book and I was dying to find out what you read at this joint, but I couldn't see the cover. This all bodes well but I was at the bar side by the bathroom,. I didn't need no sign to infer that, the odor told me. This was a long stink that wafted at least the fifteen feet I was from the bathroom. Kind of took the bloom off the rose, and everything else.

    General Impressions Its a very guy bar. Three young men were getting juiced in preparation for going to a concert at the Palladium. The other guys looked tough and talked amongst themselves. The three guys left for the concert and said they would be back, the bartender told him he would be there. This has a gritty, you come here to drink, vibe and that's cool if that's what you want. Bartender Brian told me that when he used to tend bar at the Firehouse, he would come here on his break to have a;couple drinks. It's that kind of place, On the tv, I got to watch the Sox lose badly, there are a lot of opportunities to do that on this tour it seems.

Amount of Time in the Joint 15 minutes

Will I come back No. The oldest bar (perhaps) in Worcester should be held in high regard, but really. No. Is this the sign of old age, wanting a bar that doesn't stink hard and wide? For those who want this down and dirty gin mill, this might be the thing. I am not that fella.

Stop #34 - Still and Stir

The Bar: Still and Stir

> **The Address** 120 Commercial Street
>
> **The price** 8 dollars (whoa)
>
> **Did they ask me if I wanted a lime** He just put it in
>
> **What was the type of gin** I don't know, he just made it, I am sure it was a fine brand

What was the gin and tonic like: It came in a true high ball glass, which is a pleasant surprise, but the thing is with the right type of glass, you get less drink by volume than in other places. If the drink was fantastic, that would not have been an issue, but the drink was good. That's nice to say on this tour, where in a few places I feel like I drank carbonated tree sap, but for the price and reputation I was hoping that this place was going to do more than just be good. Call me crazy, I was hoping that this mixology joint was going to knock my socks off. It didn't.

The Joint: This is part of Niche Hospitality's Exchange Group of places. There is the Citizen. The People's Kitchen. There are some restaurants in this group that I think are great. Bocado's and Mezcal are wonderful in my estimation, but there have been a few clinkers, one being the time I was at the Citizen, and had lousy service

I went in to this as the third bar on the tour for the night, but it was weird anyway you look at it. You have to follow signs to the location. You go through a nice airy outdoor atrium with diners strewn about to finally wind up at a.cramped, humid place. I have to say the decor confused the hell out of me. It felt like I was underneath a Chicago El station. Above the bartender was metal and exposed wires going nowhere. There were waffle shaped dividers between sections of the bar as if this was something a follower of Frank Lloyd Wright belched up. It was a beautiful evening out, cool and pleasant for a late July. But here in the bar, I was sweating and clammy. This should not be. The bartender was a handsome man wearing a butcher's apron. Is he making drinks or cutting up veal shanks? He was solid and professional, though a little on the other side of friendly.

General Impressions There were only a few people at the bar, but people from other restaurants connected to the bar were coming in for cocktails. It made it feel more like a bar service station than a place to hangout and have drinks. The drink was alright, but I want more than alright for eight bucks. It was dark and not very welcoming. I finished my drink and left. Perhaps if I had a wild mixology creation I would have been more excited, but all I felt was that I paid a lot for a drink in a dank humid hobbit hole and I am sure I can find a crazy libation with bacon infused aquavit somewhere else. The search continues.

Amount of Time in the Joint 15 minutes

Will I come back No

2019 Update This bar and the Citizen at the end of last year when their lease ran out. Though recently, Still and Stir has reappeared in another location near its original address.

Stop #35 - City Lights Bar and Restaurant

The Bar: City Lights Bar and Restaurant (though I didn't see much restaurant, it felt all bar to me)

The Address 395 Grafton Street

The price Four Dollars

Did they ask me if I wanted a lime Yes

What was the type of gin It was bar gin as she said. That's not the more precise of terms, because isn't any gin in the premises to be considered bar gin? I know, just call me, Dante, Barroom Lawyer.

What was the gin and tonic like It was in a ten ounce plastic cup. This is true, the moment I took the first sip, the music on the stereo had George Thoroughgood announcing his desire for "One Bourbon, One Scotch and one Beer." And I would have preferred any of those things after the first sip. It was strong and poor. As I continued on, the flavor decreased and by the end was completely bland, as if the bar gin only lives on the high end of the cup. But it is evident that this is not a mixed drink haven, this is a place where you can still get a pitcher of beer, which should be my next Blog Tour - Pitchers of Beer Across Worcester (keep your eye out for that).

The Joint Its a box with an el shaped bar. There are tables. There is a pool table in the middle of the space like a great green whale. HD televisions playing the Sox game. There is a bare thin carpet. This is the place that is a blank slate just waiting for their regulars to fill it up with noise and life and that's what the regulars, all seeming to be local to the bar, do. It was loud for eight on Friday. When I left fifteen minutes later, six or seven more came in. They all knew everyone, they ordered pitchers.

General Impressions Friday at eight. 15 or so folk. They all were talking loudly, except for the three guys by one of the large screen television, watching in disbelief as the Red Sox didn't lose the game. Everyone was friendly and intermingling between groups. A friendly Friday night out for the folk who go.

I overheard a conversation between three female friends sitting at a table as they gleefully recounted one of them finding the movie Footloose on TV the night before. This was exciting stuff it seemed. Yes friends, this is the bar where the lovers of Kevin Bacon dancing because he needs to dance, reside. Or maybe they are just big John Lithgow fans.

Amount of Time in the Joint 15 minutes. It would have been 10, but as I was getting ready to take my last sip, on the stereo, came the Mariachi Opening of Ring of Fire by Johnny Cash and I knew I had to stay until it was over. Got to love that song. It keeps me in places I am ready to leave. As I listened to it, I realized that this was the theme song to this Tour of Every Bar in Worcester. I fell into flaming ring of fire. And I left an acceptable tip.

Will I come back: No. That isn't saying its a bad bar. Its a place where locals to the area hand. Its a NB-NMO. Which is my term for Neighborhood Bar - Not My Own.

2019 Update This is gone. Well, the people are gone. The building is still there, looking dingier everytime I drive past. As of 2017, it was listed for rent as a bar property. The listing was discontinued.

Stop #36 - The Nines

The Bar: The Nines

    The Address 136 Millbury Street

    The price 5.75

    Did they ask me if I wanted a lime She did.

    What was the type of gin As the always harried, always breathless bartender said to me in a whirlwind, "Will Tanqueray be okay. It's got to be okay, its the only gin we got." I told her that that would be fine. And then she was off trying to make it and keep her balance in her way too tight and way too short black dress.

    What was the gin and tonic like Like a Jersey barrier. I don't know what that means, but I feel I have to be colorful and obscure to hide the fact that I had an almost decent though dull drink. It was just there, directing traffic.

    The Joint Can I call this place odd? I can? Well this is an odd place. It has got some floor space. It presents as run down, but it's a spacious run down. There is a pool table in the back corner and it doesn't encroach on the proceedings. The thing that does encroach is the square shaped bar, with the booze in the middle. The poor bartender has to run laps in ever more desperate circles to get everyone their drinks. Let's talk about the bartender for a moment. She was nice and friendly, but she dressed like a suburban mother out in the big city ready to have a tawdry affair. She wore a very short black dress with a mesh back. This was so odd. I mean this is a borderline dive bar and she is dressed for clubbing. There were tired men drinking near me. On the other side of the bar are a gaggle of women talking loudly about husbands and boyfriends, pausing occasionally to have group toasts and cheers. Men were playing pool. A man and a women were talking about kids these days with the woman saying that if she ever had kids she wouldn't let her hypothetical daughter wear that kind of make-up. no sir.

General Impressions After several loud country songs, another song began to play from the speakers. A guy recognized the song from the first chord and stared anger at the bartender and said, "Who the fuck played this." A woman nearby said, "It wasn't me." Then the song started in earnest and there was the song, "What Does the Fox Say" in all its sublime glory. While listening to the song, I just looked at the people around the bar, and couldn't put the two things together. Though some of the women at the other side of the bar were singing along, maybe I know who picked it on the juke box. When the song was over, no music followed it. As if nothing was worthy to follow. As if everything was said, and let's just be quiet and drink our drinks.

Amount of Time in the Joint Fifteen minutes

Will I come back What does the tourist drinker say? No, no no no no no.

Stop #37 - Park Grill and Spirits

The Bar: Park Grill and Spirits

The Address 257 Park Ave

The price $5.35 (yeah, when you are in a "restaurant bar" I guess you get kooky prices.)

Did they ask me if I wanted a lime She did.

What was the type of gin It was just well gin, like I asked for.

What was the gin and tonic like It was filled with ice and good intentions. It was decent enough, nothing great, but I must say that 36 stops on the tour means a lot of bar gin has been consumed by your kindly Dante. I am beginning to dread that first sip. This was not great, but it was okay. For a nice summer's afternoon, it was alright.

The Joint I went into the bar area. The windows were open and the tables set up by them were occupied with folks taking in the sun and the nice day. They were eating. The bar had a few people as well, mostly people sitting by themselves eating and have a drink or two. One of the HiDef televisions was showing horse racing. Horse racing. What a surprising throwback, I was expecting people in fedoras chomping on unlit cigars furiously scribbling on this day's racing form. For me, I dug it. People drank beer and debated over what the next appetizer to order should be. There was a lot of good city air and mid day light that I had to contend with as I had my drink.

General Impressions: This tour is teaching me a lot about myself and things I like. First, I still like to go to bars, which is a pleasant discovery. But I don't like bars that has too much light. Actually, I like a well lit room so that I can read the paper or the menu, but I think its natural light coming from the open patio seating that I am against. I go to bars to leave the world behind, I don't want to see the world outside on the sidewalk of Park ave. This might just be me. Most of the people here on this 2:30 on a Saturday afternoon, were eating, either alone or in groups. Those eating alone were at the bar, natch. All in all, about 15 or so at the bar area. I just wanted to be further protected from the light and the world outside. What can I say, when it comes to bars, I am a classicist.

Amount of Time in the Joint 15 minutes

Will I come back Maybe, it was a comfy place, I can see myself getting some food and a beer at the bar if I was around. I would not be averse to that.

Stop #38 - Tweed's

The Bar: Tweed's

    The Address 229 Grove Street

    The Day and the TIme Monday at 8:45

    The price 6.95 (The print out said it was a 6.50 drink with 45 cents for the man)

    Did they ask me if I wanted a lime No, he just put it in

    What was the type of gin House, by request

    What was the gin and tonic like. Is gin lighter than tonic? I don't know much about bar physics. But this was one of those drinks that had more of a gin taste on top than it did on the bottom and I don't think that it had to do with the ice melting (at least, not a lot) It was harsh to start and then got alright. Like one of those layered drinks they say is soooooo easy to do at home, yeah right/ The gin and tonic certainly didn't impress me for a drink on the pricey end of the scale.

    The Joint This is a restaurant with a large bar. The bar was a long thin oval and the bartender had a lot of real estate to contend with, he did fine. There were 10 or 12 at the bar when I got there, but petered out as I went along, just like my drink. It had sports on the TVs. He had tired waitresses wandering to the bar, cashing out.

    I am getting to the end of the neighborhood and dive bar part of the tour (though some are still waiting for me) and now we turn the corner to bar-restaurants. There seems to be people who make these bar stools their own, so it is still a valid leg of the tour, but the feel is different. People are eating and talking, there are dates going on, there are bad day at the office wind downs. It just feels like I am on a different tour now, not bad, just different. The waitresses looked tired, so did the place.

    General Impressions It was mostly folks talking among themselves. I watched some baseball while trying to listen to what

I think was two young people having a date, or it was two friends out for a drink with one of them (the guy) hoping for a little bit more. They talked about missing college, one talked about the lousy job he had at his father's company. She talked about how she had to focus in life. Why do I think this was a date like thing? They both had the same colorful mixed drink. I guess that might be adorable when you are young and in lust, having the same drink, but as you get older and you want what you want and the hell with fruity drinks with umbrellas (for me, I will have a gin and tonic, thank you). I wanted to go over to the guy, when they ordered their second fruity concoction, and tell him no! No! don't do it, have your own taste, that is more attractive in the long run. Have a beer for god's sake. Get a whiskey neat! Do it, buddy. But of course I left before the end of the evening for those two was decided.

Amount of Time in the Joint 15 or 20 minutes

Will I come back No. The place didn't appeal to me too much. It wasn't a bad place, just didn't excite me. All that wood and that old feel. I was happy to check out a place I have never been, but if I ever came back it might be to try the food, not to settle down on a bar stool.

2019 Update I never did try that food, it closed. It is now another restaurant/bar. It is the Oaken Barrel. The place was pretty snappy when I got there, but it had the same bartender I had the first time when it was Tweeds. Like they always say, you can change the decor, but the bartender stays.

Stop #39 - Center Bar and Grill

The Bar: The Center Bar and Grill

    The Address 102 -106 Green Street

    The Day and the TIme Wednesday at 9pm

    The price Five dollars

    Did they ask me if I wanted a lime No, he did not, he just put it in and not only that, he gave me a wedge of lime and a wedge of lemon. This was unexpected and unprecedented. It was more than I ever imagined possible. This was the Donnie and Marie Show of gin garnishes (it is a little bit country and a little bit rock and roll).

    What was the type of gin I asked for whatever and got whatever.

    What was the gin and tonic like It was fine. It had that syrupy feel that a lot of bar gin has, but I liked all the citrus I got from the Donnie and Marie (I'm trying to make it a thing) It had too much ice, but it was a nice drink.

    The Joint This is a restaurant bar, but the restaurant section was closed shut, so we had a dark room with a relatively short bar. There was some people there and it was mostly a young crowd. Country music was blaring. There were some tables and they were taken up with couples in conversation. One set of women held on to the styrofoam leftovers containers from dinner while still talking and drinking. The bartender went up to two young women and cajoled them pleasantly into trying a shot, it was cherry, tasted good he assured them. They came in plastic cups.

    General Impressions This was an okay place where people meet and talk and drink and no doubt shout out "Whooooo" when a favorite song comes on the jukebox machine. There is a need for this young leaning bar, and this was a decent one. This might be a staging ground bar, where folk gather and plan what to do for the evening. A good receptive bartender and an adequate selection of spirits. Not my kind of place to settle roots in, but fine for what it is.

Amount of Time in the Joint 15 minutes

Will I come back No, not a slap on the face, just a statement of preference.

2019 Update This has a storied history of closure. We will discuss some of it later in the book because it closed and opened as something else. I reviewed it and then it was closed. These things move fast, baby.

Stop #40 - The Pleasant Cafe

The Bar: The Pleasant Cafe

    The Address 318 Pleasant Street

    The Day and the Time Sunday at 7:30

    The price 3.50

    Did they ask me if I wanted a lime He did and he took it out of a Tupperware in which it was hiding out and squeezed it in for me. I could almost hear the lime slice shout "They found me! They found me!"

    What was the type of gin He just made one for me with the only type of gin they had, which was Beefeaters.

    What was the gin and tonic like He made a very strong drink, though it was a small glass thankfully. It was not a bad gin. The decent brand helped of course. I drank it quickly (get out Dante get out) so the ice didn't have time to dilute it. Yes, the scariest dive I've been too had a fine drink of gin and tonic, tell the family.

    The Joint Wow. You want to know what a Dive bar is like, go here. Wait, don't go here. Just believe it without seeing, like faith. I was anxious walking in, but this silly little project I am doing is giving me more courage than I should have. I have to be at every bar in Worcester, and nothing is going to stop me. Yes. I know. I'm an idiot.

It is small, and cramped and dirty. I sat on a stool that was made during the year they discovered Naugahyde. There is a sign saying that all cash machines are emptied every night. There was no one present who walks erect, the weight of the place brings your shoulders down. By the time I finished my drink, I think I had a stoop. The bartender was fine and people left each other alone. A weathered woman sitting at a table picked country songs from the jukebox. She listened to them with stony stoicism. By the front door, shoved in a corner, was another jukebox machine. A dead one, last year's model. Even music is unplugged here.

General Impressions I was waiting for the dessicated corpse of Charles Bukowski to amble painfully into the joint and say, "My friends, get me a beer and a shot, fuckers." This is a place that would be better if you could smoke on premises. You would finish your days faster and see nothing past five feet from your nose.

There is a need in every city and town for a joint like this. People with broken backs and broken futures need a Purgatorio to sit and drink in. There might be times when this place is dangerous, it wasn't when I was there, just a place to wait for that damned bus that don't ever come no more.

Amount of Time in the Joint 10 minutes

Will I come back No. I hope I won't. No

Stop #41 - American Legion Post

The Bar: American Legion Post

   The Address 267 Providence Street

   The Day and the TIme Wednesday at 11:50 in the morning

   The price 2.50

   Did they ask me if I wanted a lime No and I didn't get one, but that's okay, because the guy had one arm and I was happy we finished the drink mixing transaction.

   What was the type of gin It was Gordon's but that was through some talking and bandiage. I was asked what I wanted and the bartender said, "Gordon's" and there was a loud jovial guy interrupted "Tanqueray, he wants tanqueray" and I quietly said, "Gordon's sounds good."

   What was the gin and tonic like: I don't think I ever had a one armed bartender before. Nothing wrong with that, just a new experience is all. He was slow and deliberate and at times I think he had a hard go of getting the caps off the gin (not used too much) and then he had to find some bottle of tonic to open and pour. It was a long process, not like I had anywhere to go, so patience was the sidecar of the day. He got the drink poured into a 10 ounce plastic cup and he laid it in front of me and happy I was. Because it was a fine gin and tonic. This is the kind of G and T I remember having when I was a teenager and my grandmother was offended that I never had a high ball so she made a drink for me and that was the drink I was having here. It was the right mix of ice, gin and tonic. Also, the guy put more effort in my cocktail than most other practitioners of the mixing arts, so it felt practically artisanal.

   The Joint: It's an American Legion Post with a large function room and a run down bar area. It was what you want it to be. There were only a few guys there when I went in. One of the tables had a few bottles of Pepsi on it. This is where three of them sat down to play hearts. I love a place where people sit down with a deck of cards to while the day away. There needs to be more places like this. Every bar needs several Bicycle decks ready for everyone to socialize and lose money.

General Impressions The day I came in I was wearing a fedora and the loud gregarious fellow saw me and said, "Elvis Costello has entered the building." I have rarely been mistaken for post-punk era musicians so I stopped and said, "Me?" I got a nod and I said, "Wrong accent." I was worried going into a social club like this, my first club on the tour, and I was concerned how I would be received. After that crack, I realized my presence was alright. I drank and watched the end of Price is Right. It was a laid back place. People spend time there, lives are lived there. They were older, they were welcome here. It was their place after all. I was just visiting. They were happy to see me enter and wave and drink and leave.

Amount of Time in the Joint 10 minutes

Will I come back Probably not. I liked it. I liked the guy giving me guff. I liked that there is a place to play cards and feel accepted. But I have other places to do those things for me.

2019 Update I am not quite sure, but I gave up on going to social clubs. I found it a little bit of a hassle, and who needs a hassle when all you want is one mixed drink? Some social clubs require you to be a member or come in with one. Others are difficult to locate.I wish I went to more, but I got to one and it was a good little visit.

Stop #42 - Ralph's Tavern

The Bar: Ralph's Tavern

> **The Address** 117 Shrewsbury Street
>
> **The Day and the TIme** Wednesday at 12:30 in the afternoon
>
> **The price** 5
>
> **Did they ask me if I wanted a lime** She did and i got it
>
> **What was the type of gin** It was a house gin
>
> **What was the gin and tonic like** It was alright. Nothing much to say for it. I got to say, I think that's the theme of this stop of the tour, there is nothing much to say. I sat down. I ordered a drink. I had a drink. I left. Nothing much else to say.......of course I will say more (it is my curse to do so)
>
> **The Joint** It looked out of place on Shrewsbury Street. The outside appeared as if it was a very nice hardware store, or a place where you can buy large rounds of cheese. It looked big on the outside but to go in, felt cramped and small, and there was not a lot of folk there at this afternoon time, and yet it felt like there was more bar and behind the bar than there was space for customers. It was designed like a square where the bar was the large and inevitable center of the universe. You all have to flock around the large bar, like a high school exercise in gravity and force of attraction. It is strange and off putting that the bar area for staff was more than the area for us thirsty rabble. The bartender was good enough, but the place just felt odd to me. Uninviting
>
> **General Impressions** The small band of merry regulars were talking and loud about it, they filled up the joint. One guy was going on about renting properties and heading off to a place in town he didn't know. Another guy put the address into his smart phone and kept on shouting out directions that the first guy, the realtor, seemed to ignore. They talked about what properties are being developed,

what ones are being ignored and how this town ain't the way it should be. You know, fellas at a bar. Jawing.

Amount of Time in the Joint 15 minutes

Will I come back No. It had a neighborhood vibe to it, but the sense of the place was just not right for me. It didn't feel like you could settle down and take root.

DAVID MACPHERSON

Stop #43 - Loft 266

The Bar: Loft 266

> **The Address** 266 Park Ave
>
> **The Day and the TIme** Friday at 8
>
> **The price** 5
>
> **Did they ask me if I wanted a lime** No, I just got one
>
> **What was the type of gin** It was well gin
>
> **What was the gin and tonic like** It was alright, just alright.

The Joint This used to be many things, but I remember from years back it being the Above Club. What a sad place I remember that being. No one there, ever. Its on a second floor and now its very schmancy. The center of the space is the bar and two women were tending, they were wearing black. I need to tell you this, because I was the only one not wearing black in the place. There were 10 people there and I had a red shirt on, I felt like an unbeliever to a cult I forgot to join. Black never goes out of style, but that's the kind of place this is, stylish, baby. Okay, just a little bit sarcastic.

A guy was in the corner with a guitar singing songs, I didn't recognize them so they were either originals or I should branch out from listening to the all Gregorian Chants station on my radio. He was fine and had a decent voice, he was the guy you talked over to have a conversation. Folks were having food, and they kept on coming in while I was there. All in black shirts (did I miss something in the invitation?) The place is clean and shiny. It has cool cat ambience. But to me, I didn't buy it.

General Impressions A group were talking at the end of the bar about working at the DCU Center and how there is nothing booked in the summer. Others were gathering to check folk out or be checked. The people coming in were well put together. The evening might have turned into a raucous bacchanal, with hook ups happening and glances gazed at. I couldn't shake how pre-fab, how constructed this place was. There was nothing organic here. I was sitting in a piece of marketing. But then my drink was done and so was I.

Amount of Time in the Joint 15 minutes

Will I come back No, I'm fine and have a nice day.

Stop #44 - El Basha

The Bar: El Basha

The Address 256 Park Avenue

The Day and the TIme Friday at 8:30

The price Well that should be an easy answer, but in this case, it was not exactly clear. I was sitting at the bar area, minding my business, thinking about world peace (like I do). And I noticed that I was across from the ordering computer. I noticed that all of the bar orders were up on the screen with the price included. (or I think it was) There was one that said Tanqueray and Tonic and showed a charge of seven dollars. That's fine, I wasn't expecting it to be less at such a swank joint. I thought seven got me off easy actually. When i was done I handed the bartender a ten dollar bill and told her I would be settling. She didn't tell me how much it was, but I saw it on the computer, seven bucks. She took a minute and returned with my change, two dollars. Wait. Stop. Two dollars? My math sucks, I thought I was going to get three dollars back. I guess I was wrong. I guess the computer was incorrect. Maybe it had a wrong price. Because I had an eight dollar drink, despite what the new fangled computer machine would tell me. I am sure that was it, that there was nothing else occurring that I need mention.

So the easy answer is eight dollars. And don't worry about computer screens and their false testimony.

Did they ask me if I wanted a lime She did not, she just put it in. Bliss

What was the type of gin Tanqueray, that was the standard at El Basha, baby.

What was the gin and tonic like It was good. Not too strong, but also, I tasted the gin, and Tanqueray is a nice one. I know it doesn't have street cred anymore, but still, fine gin.

The Joint It is a lovely, clean, restaurant. It's fancy. The food smelled wonderful. The people eating were laughing and talking loud, it was a friendly restaurant. The bar area was divided in two, with a walk space in the middle for wait staff. It was a little cramped, but still good. When I sat down two women were next to me finishing their plates and lingering over their wine. There were others eating and drinking. The bartender looked tired and was a little hassled. She seemed put down by the man. One party in the back was very boisterous and were ordering more drinks.

General Impressions: On this tour of all the bars of Worcester, I am now only entering into the bars of restaurants. It is a different animal. There are different expectations of what the bar will do for you. This is a place for a few drinks with friends, some nice baba ganoush, a good wine, not to play darts and hit on the girl at the pool table. Under these guidelines, the place is good, it does its job. It is inviting, though I felt a little too close to the moving of wait staff and hot plates at the bar area. But that's just the nature of the beast.

If I had a complaint, it was the bartender and her friend. Near the end of my stay there, a young man sat next to me. The bartender opened up to him like fresh bread. They were good friends it seemed. And to him she complained on how tired she is, how bored she is, how she wished she was with him, hanging out and not working. And I got to say, "I can hear you." I can hear that you don't want to be here, but yet, I am your customer, paying for an 8 dollar gin and tonic, pretend that you like being here. Going out, having a drink, it's a show, it's a song and dance. The least you can do as the bartender is try to sing along, at least as long as I'm in listening range.

Amount of Time in the Joint 25 minutes.

Will I come back Yes, but not to the bar. I have eaten at one of the other El Bashas and its great. This place has a cool feel, sophisticated. I was a little put off by the bartender, so that's fine, I will just get a table instead.

Stop #45 - Anokye Krom

The Bar: Anokye Krom

    The Address 687 Millbury Street

    The Day and the TIme 2 on a Sunday afternoon

    The Story When I first came up with this tour, it was to find a reason to visit every bar in Worcester. The first idea was to write a Haiku in every bar in Worcester. I know, awful idea. But I came up with a worse one. Why don't I pick a ubiquitous drink, one you can get everywhere, and judge the experience from this commonality. I picked a gin and tonic. One, because I like gin and tonics and will find myself ordering them on occasion. And two, and most importantly, because every bar has gin and tonic water. You can get it everywhere. There is no bar in Worcester without these powers. I can go into any bar or bar restaurant in town and get this drink they call a gin and tonic. Well.

I was wrong. I went to the bar restaurant that could not do it.

I have driven by Anokye Krom almost every day since it opened. Never stopped in. But the bar I was planning on doing for the tour was closed, so I scrambled. I saw a bunch of cars parked around the restaurant, figured they were open. I guessed it was worth seeing if they had a bar. It didn't hurt to walk in and see.

It is one of the places that feels bigger than the outside would have you guess. It is brightly lit, with tables on one side and a small bar with 10 or so stools on the other. Their floor was set with large black white squares and a little girl, in Sunday best, was jumping hopscotch on them. Most of the tables were filled and the food smelled enticing. Lots of spices. The bowls were large and people were talking and laughing, shouting across the room at each other, and eating, they were doing that.

The bar had a small selection of liquor but one of them was a big bottle of Gordon's Gin. I am in! A few men were at the bar watching the first Patriots game of the season. Someone got up and shouted that I should take his seat. How could I refuse? I got the bartender's attention and told her I would like a gin and tonic and she replied, even before I was finished, with "We don't have that." I pointed to the gin and said, "Well there's gin." She asked about tonic, she didn't know what tonic was. Then I made my mistake. I said, "Soda, soda water." Yeah.

In a few minutes she poured a glass with some gin in it, and then brought over a can of Coca-Cola. "This?" she asked. What do my useless rules of this tour say about situations like this? I nodded and she spoiled the gin with coke. Yes. I drank it. It tasted as good as you would expect, but I drank it. Paid seven bucks for it to. Call it a tithing.

Luckily, I had two gregarious guys near me, talking with me, taking my mind off my drink. They asked me about the game and they were loud and funny. One was a Jets fan and wanted the Pats to lose (he got his wish). They were good company. They kept calling me boss, which made me a wee uncomfortable. One of them left and I talked to the other. His sister is the bartender and he said if I come with my wife I should have the chicken and rice. He, and most everyone here, is from Ghana. I noticed that every guy there was drinking Guinness, so I ordered one of those when my gin and coke was done (I needed to clean my palette). I chatted with him for a bit, watched the game and had a very nice time.

I do want to go back, but only to drink Guinness and try the food. Its funny that one of the worst drinks gave me a nice experience. Who knew?

Stop #46 - Ho Toy Luau Restaurant

The Bar: Ho Toy Luau Restaurant

The Address 401 Park Avenue

The Day and the TIme Wednesday at 4pm

The price 6.70

Did they ask me if I wanted a lime No, she put it in like mind reading.

What was the type of gin Well

What was the gin and tonic like It was strong. This is my first Chinese restaurant bar and I have heard that the drinks at these places can be alcohol intensive, and this made the case well. It was okay, but it felt a little like drinking aromatic lighter fluid.

The Joint I really was excited about going into this one, because I passed it for years, never seeing anyone enter or leave it. It was just this Pagoda fixture on Park Ave. So I went in and in front of me were old school red leather booths for diners, making me feel like the characters of Glen Gary Glen Ross were going to show up and start swearing in a majestically poetic manner. But my destination was to the right, the cocktail lounge. It felt like a waiting room. Kind of tight and a little shabby. There were boxes and supplies at one side (which is one of my turn-offs, please make the bar not feel like the broom closet, if you don't mind). The bar was alright, but it had a real neutral-cum-bland feel.

General Impressions This is the tough part of the tour I am on. I don't have the time or inclination to make it to the bars at times that might be their big traffic moments. Sometimes I come at off times and no one is there, so I am left with a conundrum: should I come back when it is more like itself or should I just go in and see what an off-time is like at the joint. I still don't have the answer to that. With this place, I stopped in three times, during afternoons and one early evening and saw that it was empty. The first two times, I said, I want this place to be at its best and left without stepping into the bar area. But this, the third time, I stuck my head in and said, the hell with it, I know there is only one guy at the bar, but let's get this one done and off the list.

Of course, the minute I walked in, the other guy at the bar walked out for a smoke. He was smoking his cigarette for the entirety of my stay there at Ho Toy. Leaving me alone with the bartender who was not mean or surly, but certainly not friendly, goodness no. Let us call her efficient. I watched a few minutes of Law and Order: SVU. I hate Law and Order:SVU. So the drink I had was infused with my dislike for the TV program that I was staring at.

I tried to imagine it crowded. Six o'clock on a Friday? Ten on Saturday? I don't know. I was alone with possibilities I was not offered. I am sure those happy people would be drinking Mai Tais and Scorpion Bowls. But how much of a bar is that happy raucous time and how much is the time I was sitting in? The dead time? The too early for fun time? Where are all the good time kids and where have they gone to now? If Purgatory is a real place, it would be like this waiting room shaped bar in an empty Chinese Restaurant at four o'clock in the middle of the week, in the middle of the State.

Amount of Time in the Joint 10 minutes

Will I come back: I don't know, I don't think so. Definitely not for the bar, and I have gone 15 years not eating at this restaurant, I probably can extend my streak of absenteeism.

2019 Update Ho Toy closed up last year and another Asian restaurant has been getting ready to take over and show the world how it is done. As of this writing, they are still boasting the "Coming Soon" sign.

Stop #47 - The Canal Bar and Grill

The Bar: The Canal Bar and Grill

The Address 65 Water Street

The Day and the Time Tuesday at Nine

The Price This was a process, there were three young women behind the bar, all with Russian accents, and one got me the drink and then stared at the order screen and then she disappeared. I took out my money and waited, and waited. By my watch it was 5 minutes before another woman with a very thick accent asked me what I had. I told her and through another long process she told me the drink was seven dollars. I gave her a ten dollar bill, and she gave me three dollars and a quarter for change. 3.25 change. Man, I just don't understand the new math one bit.

Did they ask me if I wanted a lime No, bartenderess number one did not ask me and I did not get one.

What was the type of gin I don't know, I think the type of gin was called tonic only.

What was the gin and tonic like Either she forgot to put the gin in or this was the most anemic weak ass gin and tonic I have ever had. Now readers of this tour through the levels of bar hell know that I am not a fan of overly alcoholic gin and tonics. I look on in horror when I just see gin and gin and gin poured into that pint glass of doom. I wonder how the hell will I stand after this, and why the hell am I going into every bar in Worcester and doing this to myself. But I am going out and getting an alcoholic beverage, and would like enough of it in the drink to taste it.

It was a tonic water.

The Joint It is a basement joint, which always is good in my book, but this is one schizophrenic place. There were college kids talking to the Russian bartenders at a small bar area. And down the hall was another world entirely in an exposed stone room that felt like it would be great for storing and aging cheese.. There was a folk open mic. I know. Run. Run fast and hard. But don't stop running. I kid. Its nice that this Folk-n-A is still going after so many years. I am glad they found a place to settle. But its a bunch of old people with guitars doing covers. It doesn't bring in the crowds. And the way that the college kids stuck to the small bar in the other room was telling.

General Impressions: There was enough weirdness that made me uncomfortable. The space felt like an old speakeasy but the happy go lucky bartenders didn't gibe. One tried to get me into small talk about football, but didn't know the terms. It took her three times of stating something before I realized what sport she was going on about. It's nice they have music, I hope that helps them. But I had a weak or non existent drink and I waited over five minutes to pay for that drink and had to go through two bartenders to do so.

Amount of Time in the Joint 20 Minutes

Will I come back No. What I said above.

2019 Update It closed last year. Only this year did a restaurant take its place. It is now an Italian joint named Russo"s. A friend ate there and said it was good.

Stop #48 - The Blarney Stone

The Bar: The Blarney Stone

The Address 79 Maywood Street

The Day and the TIme Friday at 3:45

The price 3 dollars

Did they ask me if I wanted a lime No, he just put it in

What was the type of gin It was industrial strength jet fuel. Yeesh

What was the gin and tonic like Well this one tasted of gin I can tell you. The bar I went to before, the Canal Bar and Grill, I was not sure if I got any alcohol. This one left little doubt. I like a bar that doesn't have time for subtlety.

The Joint Surprisingly roomy. The bar took up the center, though there was plenty of room around it. There were darts and games and what not. There was keno and sports. There was a taped paper saying that they had jello shots, as well as other oddly named concoctions that you can partake in a shot glass. It was a bar. It had 10 or so guys, probably just off of jobs. They had muscles and sleeves of tattoos. They swore a lot. The word fuck was the secret ingredient for this episode.

General Impressions Thank goodness for this place. For a stretch, I have had lame and dull experiences on this tour. I wasn't going to give it up, but I was wondering if I was ever to speak highly of a bar again. This felt like a bar. It acted like one too. The guys were loud and happy to be there. The bartender was chatting with regulars. People were drinking affordable beers and shots. They were bunkering down for a long night of it. I had almost forgotten this flushed camaraderie that bars can have. In my work clothes, I certainly stuck out, but there was no problem with that. I was just another person looking to have a drink, maybe play some keno.

Amount of Time in the Joint 15 minutes

Will I come back Probably not, but man, I am happy to have gotten here when I did. I needed this dose of bar-ness that the Blarney Stone had.

Stop #49 - Ken Chin's

The Bar: Ken Chin's

    The Address 272 Mill Street

    The Day and the TIme Friday 3:45

    The price 5.50

    Did they ask me if I wanted a lime She did

    What was the type of gin Well

    What was the gin and tonic like It was in a classic highball glass and it tasted sweet, but it was good. I enjoyed it. I almost wished it was in the big pint glass, but the size was fine and there is something nice about having a highball drink in a highball glass. I know, that's so twee of me, but the shape of the glass works in the hand.

    The Joint I wanted to go here because someone told me that this place was crazy. It has its regulars and they all eat the special which I hear is an egg roll with cheese in it. My friend told me it was one of the strangest places in Worcester. I think I came at the wrong time for that (I know, story of this tour) but what I got was interesting and good enough, so I forgive myself for my off-peak meanderings.

The layout for the cocktail lounge area is a little odd. That's not to say that it doesn't have a good cocktail lounge feel, with a long bar and booths behind, it does. Its just that this seems to be a Keno-centric place (or at least those that were present were Keno folk) and the Keno machine was not in the bar area. It looks like the rule is that you fill out your keno card and then you have to walk out of the cocktail lounge to the front reception desk to process the bet. What made it doubly odd is that the bartender was also the front of the restaurant person. So someone would fill out their Keno and slowly walk the length of the bar to the front of the restaurant and as they did so, the bartender would leave out a side door and take care of the transaction and then come back to the bar. It was like a long walk of shame, but with bad bets.

Two big screens had sports on, but the focus was on the screen to the side, the Keno. About five or so were there at this hour. One guy was not playing Keno, he was just slowly drinking beer, not looking at anyone, just working the bottle slowly.

General Impressions: I felt like I was in a Edward Hopper painting. People sat still and the lighting brought out that isolated in public feel. Hell, I felt myself go unmoving, I was frozen in place. The title of this work is: Still Life with Gambling Sheets.

One of the people had food and she was eating at a pace, saying she will never finish all this food. Everyone who talked didn't seem to move their mouths, it was like life sized puppets. One person commented "Where is everyone? Its empty here?" The other one responded, "Its early, its not even four." Time is fragile here. With all that, the sitting and not moving, was comforting, there was nothing odd about this slowed down world.

As I was leaving, the bartender (who I was told later was one of the owners) saw my progress and said, "Taking off?" I must say how charmed I was by the question. Who says that anymore? Taking off? You bet, I'm flying, I'm scraping tree tops. It was a friendly way to be in a such place.

Amount of Time in the Joint: 20 minutes or 17 hours, it's hard to tell when you are visiting The Cocktail Lounge Zone. I was almost expecting Rod Serling to show up behind the buffet table and give an outro.

Will I come back: You know, I might. I can see myself going for the Jimmy Chin special. I can see myself killing an afternoon at the lounge like it was a minute.

Stop #50 - The Kas Bar

The Bar: The Kas Bar

The Address 234 SW Cutoff

The Day and the TIme Monday at Five (this was a Holiday Monday)

The price 4.75

Did they ask me if I wanted a lime She did

What was the type of gin Well

What was the gin and tonic like Just a run of the mill, though kind of a strong drink.

The Joint Big roadhouse. I could believe Patrick Swayze as Dylan in the classic film would show up. There were pool tables, there was a good sized bar. Tables around the bar that gave it a pushed in feeling. The pool tables helped with that cramped feeling, which is odd in such a large place. They did have a big ballroom where bands play, though it was deserted when I was there. It has a lived in look, which is not to say it is dirty and messy, but it certainly was not pristine and orderly.

General Impressions It all seemed loud and drunken, which is interesting to note because there weren't too many people in at the time. The three playing pool would lean over to the bar and get a few shots. Shots were important, so were huge jumbo steins you could fill with beer. The bar felt like someone who had a crazy time of it the night before and didn't bother changing yesterday's clothes or do more than a cursory combing of the hair and a good breath check. That's how the bar felt. Unkempt, a little tired, but ready for the night and the possibility of shouting out Whooooo! at random people. The pool tables were very close to the path from the door to the bar and I had to walk through the game players to leave, it felt cramped for a place with a giant ballroom.

I guess this might be a good time to talk about pool tables. In my tour, I have come across 15 or 20 bars with pool tables. This is only the second time I have seen people using them. In a place like Kas Bar, it is fine, but a small place, it takes up a lot of room. In this case even, it impeded my flow to the important things, the bar with the booze. At another bar, I was talking to Saloon Owner Salvatore and he said he's against pool tables in small bars. He did comment that he has a pool table in one of his bars, his largest one, and it is a money maker. It makes money without any true work on his part. I mentioned that it took up a lot of space, and he agreed. I said wouldn't dart boards be better when it comes to space, and he shook his head, and said, "You don't make money on darts. You do on pool." Okay, more on Sal when he joins the tour for the next two bars, but for now, that's enough side talk.

Amount of Time in the Joint 15 minutes.

Will I come back Probably not. It is not my place, but how nice that there is enough variety in town that there is a true road house bar around. For those who want that feel, this might be a good place for them.

Stop #51 - Guertin's

The Bar: Guertin's

The Address 139 Grand Street

The Day and the TIme Saturday at 6:30

The price 4

Did they ask me if I wanted a lime No. I got gin. I got tonic. I got a glass. Should I expect such additional amenities? I don't think so.

What was the type of gin It was Tanqueray. This is a nice drink for the price.

What was the gin and tonic like: It was strong, but not too strong. Not a bad gin and tonic. My friend Sal was sitting next to me and said "Watch this" as it was being poured. The bartender gave me a couple inches of gin and then stopped. Sal said, "Last time we were here, the bartender didn't stop there, the booze went almost to the top of the glass. You're lucky."

The Joint When I first started this tour, my friends Saloon Owner Salvatore and Chanteuse Cheryl said I had to go to Guertin's. It is a great old bar, but I shouldn't go alone. As Sal said to me, "A lot of the bad bars in the area closed, so all those bad people go to Guertin's." That might not be nice of them to say, but I went to Pleasant Cafe by myself and I survived. Going to solo to Guertin's would have been fine, but company is always swell to have. They pointed out the great old touches of the joint, like the stainglass above the bar that seemed to have patch work penis type shapes in them. (Always a conducive sight to heavy drinking) Sal was upset that they had taken out some of the other old time touches, and put in a space devouring pool table. The bar is long and solid, its a nice place to lean against with a drink. With all these new improved detriments, the place has a great old saloon charm. I liked being there.

"You should check out the bathroom" Sal said to me. This is never something I want to be told at a dive bar (or most other places for that matter). But who I am to say no? I went in and instead of urinals there was that old style communal trough, the kind made of porcelain. Sal had a story about the bathroom here. A long time ago he was here having a few drinks with a friend who waitressed at another bar. This was the first time the friend was in Guertin's. He told her he was going to use the men's room, and that it was something to see. She said she wanted to see it then. She went in, looked around and began to lay down in the trough. She stretched out in it, she made poses in it. Afterwards, Sal was amazed, he said he couldn't believe she laid down in the urinal. The girl was aghast, that was a urinal she asked. She thought it was a bathtub.

General Impressions: There was loud people at the bar, one woman in particular was so loud I lost the conversation I was having with Cheryl and Sal. Two guys started raising voices at each other, but that soon subsided. As we were there, a handful of folk became more boisterous as the evening progressed. This was before Halloween so people were supposed to come in costume. A couple came in as a gangster and a moll. I am fascinated with costume parties at bars. That this is the place you want to dress up as a zombie in, or a naughty meter maid. This is the safe place for you to embrace your inner Gilligan or Skipper.

It was fun being there. It felt like a bar. It was loud like a bar. Too bad about the pool table though, it did eat up the floor. There was a sense of danger, of possible violence. But I have seen worse on this tour. Actually, the only bar fight I have ever witnessed was at a TGIFridays, so what's really wrong with a bar with true style?

Have I said recently that I am loving being on this tour? I never even heard of this bar before I started my gin and tonic quest, let alone gone to look for and enter it. There are people who call it home, some I might not want to hang out with, but it has enough personality to make people call it their bar, their place. Isn't that worth celebrating and discovering? It was also great to celebrate my 50th bar with friends. They asked if I had been to George's the bar attached to Coney Island Hot Dog. I told them I had not. Can you guess what will be the 51st bar on the tour?

Amount of Time in the Joint 30 minutes

Will I come back I don't think so, but I could be arm twisted into a late afternoon drink with someone interested. The place was kind of cool. Glad to have gone, but I can imagine never returning there. I am sure they will miss my company desperately.

2019 Update The "Will I come back" section of these entries is such utter rubbish. I say I will come back and never even give the bar a thought. And this one, Guertin's, a place I said I never would return to ? I was there several times. There was a year where I found myself in the area and would drink here or at Marty's or sometimes at Breen's. Guertin's is a nice solid bar to spend some afternoons in. So read these entries with a measure of caution and a jigger of gin.

Stop #52 - George's

The Bar: George's (this is the bar side of Coney Island Hot Dog)

The Address 158 Southbridge St

The Day and the Time Saturday at 7:30

The price 5

Did they ask me if I wanted a lime No. No Lime.

What was the type of gin It was well.

What was the gin and tonic like Okay. This feels like a beer place, not that mixed drinks are against the rules here, it just feels like you should order a Bud with your food.

The Joint Coney Island Hot Dog has two doors, one for the general public, and one for the general public that wants to enter into a small bar area. There is a small bar and there are booths behind it. Like the rest of the place, there is a wonderful lived in look. The bar area has newer, less carved up booths, but they have these great old art deco like paintings. Its gives it an old school grace to it. We were waited on by a guy who works both side, the dogs side and the bar side. It really feels that the bar is an afterthought, but a nice afterthought. Other people were in the bar, but they were all eating hotdogs and drinking soft drinks or chocolate milks. So this ain't a place that's Hard Drinks for Hard Living Folk. It just feels like an extension of the hot dog restaurant, but with the possibility for alcohol.

General Impressions I was with my Virgils, Saloon Owner Salvatore and Chanteuse Cheryl, and they are great company. Of course coming into this place by yourself is pretty good company as well. It really is an arms wide open joint. I had my gin and tonic and even broke my rule and had food, a grilled cheese. The place is great. Its not a hang out all night and discuss the inner worked of life join (They close at nine)t, but for a beer and some food, it's great. Sal and Cheryl seem to know everyone and several people came up and chatted with them. My one regret is that it is not open later than nine.

Amount of Time in the Joint 30 minutes or so

Will I come back This is almost not fair. I have come here for years with my son. He loves it. I try not to tell him this is where he and I will have lunch, I let it be a surprise, and he is happy every time we wind up here. This just adds another way to enjoy, sans son. I can see myself coming in with a friend for a beer and a dog as we head some place else. It has to be that way, because it does close so damned early. Sal told me that he would always come here for a drink after going to the Registry for Motor Vehicles. This was his blow off steam place after wrestling such bureaucracy. This is a real, dinner and a beer place, not a beer with some food. But you got to love the paintings, and the booths and the years it holds. And the sign, every person should have a drink and a dog just so you can walk under that amazing neon sign. Am I gushing? I guess I'm gushing. Ah the hell with it, I am so gushing, and happy to have this place in town.

Stop #53 - Electric Haze

The Bar: Electric Haze

    The Address 26 Millbury Street

    The Day and the Time Saturday at 8:40

    The price 7.50

Did they ask me if I wanted a lime He just put it in. A very thinly sliced piece, it was more a concept of a lime than an actual one

    What was the type of gin: Bombay Sapphire. No really. Very posh don't you think. He asked which one I wanted and I said (I didn't say well, because it didn't feel like the place where you say that I want well, this is a high endish place) I just said the basic. He asked if Bombay was okay and I said sure. Then he looked at the gin bottle that was in the bar well and asked again, Bombay Sapphire? I said sure. Say what you want about this Dante of Worcester, but I am one accommodating tourist.

    What was the gin and tonic like It was a 12 ounce glass and it was good. Very aromatic, as you would expect from Bombay Sapphire.

    The Joint It has exposed brick, which is always a plus in my estimation. Their bar is in the back, and there are comfortable seating areas for people to do the hooka. There is a large stage and when I got there, a celtic band was tuning up. What the hell? Will I ever get to a bar late enough for the fun to be happening? But on closer inspection, I was okay with this because in ten minutes of me coming they started getting a seven dollar cover charge, so it all worked out.

There was art on the walls but none of strong interest and all hung in a haphazard fashion, so much so that I noticed it. People were sitting in groups of twos or threes in comfortable chairs, talking about serious topics and smoking the hooka. Wow, let me just say that typing the phrase "smoking the hooka" is up there on fun things to type. You should try it.

A guy was at the bar reading a library book of Borges. How cool. Borges at a bar. Well, at a hooka bar, but still Borges. He wrote a lot of the labyrinths, both real and imagined and I had an epiphany that this tour of gin and tonics is a strange Borges Like Labyrinth, all the turns and twists and lime wedges, all the possibilities that one highball drink can provide. These were my thoughts as I wandered around the room waiting for the fun to begin, just checking out the scenery.

And then there was the giant sperm hanging from the ceiling.

This is not a very fair comment about an art piece, but I don't know what else to call it. It is a giant sperm. It is a large, three or so feet in diameter, sculpture made of thin plastic tube that changes color when light passes through it. The plastic wire like tube is twisted and entwined making a big circle with a tail. There is a light source with alternating colored filters by the tail which gives the sculpture changing colors. Big glob with tail hanging from the top of the joint. Its a big ass sperm. I would not want to have the chair underneath that. No one but me seemed bothered by this, everyone else was talking, smoking hooka,drinking beers; they were living in ignorance of the encroaching giant plastic sperm attack (call Hollywood, we have their new blockbuster).

General Impressions I feel very snarky about this place. Like I just want to shoot barbs at it, but I have to say, the staff were so nice and friendly. They were happy to chat and ask how my drink was, they made sure everyone got what they wanted. I'm sure they even had a helpful plan in case the giant sperm went rogue and started attacking the paying customers. They were that nice.

And yet the smoke headache was coming and the sense of being thrust in the middle of a participatory theater piece gave me panic. Its a happening and a bar! It was a strange coolness endurance test: how hip can you be before you rip off your corduroy clothing and run screaming into the cold darkness singing Free Bird at the top of your lungs?

Amount of Time in the Joint 20 minutes

Will I come back No. Hooka bars are not my thing. I had a headache from my time there. This is not to say that it was a bad place, perhaps a little hoity for my useless tastes, but those are my tastes and who ever has listened to me? I must say that the staff were the friendliest I have ever encountered, and that goes for a lot in my book. Not enough to return, but a lot nonetheless.

Stop #54 - The Compass Tavern

The Bar: The Compass Tavern

    The Address 90 Harding Street

    The Day and the Time Friday at four

    The price 5.50

    Did they ask me if I wanted a lime She just put it in, I like this trend.

    What was the type of gin Well

    What was the gin and tonic like Kind of like the bar, not too bad but slightly generic.

    The Joint This used to be a big ass Italian restaurant, and then a big Barbeque restaurant, now it is two bar areas. One has a clubby feel, the other a hyper extended Irish bar. Both felt a little set decorated, but still, friendly staff, and space to breathe in, way too much space to breathe, I was feeling light headed.

The bar was only two weeks past opening when I got there, so I hope it finds its people. Find those who want to call this home. At that moment, there was me and about five guys who knocked off work early. You can't make a homefront out of folk like us, but it's a start.

    General Impressions Oh, the dread of trying to get a sense of a place when it is empty. I don't know, its two large rooms. In the larger one, the bar is huge. Good luck to the bartender running around if it gets busy. This place is designed to be busy, it doesn't feel right when it is just you and five other people. Its like you are in an airplane hanger with a liquor license when its empty. When it is full, maybe it will have something fun. I am sure it would be loud. Its funny, I don't think I would enjoy myself if this place was packed, but I also felt it was pretty lonely and not too comforting with it quiet. Ah well, the great conundrum of this exercise.

I felt lonely. I wanted to see people. I wanted something to occur. I am sure that it would, but I was moving on.

Amount of Time in the Joint 15 minutes

Will I come back:I think no. Even if it was busy and filled, the place is so big that there would be no room to move and that would be its own problem as well. But I don't know. I mean this place is brand new, infant pink and unfinished. Maybe it will turn into something great and unforgettable. Maybe. Here's hoping.

Stop #55 - Scorz

The Bar: Scorz

The Address 58 Shrewsbury Street

The Day and the TIme Four o'clock or so on a Sunday afternoon, a bit before the Pats game.

The price Six

Did they ask me if I wanted a lime She didn't ask and I didn't get one.

What was the type of gin It was Gilberts, which is the standard rot gut you see around, but with that said......

What was the gin and tonic like What makes this the worst tasting gin and tonic I have had on this tour? I do not know. But it was foul. Bad gin? Flat tonic? Bad room that altered my taste buds? The funny part is a guy sitting next to me asked me what kind of gin it was and Gilbert's was mentioned. He asked me how it was, and in the nature of this exercise, where I always agree and say yes, I said it was fine. No problems. The bartender said, there really is no difference, they all taste the same. To myself, I must beg to disagree with that bar professional.

The Joint This used to be a desert place where you would find small rooms and anterooms to truly enjoy your coffee and tiramisu. But as a sport bar, its odd baby, it's odd. There is no cohesion to the place, lots of little space, cramped and filled with big leather furniture. For a sports bar an hour before the team was to play on the TV Screen Machines, it was kind of dead. Dead like the Halloween decorations from the party of the weekend before. The decorations making it look more like a construction sight than as a fun house of horror. The bar was kind of small and propped up in a corner. The bartender seemed bored. Me too.

General Impressions I have asked this before, but what is a sports bar? I came across one later on this leg of the tour, but it wasn't at this address. But here at Scorz, with the quiet volume TVs and the dour hunched people at the bar, I wondered. Where were the people dressed in Patriots blue? The bartender was wearing a fuzzy sweater, that is not sports bar. The people were talking amongst themselves and not shouting angry and jubilant at the TV. That is not sports bar. Some weirdo was sitting at the bar having a well booze gin and tonic while making mental notes for a future blog post. That is so not sports bar.

To me, I think a sports bar is a big open space to have a gathering of like minded idiots (in a good way) to drink beer and shout and cheer and swear. To show pride in your team. It is not a dark bar with a confused floor plan. You want a place where you are part of the game, because how can the Pats win if we are not at a bar 50 miles away shouting our lungs out? Now granted, the Pats game had not started,.but shouldn't we be buzzing with vicarious excitement and dread? Shouldn't we be bubbling? Not. Just talking about bad gin and long nights. That is not sports bar.

Amount of Time in the Joint 10 minutes

Will I come back No. It was nice to go here to see what a sports bar should not be so that I could compare it to a good one, which is coming in two more stops of the tour. This is the place to remind yourself what it shouldn't be.

2019 Update: It did not last another year. It was empty for a spell and now it is an eclectic neighborhood bar called the Pint.

Stop #56 - The Shisha Room

The Bar: The Shisha Room

The Address 86 Shrewsbury Street.

The Day and the TIme Sunday at 4

The price This is kind of odd. I paid ten buck for it. The itemized bill showed seven dollars for gin, one dollar for tonic, sixty cents for tax and a dollar forty for an automatic gratuity. This makes it the most expensive gin and tonic I have had on this tour. (Settle your bets, we have a winner! For now!)

Let me stop and say, one dollar for tonic? How much tonic did I have? Was this specially grown quinine? I think he would have been better off not having the tonic line itemed on the bill, let me live in wonder, I always say.

Did they ask me if I wanted a lime He didn't and I didn't

What was the type of gin I don't know, just what every gin they had.

What was the gin and tonic like It was fine. Nothing really memorable. For the price, you would expect it to be outstanding, but everything seems very pricey here. When I went to Electric Haze, another Hooka Bar, I was shocked to see the bowls of tobacco were sixteen bucks, I was aghast, but then I saw that here they were 23 bucks and a gratuity was automatically included, so it all went into perspective.

The Joint What is it with Shrewsbury Street bars, hooka and otherwise, with all their large, black leather furniture? Out of five places I have been on Shrewsbury Street, three of them had these same clunky couches and chairs. At the first meeting of the Shrewsbury Street Business Association, does a senior member tell them to get these man cave rumpus room pieces of furniture? "The customers love it, you won't go wrong." The place is well named, it felt like a room. It didn't have a strong presence. An extended living room or den where you can smoke your very expensive smoke, and don't worry about the tip, they got that covered.

Its a small place, made smaller from the big leather apparel. The bar/hooka area is a camped little space in the back where he mixes drinks and sets up smokes. I sat in a couch watching sports while I was here. I felt quite enveloped in the couch.

General Impressions: I was not planning on going in when I did, my plan was to hit a few sports bars on Shrewsbury Street. As I walked by the Shisha room I saw men, about 10 or so playing backgammon. This is not typical of a bar, so I had to enter. The guy working the bar/hooka staging area told me that this was a group of guys who booked the room this Sunday for a backgammon tournament. They were all just finishing up and they had used one set of couches to pile their coats and plastic bags on all higgely piggely, kind of added to the unkempt living room effect. The backgammon guys were not drinking or smoking, just playing. One game was still going on with one player quiet and steely and the other loud, real loud, shouting out every time he made a move. It was like they were playing two different games.

I had my drink, felt nothing about the place, I am sure on a weekend night, it could be something alright, but it didn't feel much to me. Also, the most expensive drink on the tour.

Amount of Time in the Joint 10 or 15 minutes, not long.

Will I come back No. If I had to choose between the Hooka Bars I have been to on the tour, it would be Electric Haze, but please, don't make me choose. How many more Hooka Bars do I have to do?

Stop #57 - Parkway Restaurant and Bar

The Bar: Parkway Restaurant and Bar

The Address 148 Shrewsbury Street

The Day and the Time Four on a Sunday

The price 6.75.

Did they ask me if I wanted a lime No, he put it in, with no problem all by himself. The clever lad.

What was the type of gin He was looking for well drink, like I asked, and he shrugged and took out the Tanqueray. That was nice. I got a better drink out of convenience!

What was the gin and tonic like It was good, I liked it. It had a kick but it had flavor. But let's be fair and true here, I liked being at this place, and surprise surprise surprise (say that like Gomer Pyle) I liked the drink. Like the place-like the drink. Coincidence?

The Joint This is a clean, straight forward restaurant with an el shaped bar. The tables are basic, so are the chairs. The walls have sports memorabilia on it. It looks like a basic diner style joint, because brother it is a basic diner. And that's good. There is nothing here you haven't seen in a bunch of other places, but those other places are probably where you like going for breakfast or lunch. This is a place to drink as well, this joint swiss army knifes!

General Impressions A sports bar! A sports bar! A sports bar! What a joy to see a decent exemplar of the idea. Yeah, its a diner restaurant, but what a nice thing. People were here to see the Pats play the Broncos and they were all invested and happy and wearing the correct colors, there was no Denver orange in this place, bucko. A couple stops on the tour ago I was at Scorz, and I thought that that was not a good sports bar, but I couldn't say exactly what the key points of good sports barness could be. I now have a good one to compare and contrast with. When I got in there, the Patriots and Broncos game was getting close to start. There were three people working the bar, all in official Pats gear. The bar was mostly full. The tables had groups getting pitchers and food. They were busy, but there was no wait time for my drink. All the people at the tables were sitting in a way to see the screens behind the bar. There was shouting and talking and a general feeling of goodwill. The bartenders were good and attentive, even though they had no slack time.

Everyone here was present for one thing, to have a good time. And this group had decided that a good time was gathering here, in a brightly lit space, with room enough to sit and stand, to watch a game and shout together. To triumph together, to (we hope not) lose and blame the team together. It was a raucous welcome.

Amount of Time in the Joint 20 minutes

Will I come back You bet. A good time. The food looked good. The staff were on their game and the place was open and fun. I guess the real clue to how I felt was that I debated staying, about getting another beer and pushing down roots. Can't have a better recommendation then that in these parts.

Stop #58 - Peppercorns

The Bar: Peppercorns

The Address 455 Park Avenue

The Day and the Time Friday at 4

The price 6.69 (that's right, 6.69, just three cents more valuable than the sign of Satan, I feel quite expansively evil when I consider that point)

Did they ask me if I wanted a lime Nope, he put it in with no muss and fuss.

What was the type of gin I think it was a well gin.

What was the gin and tonic like It was good. It was fine. It was adequate. It was sufficient. It was.

The Joint They did something to the bar area, which is a good sized room and a decent bar. I think it looked better before. I think they refurbished it. It is very light fake wood. Even the walls have that light wood paneling thing. Okay, let me say it, the place looked and felt beige. It might not have been exactly beige, but that is what I would say if asked ten seconds after leaving. I would have said, "The place? The place? Beige, right?"

General Impressions I used to like this place. That is not a stick in the eye. Just a statement of fact. I used to like going here. Hell, I had the rehearsal dinner for my wedding here. I liked it. But it went through changes. It built a front room that for a while was an ice cream place and then it was Wormtown Brewery. They changed their menu. They upped their prices. I didn't really enjoy the last time I was there. My wife met friends a few months back there and was shocked at how pricey it had gotten and it wasn't that great. That kind of thing. Nothing terrible, but it was easy to find myself not going. There were other places to be and call "my place."

For early Friday happy time, it was alright with 10 or 15 people. Near me at the bar, two people were talking about their kids and things at work, which was obviously Clark University. This ain't a Clark bar, but a Clark faculty bar. Two young guys at the bar both got a flight of beers and were both consulting the beer menu and their smart phones, and taking pictures of beers after they tried them. Hey! Wait a minute. I'm the only one blogging about bars here, buddy! Just kidding, they were beer folk getting all foodie on their hops and malt. They were quiet and didn't seem to be having too much fun while doing this.

I listened to after work conversation and kvetching. I watched serious beer drinkers drink seriously. I waited for the paint to peel. The bartender was good, checking to see how I was, making sure no one was left adrift.

Amount of Time in the Joint: More than 10 minutes less than 15. I pinched myself to attention and got out.

Will I come back: Huh, what wait, I drifted off, what? Oh can you ask that again, I missed what you said.

Will I come back: No.

Stop #59 - 7NaNa Japanese Steakhouse

The Bar: 7NaNa Japanese Steakhouse

The Address 60 Shrewsbury Street

The Day and the Time Friday at 10pm. And yet, I still missed the party. When I came in, the hibachi chefs were cleaning all their stations and what was left were people in the main front room at the bar and four or five of the outlying tables.

The price Nine dollars. Then with charged tax it was 9.60. Then we had to leave a tip. I should stop saying what the most expensive gin and tonic will be, I mean I still have a score or so of bars to visit on Shrewsbury Street and that restaurant row is going to surprise me with the exponential nature of pricing, I think.

Did they ask me if I wanted a lime No. I got one though.

What was the type of gin I asked for the basic and she said "Tanqueray" and I nodded. Who I am to doubt the acumen of alcohol technicians?

What was the gin and tonic like: For the most expensive gin and tonic (for now) on this tour, it was kind of light of flavor, and when I went to the bathroom and came back two minutes later they had already cleared my drink, which was half filled. I saw it on the well and asked, is that my drink. I got it back and it had watered down to no flavor in just those two minutes. How is that possible?

The Joint Let me be blunt. I knew I didn't like the look of the place as soon as I approached the bar stools. The place is attempting a high end ultra modern look and esthetic with high ceiling, indirect lighting and a huge glass bead chandelier over the large oval bar. Actually the chandelier reminded me of the fringe on a go-go dancer. ("Attack of the 50 Foot Go-Go Girl!!!! The Thrills! The Chills! The Maki Rolls!") They have large hibachi rooms in the back and a sushi chef working the side of the bar. I approached the bar stool and saw that it was worn and some of the fake leather of the seat was gone. I looked around and all the other stools I examined were similarly worn. So you have a swank place with last year's stools. It's like a dowager getting her fifth facelift and two months later already getting new wrinkle lines. Friends, the stools at some of the dive bars I have been to, like the Nines or even Pleasant Cafe, were in the same shape if not a little better. And I paid a hell of a lot less for my opportunity to sit there at their bar.

General Impressions Couples were having drinks and food in amorphous dishes. One couple were bravely having a scorpion bowl with neon shaded three foot straws. Three folk at a table took a selfie of themselves. The bartender had a friend at the bar and that was her focus. He received the bulk of the conversation and her attention. I was not asked if I wanted anything else. But of course, I went to the bathroom and they took my drink away, so I think they were happy I didn't stay any longer than I did. I am sure the food is nice. I am sure the prices are insane. I am sure the staff would be friendlier if I came in with an expense account.

Amount of Time in the Joint 10 minutes

Will I come back (Sing it with me now) Na-na-na-na Na-na-na-na Hey Hey Hey No way!

2019 Update *This place is gone. From what I gathered, it lost its liquor license and it was out of business soon after that.*

Stop #60 - Bennie's

The Bar: Bennie's

The Address 13 East Mountain Road. This is off of West Boylston Street, not far from the Worcester North Movie Theater and the 99 and the Community College. I don't know, I just want to put it in its place. It's one of those little known bars, that I figured I might want to give you an idea of its location.

The Day and the Time Sunday at 5. It was a game day, but the Patriots had already finished the game and their opponent. So the mood was high and airy.

The price 6

Did they ask me if I wanted a lime She did and I got it

What was the type of gin It was well gin

What was the gin and tonic like It was a little harsh, but I liked it. Go figure. I like the bar and I tend to like the drink. You don't need deep psychological knowledge to suss that out.

The Joint A narrow place that is divided in two, with a bar on one side and tables on the other. The bar is just a long lunch counter with a classic old bar railing in front of it, it does look a little odd having a bar staple attached to a formica counter, but hey, that's what this place is, you got a problem with that, go somewhere else buddy-o. What I really like about the layout is that the grill part is just the front part of the bar area, right by the window. There is a microwave and a grill and a place to make sandwiches. That is all. The menu is based on things that can be made there. I love it, so old school. Burger and a beer joint. And sports. The place is about those three things, at least for my visit. It is an older crowd, all talking and discussing football. They kind of all know each other, but that's not to say the place was exclusionary. There were a bunch of flat screens above the bar that played the games. It all felt like a lunch counter from an old movie, I liked the feel. On the other side, people were ordering and eating burgers. I think they could see the tvs as well, so no one was left out of the fun.

General Impressions There is something quite nice about a place where people know that this is their kind of place. You are of a certain age and want a no fuss place for some drinks and some grub? Well this is the place for you, welcome. You like sports? Bonus! I am not quite sure how it works that this is a bar for older sports fans while others places will be for the younger sports freaks. I am not quite sure how that self-selection works, but people go to where they are most comfortable and this joint is definitely old school, hence the old school clientele. But you don't need your AARP card to come in, it's here and happy to help. Okay, I like these throwback places, sue me.

Amount of Time in the Joint 15 minutes.

Will I come back I don't know, I am not in that area often. But I liked it. I liked leaning on a lunch counter with a drink to watch the game, knowing I can get a burger. Knowing that if I had an obscure question about a Pats game from 18 years ago, the fella next to me would have the answer, or at least give a decent bullshit response. Who can ask for more?

Stop #61 - Smokey Joe's Cigar Bar

The Bar: Smokey Joe's Cigar Bar

    The Address 373 Park Avenue

    The Day and the Time Sunday at 5:45

    The price: It is of two prices. I went in, ordered my drink (it was a gin and tonic, if you were curious) and she poured it and then she asked for 4 dollars. This was surprising, because I figured this place was going to gouge, and here I was paying small change. I paid and started drinking (slowly, but more on that later) and then she came back and said, "It's really eight bucks, but between 4 and 6 we have half priced drinks, so that's why I charged you four. But it's almost six and I didn't want you surprised when you ordered another and got charged eight." That was really nice of her, I must say. So the answer for price is 8 bucks, mostly, but come at the right time and its 4. Of course, the way she poured her drink, you don't need a second one.

    Did they ask me if I wanted a lime No. She just put it in. I really like how that's happening more often. I mean I look like a lime wedge kind of guy, they should just know.

    What was the type of gin I think it was Tanqueray

    What was the gin and tonic like Alcoholic. It was a hell of a lot of gin. She took out a pint glass, put in ice and then poured the gin. And kept on going. There was only an inch and a half of pint glass remaining before she stopped the gin bottle and squeezed in the small amount of tonic. It was a fine glass of gin, not a gin and tonic. And I was wobbly. There were diet cokes in my future. It was fine for what it was, but what it was was a hell of a lot of booze. As I valiantly had at the drink I thought of an open letter to bartenders. (which I wrote and I cut out of this post and will post down below in the 2019 Updates. It's not a 2019 update, but I need to put it somewhere.)

    The Joint It has signs outside declaring it as Rumors Night Club and Smokey Joes, and it has a giant phallic cigar sticking out from the building, menacing the people walking on Park Avenue. Inside, it is all cigar bar. They have a room where cigars are purchased, that was not opened or used the time I was there. It is a good sized room with a few seating areas. By the windows are groups of leather chairs where people can sit, smoke and chat. In the center of the room, in a large area, there are couches set up in a U shape. This area was taken up with gentlemen speaking Russian. The front area had a young-ish group of folk smoking and kibbitzing. Then there was a smallish bar. I sat there with a few others. They had hookahs but no one was using them at the time (does that make this my third Hookah bar of the tour?) The guy next to me had a pipe. Most everyone else was smoking their own packs of cigarettes.

Which brings up my ignorance about cigar bars in this new era of anti-smoking. When I first started going to bars, a quarter century ago, all bars were this cigarette centered. But times, they have changed. The only other cigar bar i have been to, which was quite some time ago, had a policy of charging you for smoking your own pack. I thought this was the norm. I guess this is not the case, for people were coming in here with their packs and smoking with no worries. No one was buying cigars, They were getting drinks and holding their packs for the world to see. I guess the high price of drinks is to pay for the privilege of smoking and drinking. It's like a natural wildlife preserve for smokers. The air filters did a decent job, I could see everything, nothing was hidden away through a fog of smoke, but I still left there with my clothes smelling of cigarette.

General Impressions If my question is, why do people go to certain bars, the answer to this one is easy. Because I can smoke my Newport's here. There was a big age range here. Next to me were two older people, then young folk at the chairs upfront. The older woman near me was going on to her companion about how she wouldn't use a hookah, doesn't like them, doesn't trust them. I'm with her. Like I said, this has a feel of a last outpost, a stronghold of smokers fighting back against the tide of unwanted public opinion. The bartender was good and friendly. She made strong drinks for everyone asking and even had to make an espresso. People greeted her with familiarity, this place has its regulars.

Amount of Time in the Joint 25 minutes (took a while to finish my drink)

Will I come back No. Not my place. We select the places we need, and I don't need a bar I can smoke in. I don't need to pay high prices for my drink for that opportunity. For those who do, I think it is decent enough.

2019 Update. The bar is still around. I just have this extra post I want to include in this book and I am trying to figure out the best way. I wrote other things during the time the blog was lively. I wrote about bars that closed before I got to them. I wrote about bars that were never open. I wrote about the newspaper articles about the blog. I have saved you from all of that. But there is one addendum post I think is worth including and it is tied in with this bar. So, here is my open letter to bartenders.

Dear Bartender,

There are a lot of words for being inebriated: drunk, wasted, blotto, gone, pissed, smashed, sloshed, shitfaced, plastered etc, etc, etc. So many names for something that happens so often. In the bar world, it's the equivalent for the 50 words of snow in the Inuit language. But just because its so prevalent, doesn't mean you have to contribute to it.

What I mean to say is, don't make the drink so strong I won't be able to stand afterwards. You don't have to overload your cocktail for me to like it. I like cocktails. I like bars. I like remembering where I live and the names of my loved ones. Those three things can co-exist together.

Yes, I am at a bar ordering a drink which can cause intoxication, but you are working for a business, why make a drink so strong that I won't be able to order more than one before I am legally cut off? If its decently poured, then I can have a couple. Maybe order some food. Talk to the other patrons and be a positive part of the bar scene. Which won't happen if I'm shitfaced. If I'm shitfaced, I will yell at the TV screen, even though I am looking at a mirror. If I'm shitfaced, I will start fights, cry over the friends I don't have anymore, or worse, I might quote you favorite scenes from Anchorman or Monty Python and the Holy Grail. If I am shitfaced, I am not a paying customer, I am a lump you have to deal with and trundle into a cab later on.

These things happen of course just through the course of working at a bar, but you don't have to contribute to the problem. Don't over pour my drink. I ordered this drink because I like the taste of the spirits and the mixers combined. i like the way it looks, feels and tastes. I like the way it warms me. I am ordering an item that has measured parts. Let me enjoy the proper flavor. Let me be able to have more than one. Please.

I am aware that some of your customers will come in annoyed that you are making a weak drink. That they want a stiff one, they want a man's drink. The kind of a man's drink that turns you into a blubbering little child. I know these guys exist. They will not tip well if you don't over pour. For these monsters, do what you need to do. But remember, we are not all these Cro-Magnons. To lump us all together as a wannabe lushes is unfair and unwise. If I was looking to just get wasted, I would lock myself at home with a bottle of vodka and watch ESPN or Lifetime Movie Channel all day until I woke up in the next century. But I choose to go to a public space to drink, not just for the drinks, but for the company. Let me be able to recall both.

Now, nobody appreciates a weak drink, but it takes a true drinker to appreciate a well proportioned one. Let us strive to be that drinker.

Thank you for your time, and your judicious pouring of my next drink.

Sincerely, Dante of Worcester

Stop #62 - Birkbeck's Waterfront Grill

The Bar: Birkbeck's Waterfront Grill

The Address 242 Mill Street

The Day and the Time Friday after Thanksgiving at 8:45

The price 5 bucks (but I don't know if that's what it will say at)

Did they ask me if I wanted a lime No, it just came with it, like peanut butter and jelly, like ham and eggs, like Cagney and Lacey (they just are inseparable.)

What was the type of gin Well

What was the gin and tonic like: It was a fine sweet gin and tonic. Nothing special, but fine.

The Story: I was driving around, looking for a place to go, because the place I intended on going to was open, but no one was in, not even staff. There was a big open sign all red neon and there were lights on and a sense of bar readiness,, just add people, and bartenders. I didn't know what to do about that, so I left without evening trying the door (more on that place another time) and got in my car and saw this place.

This used to be a few other restaurants right on the lake. It was Joey's, and then it was Lago's and then when that placed was forced to close, it has been empty for something like two years. Good to have something there. I saw lights on, I saw people at the bar. I went in and I could tell that something was off. Not bad, but off. What I mean is that there was no one in the dining area, only the bar was inhabited, and the kitchen looked unused. Almost unfinished. Not all the shelves on the bar were filled with glasses or bottles. There were some holes in the walls. It felt like the paint was still wet on the High School Play sets. There were about 10 or so people there. All talking to the bartender. One group of three guys were loudly talking near me, which makes it a bar. One of the them seemed to be trying to leave the entire time I was there (he never did).

The bartender came over and asked how I came here. I said I saw the lights and decided to try it. He told me that they just had a soft opening two days ago and right now they only have drinks, five dollars a drink, cash only. I complied, which is also why I think if you come back to this place the drinks might not be that price. I liked the place from what I could imagine when it was finished and full of folk. My one complaint is that the bar was sparkly, there was some kind of shiny stone thing going on I think. It was the glitter bar. The picture I posted on the blogsite is from a search of the former iteration, Lago's and the place looks very similar. The lights and the set up seem identical. If it ain't broke.....

Now I don't know if this is going to be an awesome place (the location is great) but I won't be checking it out for another review. This is not the way to be a bar reviewer, but I am not a reviewer, just a tourist. I got my gin and tonic, and that's all that matters to this endeavor. It is a strange list of activities I set out for myself, but that's what I created. Who did I see here, friends of the owner, people who want a bar in the area. I wish it well, I hope it all goes off they way they want it to.

2019 Update *It didn't. It was closed in under a year. Running a restaurant is hard. It is now the site a popular BBQ place, Big T's,*

Stop #63 - Sakura Tokyo

The Bar: Sakura Tokyo

    The Address 640 Park Avenue

    The Day and the Time 9 on Friday after Thanksgiving

    The price 5.35

    Did they ask me if I wanted a lime No. I just got it.

    What was the type of gin Well

    What was the gin and tonic like Kind of strong, kind of edgy. It was not a great gin and tonic. I talked to someone afterwards and he said that they don't make those drinks, they make Mai Tais and Scorpions bowls. I get it, you don't go to an Irish Bar for a Singapore Sling, but come on, a gin and tonic. We are not talking about a complicated mixological creation. And if you google a little you will find many bars in Tokyo that make this particular high ball. No, I don't think its cultural. I mean,I am in a cocktail lounge in Worcester Massachusetts listening to a cover band doing Tom Petty tunes, I don't think its because of culture. I think I just got a fair to middling drink. It happens.

The Joint It is a very large restaurant. There are three huge sections. One for Hibachi. One for the Sushi Bar and the general japanese restaurant and then there is the cocktail lounge. This is the kind of cocktail lounge that I imagined when I think of the late 70s swinging life. It is big with a large stage where the band can stretch out. There are booths and tables and a dance floor and there is a good sized bar. Close to 200 folks can be here. Not that there were 200 people when I was there, more like 25. This ain't a bad number, but the space drowned us all.

This is a place where good bands play covers. The band was decent, they had nice chops, but they started up on Tom Petty and I was shrugging my coat on and getting ready to get. I don't have much against classic rock or those young fellas who play it in Asian

Restaurant Cocktail Lounges, I just wasn't feeling it. My loss I am sure.

General Impressions As I came in, the band had just finished sound check and were now back with their friends at a table. The band and their "entourage" were more than half of the people there. This was changing when they got up to do their first set. Folks were coming in and getting scorpion bowls. A few solitary men and women were peaking in, waiting to see if there were people to check out, to talk to, to a make a scene to. I don't know how busy it gets, but I hope it takes care of the needs of all these divergent peoples and groups. That you can meet and hook up and you can also go and share a ridiculous looking drink with a couple friends. Its big enough for all kinds.

As the band played a couple of the women who came with them started dancing crazy to each other. Acting all mad and bohemian.

The bartender was good. The evening seemed thin so one of the waitresses went home, she talked about going home and getting out of there for 10 minutes before she actually did. The remaining cocktail waitress seemed to have her work cut out for her, even though the crowd was still light. She was moving, but I guess not fast enough for some people. One guy, who was hanging at the band's table came over to the bar to get a drink. The bartender asked him if he was with the band's table, and the guy said he was. The bartender told him that he had to order his drink at the table, that he couldn't help him here. The guy tried for a little bit to get his drink at the bar but soon surrendered and went back to the table and the hope of the emergence of the cocktail waitress. I felt for that guy. That has happened to me too over the years. I never quite understood why I just couldn't jump over the waitress-table customer relationship and get my drink at the bar? Tips, I know, but I still felt for the dude.

Amount of Time in the Joint 35 minutes. I was waiting for the band to start to get a good feel for the cocktail lounge experience. The band started and I now was experienced and ready to leave.

Will I come back For the restaurant, I like going and will continue. For the cocktail lounge, I don't know. I don't think so. Like the Kas Bar, I am happy we have a hyper huge cocktail lounge in town, I just don't think I am the guy who wants to go to them. For those who want that Mai Tai and 70s rock cover tunes elan all tied up with the chance of getting lucky, go for it.

2019 Update The owner decided to retire a couple years ago and sold the building and the land. The restaurant was torn down and now instead of a huge restaurant and lounge we have a convenience store with a Dunkin Donuts. This one hurt a little. We should have more lounges and joints to get maki rolls and just a few less Dunkins.

DAVID MACPHERSON

Stop #64 - Blue Jeans Bistro

The Bar: Blue Jeans Bistro

The Address 266 Park Avenue

The Day and the Time Sunday at seven, a Patriots game was on, though it was pretty obvious that they were going to lose. Just to put the right mood on a game night moment.

Musical Recommendation While Reading this Post: It has to be Jazzin for Blue Jeans by David Bowie. You can find it on Spotify I'm sure.

The price: 5.50

Did they ask me if I wanted a lime No, he put it right in like he had been practicing all his professional life.

What was the type of gin. Well. It was Gilberts. Which is becoming my arch nemesis.

What was the gin and tonic like It was okay. After 63 gin and tonics on this tour, I am getting a little tired in the pallette area of Gilberts and Tonic, but it was a well put together drink. The right amount of tonic to gin. Ice and Lime. For the lowest common denominator drink (which is what I asked for) it was all good.

The Joint Wouldn't it be awesome if Blue Jeans Bistro had a dress code of only formal clothes? I know, silly, but this is how my mind works sometimes. But I can see it "I was thrown out of Blue Jeans Bistro for not wearing slacks and a dress shirt." Okay, I'm done.

This is a nice new place to have on Park Avenue. This is next to Blue Jeans Pizza and underneath 266 Club. This used to be a variety of Asian places, I know it was Thai Cha-Da, but I couldn't find all the info if the location had another name or iteration. So the Blue Jeans Pizza people took it over and now they have a pub restaurant next to the pizza joint (which is pretty decent). The place is classic pub bar decor of wood finish and railings and tables with big chairs. What surprised me and was kind of nice, was that the tables were spread out, they could have put more tables crunched in, but they went for space. I really like that. You don't see that too often and it was nice to notice. Also, they had two areas where instead of dinner table and chairs there was a low coffee table and leather chairs for people to relax with pitchers of beer and have the apps or whatever. This was cool too. When I came in the place had about 10 or 15 in the dining area and another 10 or so at the bar. Which was alright for a game night.

General Impressions The bartender was good and he was pouring a lot of very large beer pitchers, larger than I have seen at the other bars on the tour. He kept things going. The food looked good in a "I got a buzz and I want some fried food and carbs" sort of way. The crowd at the bar was older, and more female than male. It felt like a very open available place. It was really a food and then drink place, but we will forgive it.

Amount of Time in the Joint 15 minutes

Will I come back I think so, why not. This could be a place me and Epicurean Eric and I can go for a beer and fries. We have noticed that some of our favorite bars don't have fries on the menu. This can handle the dilemma quite well. You hear that Eric? Wanna get some grub and a beer?

2019 Update It stopped being Blue Jeans Bistro very quickly. I don't know if anything is in this space now. It's just a door that doesn't open on a street with many choices.

Stop #65 - Funky Murphy's

The Bar: Funky Murphy's

The Location: 305 Shrewsbury Street

The Day and Time: Sunday around five-ish

The Price I think it was around six bucks. I can't find my notes and my memory is not clear past around six bucks or so. Give or take fifty cents.

Did they ask me if I wanted a lime: No, they just put that bad boy in. We are on a definite streak with this, I like.

What was the type of gin: It was well.

What was the gin and tonic like: It was decent. I think it was a little harsh, but it was decent. I didn't complain. I drank it all up, like every good little boy should.

The Joint: A Shrewsbury Street stand by. I have never been here, probably because I am not insanely enamored with chicken wings. Don't get me wrong, I like chicken wings. I have eaten my share. But I am not a crazed wing head. It is a bar that skews young. The bar is long and there are a good amount of tables in the bar area. A band was setting up in a corner when I was there, but it was not crowding the place at all. There were rooms in back but they were taken up with a holiday party at the time. It was a good professional sports leaning bar with TVs showing the games going on. I should say that as soon as I walked in, I was assaulted with the smell of buffalo wing sauce. It was the perfume of the joint. I never thought I would want to be bathed in hot sauce before, but if I ever did, I know what my piquant aroma would be like. Almost every table had a large heaping plateful of wings. Some with different sauces, but the wings were ever present.

There were groups of guys at the bar. There were groups of women at the tables. There were even mixed groupings, this place takes all kinds.

General Impression: It's a good young folk place, where fancy popular drinks are mixed and beers are poured. There was a group of guys near me and one was pissed because he left for a few minutes and when he came back his drink had been cleared. His friends apologized and said they told the bartender that they can clear the drinks, because they were heading to a table. The guy kept on going on talking about this lost well remembered drink. The guys went to a table and the guy mentioned to the waitress that his drink was cleared before he was done with it. The waitress smiled and nodded sagely and said, "Well, that's too bad." And said no more. The guy got the hint and ordered another drink. I must say that I loved that waitress and her batten down the hatches attitude. She knows what she's doing and the place is the better for it.

Amount of time in the joint: 15 minutes.

WIll I come back: I don't think so. It's a good place for a young person's sports bar. But I don't need a young person's sports bar. I also want to smell more than buffalo wing sauce when I am at a joint. But for its type, its good and the people who want that kind of thing will want to go there, if they don't already.

Stop #66 - Vintage Grille and Gourmet Pizza

The Bar: Vintage Grille and Gourmet Pizza

The Address 346 Shrewsbury Street

The Day and the Time Sunday around five or so. Not sure,

The price Six bucks-ish. Like the last stop on the tour, I don't know where I put the notes on this one. It was either six or six fifty. For being on Shrewsbury Street, this is practically free.

Did they ask me if I wanted a lime She just put it in. This is getting to be the new thing, the thing I always wanted. To get a gin and tonic by just saying those simple words and getting everything I would want, which would be gin, tonic, ice and a lime. Inalienable rights, dontcha know.

What was the type of gin It was well.

What was the gin and tonic like This was a harsh drink, nothing to write home about, but it was decent. The old adage, nice enough place, makes a nice enough drink.

The Joint This once was a pizza joint named Junior's which I had been too. But then before that it was a garage, for cars, ya know. This is the new iteration, and it feels better. They fixed up the walls to be less garage bay like and filled the place with old car and oil signage. It's the place American Pickers would decorate. There were people here on this off time. Five at the bar, a few couples at the table. All drinking and eating. The bartender was friendly and the place was comfortable, though it did feel a tad bit too much like a set of a retro bar, and not the actual retro bar itself.

General Impressions It was a nice place. Food and drinks. You get pizza. You get beer. You can even get a gin and tonic. But then I watched one of the platters of food arrive for a fella a the bar. He ordered a burger with onion rings. What he got was some kind of pop art. There was the bottom bun, there was the burger patty and then on top of that was a tower of onion rings that tapered off until it towered five inches above the patty and then the top bun was placed on it. It was like a telescope burger. It's like the burger had some teenaged impure thoughts and expanded up. It was an oniongasm. It was weird art that the guy didn't know how to eat.

The staff told him to either take the onion rings off or scrunch it down, collapsing the creation. And I have to ask, despite the fact that it looks cool, wouldn't it have just been better if the onion rings were on the side? Is the shock of the first image worth the work you have to do to have it ready to be eaten? I don't know, but I feel the same way about complicated drinks where you have to mix this and then take this first sip and then that second sip. I just want a drink to enjoy. A burger I know how to navigate. Perhaps I am a culinary luddite, but I am okay with that. To answer the question, the guy took off the onion rings and ate them separately. They looked good, but believe me, kind of daunting when it came from the kitchen.

Amount of Time in the Joint 15 Minutes, I spent a good chunk of that time just staring mesmerized at the telescope burger installation.

Will I come back Maybe. The food looked good. The place was friendly. The drinks were decent, but the thing is, I am now at 65 bars, that's a lot of places to chose from. This place was good, but it just might not be mine.

2019 Update I did go back one afternoon for a bite to eat. Whatever I had was tasty. I don't think I ordered a gin and tonic, I was kind of done with gin and tonics.

Stop #67 - Plaza Azteca

The Bar Plaza Azteca:

The Address 539 Lincoln Street

The Day and the Time Friday at 10

The price Ten bucks. Oh, yes, ten bucks. The music was blaring so conversation was tough. I asked how much and she said ten and I looked at her puzzled, because I saw the plastic cup of booze she gave me and then she brought up her two hands and shot out all her fingers. I was hoping this was a muscle spasm and not her telling how much it was. Ah well, it was no muscle spasm. Darn.

Did they ask me if I wanted a lime I don't know, it was so loud, she asked something, I said what, she asked it again and I still heard nothing, so I said yes and shook my head emphatically. I got a lime.

What was the type of gin. Well

What was the gin and tonic like For a ten dollar drink, this was pretty paltry. It was well gin in a 10 ounce plastic cup. The drink tasted of the ice. It was okay at best. But at this place I guess you are paying your admittance and not for the drink.

The Joint This is a big Mexican restaurant in the Lincoln Square area. It used to be a Bickford's. Ah, how I miss those greasy Bickford breakfast specials, but never mind. Now it is a fairly busy Mexican place, I have not eaten here, but my friends say it is alright. When I went in, people were still dining. One large party, all Spanish speakers, had taken over one of the rooms and was having a raucous pre-Christmas dinner. I had to go through the entire restaurant before I got to the bar. The bar room was a good sized square of a room. I think they took out tables to allow for dancing. So it was pretty hollow in the middle. The DJ in the corner was blaring salsa and lights were flashing. About 20 people were there, still too early for the real fun to start. People were trickling in as I drank. Only one couple was dancing, and they looked good. A joy to watch two people who know how to move, actually do it. The man seemed to want to hold back and wait for more people to show, but the woman kept dragging him out to dance and he was happy to oblige.

General Impressions As far as I could hear, I was the only English only speaker in the joint, That's cool. Let the cultures of Worcester find a place to hang out and dance. They were happy to see who came through the door. They were excited to have the evening begin. They were all dressed up. One woman didn't take off her coat, she de-armored, it was ritualistic how she took off her coat to show off her dancing rags. It was like she was in a slo-mo scene from an eighties movie. She was in five inch red wedge shoes and I thought she was going to teeter over and hit the ground, but this was not her first rodeo, or salsa dance and she was fine. Everyone was at the bar or in the chairs and tables around the perimeter. All waiting for the critical mass of people and need when there was no choice but to hit the floor and dance. It was time for me to move on.

Amount of Time in the Joint 10 or 15 minutes. When the music is blaring, time becomes more flexible. So does anyone really know what time it is (as the Chicago singer so sagely asked)?

Will I come back Probably not. I have Mexican places I like and the bar was crazy expensive. It was lovely to be aware that we have such a thing in town but not for me. This is how people pick where they want to go and who they want to be with. This is a place for a group of Worcester folk to feel comfortable, dance, and look good. And besides, 10 bucks for 10 ounces of gin and tonic in a plastic chinet cup, a wee steep for me.

2019 Update It closed about a year later. I don't think anything has filled the place.

Stop #68 - Nancy Chang's

The Bar: Nancy Chang's

    The Address 372 Chandler Street

    The Day and the Time Sunday around five or so

    The price 5.75

    Did they ask me if I wanted a lime She just put it in

    What was the type of gin Well

    What was the gin and tonic like. Eh. There has been worse. There have been better.

The Joint This is the first Chinese Restaurant I ever went to in Worcester about 15 years ago. I liked the food then, still do. Though they changed the set up in the place recently. The front door is in a different location, and its kind of weird. You have to walk through the outside eating area to get into the inside eating area, The big change for this blog is the bar, It used to be bigger. But it also had an area to pay and to get takeout. Now it is just a small oval bar. 12 can sit there and when I showed there were five. One guy was waiting for takeout and having a beer. Two were having food and mai tais. All the drinks, including mine, were in silly mason jars that had handles. Not a cool way to have a tropical drink or even a gin and tonic. So the Mai Tais come in mason jars, do the scorpion bowls get served in a moonshine jug?

General Impressions I can talk about how creepy the guy at the bar was with his "I'm just kidding" method he had of blatantly hitting on the bartender. But I want to spend my brief time talking about how the restaurant redesign completely took away the ability of the bartender to be a bartender. The way it is now, she has no control of the cash register. She has to go to the lobby to process the bar payments. I gave her the money for my drink and she took it, left the bar, went over for two or so minutes to have the cashier process it and then come back to the bar with my change. That sucks for her. She is not a bartender, she's a waitress with an oval shaped section. Up until this moment did I not consider one of the powers the bartender has, the control of the till for the bar. I know that a bad bartender can ruin a business, but to take away all of her ability to run a bar, its crazy. Before I left, she had to go and take care of a credit card payment for some food and a couple drinks. She was gone for another two or three minutes. I want my bartenders to be the rulers of their tiny domains, not subservient to the girl at the cash register.

Amount of Time in the Joint 15 minutes. But much of that time was waiting for the waitress, I mean bartender to return from her visits to the cashier.

Will I come back No, not for bar only. I have always liked the restaurant. I don't like the new renovation set-up, its cumbersome and confusing. But I still like the food. The bar was just a laughable way-station. If you want a mai tai, go a place with some sense of fun. Sakura Tokyo or Ho Toy. Those places the bartender can take money and give change right at the bar, its nice. You don't know how nice it is until you are deprived of it.

2019 Update It's amusing to consider that the two places I mentioned as places to get Mai Tais are both gone. This place is still around. I have no skill in figuring out what place will thrive.

Stop #69 - Sake Bomb

The Bar: Sake Bomb, this is up there as one of the establishments with one of the worst names. Sake Bomb, its just taunting for a bad review, ain't it? (and, spoiler, it gets one!) Yes. I know it is the name of a cocktail. It is the Asian restaurant equivalent of a boiler maker. It is a glass of Red Bull where a shot glass of sake is dropped and submerged into it (thank you wikipedia) I acknowledge, it is a drink a fella can order. But, there is a drink called Sex on the Beach, but I don't need to go to that bar. This used to be where the sushi bar Haiku was. That's a nice name. Now its a place called Rum and Coke, I mean Sake Bomb.

The Address 258 Park Avenue

The Day and the Time Six-ish on Sunday before Christmas

The price 5.89. Tax is so silly, why don't they just charge me six bucks and be done?

Did they ask me if I wanted a lime No, she just put it in.

What was the type of gin It was well.

What was the gin and tonic like It was good. Nothing special, but good. It was in a lovely high ball glass with a tapered top. It was a nice glass to hold as I drank. You might think that glass shape doesn't matter in enjoyment of a beverage, but then you would be a philistine.

The Joint It is a narrow restaurant with tables on one side and a restaurant length bar on the other. There were people at the bar eating and drinking. It was certainly not a rush time but still pleasant to see people there. At the end of the bar was the area where they made the sushi. One of the dishes came out for a customer and it had blinking LED lights underneath shredded cabbage on the side. What's the deal with inedible plate elements?

Besides me at the bar were three guys drinking and eating and talking, about cigars, cars, vacation spots they have been to. One was slightly annoyed that the bartender could not make him a white russian, because they don't have milk or cream as part of their bar set-up. The guy said he will go to the Exxon and buy a quart. He didn't. The bartender said that the next time they come they should call ahead so she can pick some milk up. She offered him a black russian, but he declined, I guess the moment was gone.

General Impressions I was going to say it was alright. That it had a sense of bar-ness to it. That it was cool to see the sushi chef come over to a customer to ask how she liked what he did. But then I tried to pay and leave, and suddenly I was stuck in a Luis Bunuel film or in the ending of Waiting for Godot. I was not allowed to leave.

When I was done with my drink, I waited a couple minutes for the bartender to notice me and I asked for my bill. She went and did a few other things, talked to a few other customers and came back in a few minutes with my bill and then she was gone before I could give her my money, which was out and waiting.

She came back to my general vicinity and walked right past me, the guy next to me asked for his check. She went and printed out his bill and gave it to him, and then he took out his credit card and she took it and processed it. I am still sitting there with my money and bill in my hand. She finishes that and then the guy two down from me asks for his bill and she does the whole thing again.

I am still there with my money out. I didn't know there was a third guy in that group but before she even noticed me she printed out his bill and processed his credit card. All these guys had their cards out and pointing before she went to them. I only had cash (poor Dante). She finished the bill of this third guy, these guys had drinks and food and probably tipped well, at least I hope they did.

So now there was no one but me and she walked right by me and went into the back. I was pissed. I got up and looked for the cash in my pockets to see if I could pay and leave. I had enough money for the drink but not enough exact change for the tip, and here is the funny part, I couldn't see myself leaving without tipping (even though the bartender ignored me for five minutes over perhaps more preferred clientele) I couldn't leave. Crazy.

Let me state again, I was the first out of the four customers who asked for the bill. At this point I was standing up and looking manic, trying to find a way to pay and leave without needing to include her in the process. She either noticed this mad man or someone pointed out this mad man and she came over, took my money, gave me change and quietly mumbled, "Sorry." I tipped her. More than twenty percent. Its what us tourists do. I left fuming. I know its petty, but man, it was so obvious and annoying. The guy with only one drink on the tab gets bottom of the barrel service. The high rollers get preferential treatment.

Amount of Time in the Joint 20 minutes. Most of those waiting for her to deign to notice me to allow me to leave this crappy ass place (sorry, I usually am not this annoyed at a joint, but I watched her ignore me over three other customers and then not even come by after that to take my money. Did I get leprosy recently and didn't notice?)

Will I come back No. Never. Even if my great friends tell me that what happened to me was an aberration and its a great place. But I know my great friends, and I think they would have issue having food at a place called Sake Bomb. I'm sorry to say this, please avoid. I don't know if it will be you who will be snubbed there next.

2019 Update Sake Bomb is still there. And so is my ire toward the place. It is astounding how annoyed I got from being there. Just editing it for this book, I got angry all over again. To be fair, it might not be the bar, it might be me.

Stop #70 - The Smokestack Urban BBQ

The Bar: The Smokestack Urban BBQ

The Address 139 Green Street

The Day and the Time 2 o'clock on Wednesday, Christmas Eve

The price 7.49 (you know, I would have paid for the extra penny. Really, I would)

Did they ask me if I wanted a lime Yes, this is awesome. Yes Virginia, there is a Santa Claus, and he likes limes put in his highball cocktails without being asked. (Yeah, I believe in a sophisticated, erudite St. Nick)

What was the type of gin It was well, but it was not Gilberts (Once again, the joy of the Christmas season)

What was the gin and tonic like It was okay. A little on the light (weak) side, but tasty nonetheless. I drank it quickly and didn't feel light headed. It was an acceptable cocktail. This is not a place to get fine drinks, but have something to go with the barbeque ribs and mac and cheese they have there. And taking that into account, the drink was perfect.

The Joint This used to be a few places in the past, notably Block Five. But now it is the smaller location for Smokestack and its a good setting. There is a nice sized bar area where folk can sit and eat. and they were. It has that urban upscale thing going, but still, its BBQ and that has a humble feel as well. The place was busy in the bar with groups of workers cutting out work early for the holiday and having one more little meal-party together. There was a really nice aura of congeniality. Lots of beers were being drunk. Ribs were being consumed.

General Impressions The bartenders were very nice and friendly, attentive and quick. Maybe they were pleased with the sudden amount of business. The joint is clean and the food smelled really good, especially to the nostrils of this one tourist who was

Christmas shopping and skipping lunch. This is a bar restaurant and works well with that. You come for food. You might come for a beer and an appetizer. With the good bar staff they had, even the busy times would be a decent time to come.

Amount of Time in the Joint: Only five minutes but that's because this was just a quick respite on a busy day for me. I had other places to go. I'm a guy, of course I didn't complete my Christmas shopping until the last moment. It's in the genes.

Will I come back Yeah, I have eaten here before and liked it. I have another BBQ joint that's my favorite in town, but this one is good, though a little pricier. The drink was good and I liked the way the bar area was, I can see myself having lunch and a beer there.

Stop #71 - Pepe's

The Bar: Pepe's

    The Address 274 Franklin Street

    The Day and the Time Friday around eight thirty.

    The price Six bucks

    Did they ask me if I wanted a lime She just put it in.

    What was the type of gin It was well.

    What was the gin and tonic like A little flavorless. It was fine. I liked the wide bar and the comfort of it, and that certainly helped with my enjoying the drink.

    The Joint Its a big old room of an Italian joint with a good sized bar. Friendly and brightly lit. There was exposed bricks but there was Digital TVs too. I don't know, but I wouldn't mind a bar without three or four TVs going, ready to be seen by anyone's eyeline. I know, Luddite Dante, this is the way for a bar. Even restaurants have to have the sports going at all times. There was a huge family that took up most of the tables into one large table. About 20 or so. A couple of 10 year old boys wandered around, bored with all the familial congeniality (which is how the ten year old boys would put it, those loquacious little scamps.) Most of them had to go pizza boxes in front of them. It was a nice warm joint, I could see people coming in after work for a couple beers and maybe an appetizer. I have been thinking that some restaurants with liquor licenses are not really bars, that bars need people to want to settle in and spend some time at that long plank of wood, and this place fits that (more about this when I write up about Sweet and The Fix)

    General Impressions A nice place, the pizza looked good. Though I know no one who has eaten here, so I don't know how it is. I watched the large family party leaving, it took up almost my entire time at the bar. Everyone had to go around the table and hug the next person they came across and say how great it was to see them and don't be a stranger, and then they were on to the next person to say farewell to. It was like the Stations of the Cross, with leftovers. One guy had his girlfriend with him, she not knowing anyone, and yet she found herself hugged a lot by relatives or her boyfriend. The first time I saw it happen I watched her eyes bulge in surprise, it being a sneak attack hug from a little woman who didn't seem to have it in her. By the third time she was hugged, she was cool with it, with a smile and a hug back, she was turning into a family reunion veteran.

Amount of Time in the Joint 15 or 20 minutes

Will I come back I don't think this is fair because I read in Pulse that Pepe's is moving. That's how I first heard about Pepe's. So how will it be in the new joint? It could be the same, it could be better, or it could be that all the energy of the place might not have made the move. Who knows. Where it is now, I think its a nice decent place. I might go back, if they are still there.

2019 Update They never moved. They are still in the same location.

Stop #72 - Sweet

The Bar: Sweet

The Address 72 Shrewsbury Street

The Day and the Time Friday at 8:50

The price It was 9.60. Now there might have been a cheaper drink, but I went in and saw the nice selection of gins and scotches and just didn't want to dive into the Well, if you will, so instead of saying Well, or Basic. I told the bartender, "Your choice." And he chose. So I paid for my request. I know, I know, I broke my rule, but after so many Gilbert's Gin and Tonic, I just couldn't make myself do it in a shmancy place like this, consider me chastised.

Did they ask me if I wanted a lime He just put it in

What was the type of gin This was funny, I never had anyone do this before. But the bartender twisted it open and sniffed the bottle. He nodded approval and poured it for me. When he sniffed it I had an instant thought he was going to recoil as if he had just smelled toxic fumes or Gilbert's. The gin was a brand called Old Grove. I looked it up and it is a nice small brand. I can recommend it.

What was the gin and tonic like It was good. Let's hear it for breaking the rules from time to time and getting yourself a self respecting shot of gin. And it was a shot, for not only was this the first place where the bartender sniffed the bottle, it was the first place in all this tour where someone used a measurer. Nothing wrong with that, that way I won't get too strong a drink, but it's funny it took until the 71st joint on the tour before I came across this practice.

The Joint I think this used to be part of an old car dealership (someone can correct me if I am wrong) but that's what it looks like. The ceiling is way up there, there is even a second floor, like a small loft area. Most people were at tables eating desserts, which is what it is known for. I don't know if they have entrees or not. I was just there for the gin, thanks. The crowd was all ages, but skewed young.

Exposed brick, wait staff in black shirts and blue jeans (the 90's, they have returned!) Not very many people at the bar, but that's what you would expect, this is not a bar to hang out in, read the paper in, watch the keno in. This is a high end dessert place with fine drinks that happen to have a bar like seating area.

General Impressions: At the bar in places like this, I am always near the area where the wait staff gather like migrating birds, where they wait for drink orders, and natter about the people they have to serve, or about a wait staff who isn't here that day. I wanted to shoo them from their roost, to send them out to their tables, do something. One young woman was particularly loud and annoyed at something or other. I liked my drink, but I didn't feel like I was in a bar. I felt like I was waiting for a taxi to come and killing time at the closest bench. It's a nice place, but I felt that without a plate of Creme Brule in front of me, something was wrong.

Amount of Time in the Joint 15 minutes

Will I come back I can see myself coming with the wife for dessert. It's great to see this place morph from a small storefront to this huge thing. But maybe not on any solo excursion, and I doubt I would get a cocktail. I like coffee with my sweets.

2019 Update They closed a while back. There is a very good Korean joint in its place.

Stop #73 - The Fix

The Bar: The Fix

> **The Address** 166 Shrewsbury Street
>
> **The Day and the Time** Friday at 9:20
>
> **The price** Eight bucks
>
> **Did they ask me if I wanted a lime** She just put it in.

What was the type of gin I had a sip and was impressed and asked the bartender what it was and she said it was a Small Batch gin called Journeyman Bilberry Black Hearts Gin. They use Journeyman distillery as their basic liquor. I get a chuckle over the use of small batch. It's the "Organic" "Farm to table" "hormone free" for the booze world. Now I could be told that Gilbert's Gin is made in small batch, it is still lousy syrupy swill.

What was the gin and tonic like Hands down, this was the best gin and tonic I have had during this tour. It was delicious. It had good flavor, it was the right combo of tonic to gin, it was a hell of a drink, and I was so happy. The bartender told me that they always use Fever Tree tonic water, which is very popular in Europe (hey, I do my research). Now my friend Epicurean Eric reported to me that he went here and he was asked if he wanted their homemade tonic, he did and he thought it strange. I was not offered that, I was just given their standard eight buck gin and tonic. Which was Journeyman Bilberry Gin and Fever Tree tonic. This was good.

The Joint This was the location for the Niche Group's Mezcal Cafe, but that moved and now they put in a burger joint. It still has the small bar and small eating area. It is kind of bland in the land of decoration, though they have some crazy Chalk drawing, but its a burger joint, you are there for the burgers not for wall hangings. You can also be there for good drinks, as I said.

General Impressions With the best gin and tonic of the tour, I must say that I was disappointed by the time I was here. Though there is a metal table where people can sit and eat and drink, this place is not a bar. Its just a restaurant with booze. There was no sense of community or comfort in the bar area. I wanted to talk to people about how good my drink was, but I was alone, even the friendly bartender who told me about my drink was gone, off shift I guess. She was replaced by another bartender looking at the clock, waiting for the day to end. Ultimately the Fix is a restaurant, that's what they want to be, but the bar is just a place to mix nice drinks. It takes more than stools and a flat surface to make a bar. You need people invested in spending time in that space. Hell, the bartenders split fast too. Pity. Almost a waste of a killer drink.

Amount of Time in the Joint 15 minutes

Will I come back Yes. People tell me the food is great. I can tell you they care about their spirits. But don't go to the bar thinking you will have a fun relaxing time. Go to a table. Get some food. Get some drinks. Go somewhere else if you want a bar. The funny thing about the Niche Group is that I went to one of their other properties that is more like a bar: Still and Stir and it had gin and tonic that was inferior to the one at their burger restaurant. Its odd, but true.

2019 Update The Fix is still thriving, but it is now in a bigger location. The food, by the way, is pretty good. This location has gone through a lot of names and dishes since the Fix left. It was the Usual. It was the Chameleon. It is now Meze Estiatorio. By the time you read this, who knows what amazing place will be there.

Stop #74 - Ralph's Chadwick Square Diner

The Bar: Ralph's Chadwick Square Diner

    The Address 95 Prescott Street

    The Day and the Time Tuesday at five

    The price Eight Bucks

    Did they ask me if I wanted a lime No, he just put it in

    What was the type of gin Well

    What was the gin and tonic like It was fine. Pretty strong, but not over the top.

The Story So Victor Infante from the Telegram and Gazette contacted me about a website ranking Ralph's one of the best Dive Bars in the country and asked me to see if I agreed, and asked what I define a dive bar and what are the dive bars of Worcester. Here is my reply to him, which will count as my write up for Ralph's. I know it deserves more, but I am happy with this letter and I think it will suffice.

Dear Victor,

I got word you wanted me to respond to Impulcity.com ranking Ralph's Chadwick Square Diner as one of the 32 diviest bars in the country. I looked at what they wrote, but realized the best way to figure out if Ralph's is a Dive Bar is to go there. I am at Ralph's now, having a gin and tonic. It is mostly quiet here at the moment, but it is great to be here. I love this place. I am happy that they have a good gin and tonic (which for me is a definite plus) but on the question of whether Ralph's is a dive bar, I have to say no. But that's how I define what a dive bar is.

What is a dive bar, that is a personal question. To those who like the frozen daiquiris at TGIFriday, then O'Connors or Nick's or anywhere you might see a leather jacket or a full sleeve of tattoos would be a dive bar. Also, I don't like the idea of a dive bar being a slightly run down joint with cheap beer that the college kids go to to give themselves some sense of cred. Dive bars are not for tourists. Dive bars are for people who consider the bar not only their favorite joint, but their office. This is where they believe they should be.

To me, a dive bar is seen from the outside. Tell a regular at a dive bar that its a dive and they will get so upset that they will probably harm you. A dive bar is a run down joint where people drink. Where they see themselves as drinkers and this is the place they punch the clock for that calling. There is nothing wrong with a city the size of Worcester to have a few dive bars. A dive is a down and dirty place for people who want a little anesthetic to get through the day and do it with others who feel the same. We have those places, I don't mean to offend the regulars of them, but to me they are the Pleasant Cafe, Guertin's Cafe and the Hotel Vernon during the week or during the day, on the weekends it has turned hipster. But the hipsters will soon tire of the Vernon and it will go back to its run down and dirty glory. Where people drink and sit and stare at the TV and play a little keno.

The article from Impulcity.com said that the patrons of Ralph's are rough around the edges. Since when? Maybe back in the day, but now, where I am standing and typing this, that's not the case. This is a local joint with good burgers and crazy things on the wall, where you can hear good bands. Its a local music bar. It has neon on the outside, its cool to be here. I can imagine some people saying its a dive, because things are old and the bathrooms are an adventure. It has its own personality, but that does not make it scary. That does not make it disreputable. I love that a national article is praising Ralph's. It is a wonderful place, but it ain't no dive bar. I know dive bars. I had a gin and tonic at Pleasant Cafe (which I don't recommend you do) and that's a dive bar. But people who need that kind of place will find it.

Ralph's is a local music bar with great panache. You want to go to a dive bar. Skip work and get a dollar Gansett from a dirty glass at the Vernon some random Wednesday at two in the afternoon. Or go to Main South and walk into Moynihan's and get a beer and a pickled egg. You will see the difference. Those two are worth trying out, and maybe an after work beer at Guertin's. Those should be experienced.

I hope that answers your questions, Victor. Thanks for asking and for supporting my useless tour of every bar in Worcester.

Dante of Worcester

Stop #75 - Northworks Bar and Grill

The Bar: Northworks Bar and Grill

 The Address 106 Grove Street

 The Day and the Time Tuesday at 6

 The price $6.45

 Did they ask me if I wanted a lime She just put it in.

 What was the type of gin It was Gordon's.

 What was the gin and tonic like I thought it was decent, there was some nice notes to it that didn't make me want to weep once again.

The Joint: This is one of those stealth joints that is a hell of a lot bigger than it seems from the outside. Its a good long bar area with several connecting dining areas. The place was a little more than half full, decent for Tuesday. The bar was a classic style, read slightly generic. It was clean, it had booze, it had signs and pictures. Been there, seen that. Nothing wrong, for some this familiarity can be very comforting.

Can I make a dumb statement? I know I don't have to ask, if you have read this tour, you know I ask a lot of dumb questions, and respond with even more idiotic answers. So here is the question, what's the deal with all the TVs? At a bar I guess that's just how it is, but not only did Northworks have TVs in the bar area, they had TVs hanging above the dining areas as well. Heaven forbid that you are at a bar and cannot see Sports Center (without sound) playing when you are having your highball cocktail, but to have it on while you are out with your family eating dinner, must we have Reality Programming in our eyesight? Is it crazy for me to dream of a bar without a TV going, maybe I would look at the paper. Maybe I would concentrate on my drink. Maybe I would have a conversation with someone nearby? In my memory, I have only been to one bar in this tour without a TV (one in seventy four) and I didn't even like that bar, go figure.

General Impressions The bar was full and that was surprising. It was December 30th and I think a lot of people were ramping up for New Year's. Near me, at the bar were a group of older men who all seemed to know each other. They talked about work, and some were doctors, bankers and other things out of my pay grade. They complained about how hard their work was. One said, "I am working harder than I ever had. I always thought when I got to this age, it would be easier, but I'm working harder now." All the other men nodded understanding and got more drinks. One of the guys was all hands with the female wait staff. One waitress was leaning over the bar, getting a bar order, and this old spry fellow had his arms around her and she tried valiantly to not offend him but still get the beers she needed for her tables. She had a resigned look, like this was not the first time the old guy regular did this. All the waitresses and bar staff knew his name. The bartenders were good, gregarious and just on it. They created a friendly atmosphere. Too friendly for one guy sitting near me though. I was tempted to tell this guy, leave the staff alone, they are trying to work here. Of course I didn't. I didn't eat the food but I had a friend who said he didn't like the place, that the service was poor and the food mediocre. I thought my drink and the service was good.

Amount of Time in the Joint 20 minutes

Will I come back No. Not my people. I am not the right age and not the right tax bracket.

2019 Update The owners couldn't make the new rent agreement work and so they closed. Soon after, the Fix moved in and are doing amazing business.

Stop #76 - Ritual

The Bar: Ritual

The Address 281 Main Street

The Day and the Time 8:30 on Friday

The price Six bucks, which surprised me, but that's what this tour is, nothing but surprises.

Did they ask me if I wanted a lime She just put it in.

What was the type of gin Bombay Sapphire. No shit. Really, a six dollar g and t with Bombay. I didn't see her put it in, but when I looked up I saw that the liquid level in the Bombay bottle was rocking like a wave. Call me Sherlock Dante, I notice things.

What was the gin and tonic like Alcoholic. Did she not see my Open Letter to Bartenders? I am already at the bar, I don't need to stay to buy a drink that is all booze and no panache. Wow. I didn't even taste the florals of the Bombay, I just tasted the fact that I was getting shitfaced.

The Joint What an odd place. With a name like Ritual I would want to see some kind of altar, some area where there can be a blood sacrifice for those who don't tip the servers. At happy hour, they perform the final scene of Shirley Jackson's story the Lottery, where everyone at the bar is given a folded piece of paper and the one with the paper with the black dot gets their Buffalo Wings appetizer free on the house, and then they are stoned to death. That's what I want a Ritual restaurant to be. They can get a Zagats rating and a FBI Most Wanted posting.

But what we have here is a concrete block with high walls. There are idols around the room that range from Buddhist statues to some angry Island God of Vengeance and Hotel Hospitality. But there is a little wear and tear in the place, some of the walls are marked with nicks to the exterior, like someone hit it with a ball peen hammer indiscriminately. The staff were either dressed in restaurant server black or go-go dancer regalia. I am talking about the woman who served me my drink, she had go-go boots and a dress that looked more like a doily. It was short, and then some. Making me wonder what the targeted audience is for the place. There was a serious, almost dire decorative idea mixed up with sexy girl server. Weird.

General Impressions The place is a restaurant that happens to have a bar in the middle of the joint. But the restaurant was odd. I don't know what kind of food it had or how good it was, but it was dark, foreboding and then there was dance music playing, sports on the four large screen HD TVs and who the hell knows what the esthetic is? They had a couple at the bar who were very dressed up and ready for a night out. Then there were others at the tables dressed for Mozzarella Sticks at Appleby's.

Then there were the two little kids walking around the bar area. Behind the bar. I guess they were the children of an employee (I saw what looked like the mother cashing out at the register behind the bar), but for a drinking tourist such as myself, you don't see seven year olds in the bar area of a place. I wondered how the kid would do making a Whiskey Sour, they teach that as part of the Massachusetts Education Core requirements for third grade. It's part of MCAS, isn't it?

Amount of Time in the Joint 15 Minutes
Will I come back No.
2019 Update This place closed. Not a shock. It is now the site of a pretty popular restaurant, Deal Horse Hill. I know. Crazy name, but decent place.

Stop #77 - Michael's Cigar Bar

The Bar: Michael's Cigar Bar

    The Address 1 Exchange Street

    The Day and the Time 8:45 Friday

    The price Eight Dollars

    Did they ask me if I wanted a lime He just put it in and it was a whale of a lime slice. I had apartments smaller than this lime slice.

    What was the type of gin Well

    What was the gin and tonic like It was alright, but not mixed well, I think. By the end of the drink, it was quite weak.

    The Joint. I believe (and you know me and my thorough research of this tour) this was the Firehouse bar. This is a big place with plenty of space to recline and hookah and smoke cigars. Their cigar room, where you buy your stogies, was a handsome space. The whole thing has a men's club feel. Dark wood, leather chairs. A guy was setting up to play some music when I was there, but I missed his brilliant performance (darn). This is the first smoking bar where it was smokey. Maybe their air filters were down or something. But I watched a low flying nicotine cloud travel from the low pressure front of the bar area to the high pressure cigar room. There was a nice crowd of people, but not too crowded.

    General Impressions: The first conversation I heard was a guy at the bar talking to a woman about the sales job he has, and she said she was in marketing and there was something about strategies and what not. This is no dive bar, buddy. This is affluent younguns and their toys, which seemed to be fine scotch and cigars. The class aspect of the place was interesting to me. I didn't feel like they were my people. The bar staff was decent.

    Any First Date Horror Stories?: Why yes, there was behind me. A man and woman were heading to the bar. She asked him what he was going to have and he said he was going to have a Jameson's and coke. She asked what Jameson's was and he said it was whisky. She said, "Oh. Hard liquor." The date should have ended at that time. but yet they didn't play the "Run Out As Quick as You Can" Card and he ordered a Jack and Coke (I know, he changed his order) and she had a wine. They talked about the shifts they had at work. He didn't seem to understand what second shift meant. In the space of three minutes the date was spiraling down, the repartee was getting more stilted, the conversation drying up like a puddle in the Mohave. He stated that it looks like there is going to be some music, maybe they should find a seat near and listen. She shrugged. They went to find seats to have a wonderful experience. Oh, this one is going to end badly.

Amount of Time in the Joint 15 minutes

Will I come back No. Cigar Bar meet Non-Smoker, Non-Smoker meet Cigar Bar, now go out and never see each other again. For its type, it seemed nice. I liked it a little more than Smokey Joe's. But I ain't going back to either one.

Stop #78 - 3Gs Sports Bar

The Bar 3Gs Sports Bar

The Address 152 Millbury Street

The Time 8:10 in the morning (That's right, the morning.)

The price 3.75 (I had a choice and had the short gin and tonic)

Did they ask me if I wanted a lime He did and he put it in

What was the type of gin Well.

What was the gin and tonic like I got a short one, about 10 ounces or so. It was fine for its kind. Nothing wrong with it.

The story: So, on this day, everything went pear shaped and I didn't have any place to go for the entire day. No commitments. No family obligations. Nothing. So after finding this out, I was heading home, driving through Worcester. And it hit me. I remembered years ago, talking to this woman who was a daytime bartender at a dive bar that no longer exists. She said that when she opened at eight in the morning, there were a small gaggle of people waiting for her to unlock the door. Just waiting there. Now most of those places are gone.

I was just thinking about it and thought, I bet 3Gs is one of those that opens in the morning. They were still on my list for this tour and in a fit of poor judgement, I turned a few corners and was there. The lights were on, but could I go in? I debated this like a mad man for a while and then said the hell with it, its for the blog. I have to do it for the blog. I have to have a gin and tonic in a joint that opens at 8am. For the kids. I mean the blog.

Okay, I was bummed, because I went in and it was just me, a bartender and a guy cleaning and stocking. I can't win. But I was lucky in that the bartender was also a little disappointed that no one was around and spent the time chatting with me. And chatting with me. He was amiable, and how.

The place is a run down dive from central casting. Dart boards? Check. Pool table? Check. Separate room with a stage? Check. Galaga Game? You betcha. They have keno and dart supplies and sheen of age and use. It ain't dirty, but this place is worn, you know.

The bartender and I talked about how it was probably the cold weather that was keeping the folks away, but this place is usually packed. All day, from eight until close, this place is filled with people, all nice folk. It's a great place. I asked if people come in after third shift and he shook his head, there ain't no third shifts left in Worcester. People come in because its eight in the morning and what else are they going to do? He told me that people play keno here. That this place has the second highest keno sales in Worcester. I'm not quite sure if that is something to go crazy proud about. He told me that the first of the month, when the government checks came in, the place was filled and then some.

He waxed nostalgia about how there used to be a lot of bars open all day. Now we could only think of this place and the Nines. The Nines, he said, has good looking day bartenders. He goes there on his day off. He doesn't go to 3Gs. I mean he needs a break from the old workplace, best to go half a block down to the only other morning hours bar in the city. But 3Gs is great and is usually packed and he was sure they were all going to come in soon. This place is worth staying at. But I had lingered for forty minutes and had nursed my gin and tonic. Now it was not even nine in the morning and I had finished my drinking for the day. It was a weird sensation. I would have loved to be there with people, but still, it was a nice dive bar experience. I doubt I will come back, despite the friendly bartender and his positive spin on the joint.

So I drank at a bar at the eight am opening. Did that, and now on to the usual time frame for this tour.

Stop #79 - Zorba's

The Bar Zorba's

    The Address 97 Stafford Street

    The Day and the Time 3:45 on a Friday

    The price 6.96. Really? Six dollars and ninety six cents? This is the sign you are not partaking at a neighborhood bar and at a restaurant, you get mashugana prices for your drinks. I want a place that would charge me seven bucks. Actually, I would like a place to charge me four bucks, but either way, rounded off prices, please.

    Did they ask me if I wanted a lime No, she just put it in. Yah!!!!!!

    What was the type of gin Well

    What was the gin and tonic like It was in a pint glass and it was fine. Not much flavor, it was alright for what I ordered.

    The Joint This big old restaurant has been Zorba's for a while, though with the plastic front, to keep out the cold I think, it feels temporary. The bar is big. The music is classic Greek. It was what you expect from a bar/restaurant. Dark wood. Sports on the TV screens. This was still early on Friday, The hour was not happying yet. A few groups were sitting at the bar. Two women were talking about work, they were teachers, probably from Gates Lane, which is one parking lot away from Zorba's. Another two-some looked like they were on an early stage date. They were cuddly and rapt in each other's eyes (cue romantic Bouzouki music, baby!)

    General Impressions It's nice to have a neutral place to meet after work and complain and find common enemies. This seems like a fine, though undistinguished, place for that. This is where the workers of nearby businesses can go, have a beer or a drink and some humus. I am sure it can get thick and busy around five after work ends for most.

    Amount of Time in the Joint 15 minutes

Will I come back Probably not.

Stop #80 - La Scala

The Bar La Scala

The Address 183 Shrewsbury Street

The Day and the Time Saturday at 12:30 in the afternoon

The price Eight Dollars

Did they ask me if I wanted a lime He just put it in

What was the type of gin Tanqueray. Lovely.

What was the gin and tonic like It was good, I like Tanqueray. The bartender did have difficulty finding the button on the tap that would give tonic. Part of me was afraid he would pick the wrong button, that I would get gin and Coca-Cola. Which I have had before, and really rather not have again.

The Joint This is a small Italian joint on Shrewsbury street that seems to hide every time I come in the area. I always forget about it. It has been around for years, but it doesn't stick in the mind. The place is small but comfortable. A medium sized bar. There was just me and another couple at the bar. They were having lunch, which was sandwiches. The sign outside did say they had Tripe on the menu. How cool, a place proudly selling tripe. I won't eat tripe, but its the kind of place I want to hang out in, Tripe Friendly Locations.

General Impressions The couple were watching a program focusing on the wonderful life of professional athletes, you know, true to life stuff. They ate their sandwiches. They lingered. They talked to the handsome young bartender. It was a cold Saturday, people were very relaxed, and the tripe was waiting in the back, for its time to at last to come. Time to shine little tripelette, time to shine.

Amount of Time in the Joint 10 minutes

Will I come back Maybe. It has the feel of a nice hole in the wall Italian place where the food is the star. It is a place I can see you sitting down at the bar for lunch and maybe a beer. I can think of worse places to do such a thing.

Stop #81 - Padavano's Place

The Bar Padavano's Place

The Address 358 Shrewsbury Street

The Day and the Time Sunday at six. The Patriots game had just started (the deflated balls game, wow, typing that makes me feel dirty).

The price 7.50

Did they ask me if I wanted a lime He just put it in. The bartender was pretty good.

What was the type of gin I asked for the basic and he gave me the Tanqueray. Nice.

What was the gin and tonic like It was good. A little flat, but it was good. I didn't care for the place too much, so I found myself not enjoying the drink as much. What can I say, a gin and tonic is really an alcoholic mood ring. Happy Dante, good drink. Unhappy Dante, a very long slog through a pint glass.

The Joint This is a new place, officially part of Shrewsbury street, but off the road in a parking lot. It is a large ceiling place with a small loft area. The bar is a big u shaped number. There are tables around it and in a area to the left. It was not too busy at the time. There was about 10 people at the bar, a few in Patriots shirts. A family in the Pats .blue.was eating and watching at a nearby table. The place looked kind of nice, but it felt sterile to me. And then going to the bathroom, only one bathroom which is fine, the door was almost blocked by a dough making machine. It was just there in the hallway taking up space. In a low rent bakery or a greasy spoon, that would be fine, but here in a place trying to look cool and slightly upscale, it kind of stuck out. A lot of the people at the bar knew each other, many of them, it seemed, worked there, ending work early due to the Pats game killing the business. I didn't feel fantastically welcome at the bar, nothing mean about anyone, just not too welcoming a place. Everyone knew everyone, and too bad for me.

General Impressions Here is how I felt about the place. At the bar was a young woman wearing very tight clothing that did not allow much to go unnoticed. She was sitting by herself, talking to two older men across the bar, as well as the bartender. My guess is that she was a waitress for the place, now off shift. After a few minutes, she took the offer of the two older men and joined them on the other side of the bar (actually, I can't recall if she just went over or if they asked her to). She sat in between the two men. She talked and smiled and laughed. We might call it flirting, but who am I to know these terms? Another woman came from the back and sat at the bar. going over figures in a ledger. She was an owner or manager. She talked to all the people she knew (I was ignored, I was like the invisible man, amazing powers that I have). She saw the two older men with the young waitress sitting between them and the manager woman said to one of the men, "You're a pimp daddy." The man laughed, shook his head and said, "No, pimp grand daddy."

And that's when Dante declared this stop on the tour over.

Yes, I have heard worse and raunchier. But is this what the place wants to be? May-December jokes among the regulars? And maybe that's the problem with Padavano's Place, what does it want to be? Is it a high end Italian Eatery? Is it a local watering hole? Is it a hook up joint? Is it a place where mixing equipment is left right outside the bathroom like an industrial bakery? It can be whatever it wants to be, just not with me.

Amount of Time in the Joint 20 minutes

Will I come back No. I hear the food is quite good. That's nice. But still, no.

Stop #82 - Fiddler's Green

The Bar Fiddler's Green. It is nestled deep in the breast of the Worcester Hibernian Cultural Centre.

The Address 19 Temple Street

The Day and the Time Sunday at seven during the Deflated Ball Pats Game. I hope that in three years, someone might read this blog and have no idea what I am talking about. These are pleasant dreams that I hope to come true.

The price Four Dollars (haven't seen a gin and tonic below the five dollar border in a while and what a pleasure it was.)

Did they ask me if I wanted a lime She just put it in

What was the type of gin Well

What was the gin and tonic like Alllllllllright. It was oooooooookay. It was another word with too many letters put in to signify inconsequence.

The Joint: It is a nice room. A very nice warm room suitable for people sitting and having a pint of dark and perhaps a wee dram. That's what it looks like. You have to walk through a few hallways and up a stairwell and there is the bar in this Irish Club. It feels like a real Irish Bar. It had all the attributes of a fine Irish Bar, save for just one wee thing. It was devoid of people.

General Impressions This is the third time I have come to this place, wanting to put it on the tour, and finding the bar completely empty. The first two times, I saw what was what, and split, because I want this place to be amazing. I know, I shouldn't put bet on the worth of a bar on this tour, but I don't know, I wanted this place to be amazing. This time, I came in, thinking that a big ball game would get people. I was wrong. What the hell. Can I never get it right? Don't comment, I know what the answer is. It's no.

I was about to turn tail and run, waiting for a better moment, but the bartender smiled and said hello and said she was about to close up. I told her, that I shouldn't stop her. She then said it's better to have someone there then close early. So damn. I had to get my gin and tonic. She chatted with me, killing time. She said that every other Sunday it was packed with Irish musicians. Not this Sunday. And Fridays are good too. Everyone was home watching the game she figured. We chatted for a bit while as I finished my drink and it was pleasant enough in a Bartender and Strange Fellow Having an English Drink at an Irish Bar sort of way. She was nice, she made the place appealing, even without people.

Amount of Time in the Joint 20 minutes

Will I come back Yes. I want to see it filled with Irish musicians singing and drinking and getting sloppy like they did in the Olde Country. I know this is not usually my MO, but damn, I want the bar in the Hibernian Cultural Centre to shine its best.

Stop #83 - Joey's Bar and Grill

The Bar Joey's Bar and Grill

The Address 344 Chandler Street

The Day and the Time Thursday at four thirty, a couple days after the big winter storm

The price Oh crap, I can't remember and I didn't write it down. Damn. I think it was something around 6.50

Did they ask me if I wanted a lime Yes, she did and she put it in

What was the type of gin It was Beefeaters

What was the gin and tonic like It was a decent drink. I liked it. Nothing wrong about it.

The Joint This is a long time restaurant, though not all in this location. It has a nice sized bar and a lot of tables for dining. I went on a off time, but people were there, which is always nice, though the number of folk were swallowed up in the space. The place has eclectic art on the wall, I enjoyed looking at it, I didn't like the art, but it definitely had a personality. One of the walls was painted light blue and in the middle of the wall in a long streak were glued little crystals, like there was a slash of stars in the middle of the restaurant. It was crafty, like the thing one of the designers from Trading Places would force on a contestant. With that said, I liked a place with a sense of style, even if it wasn't mine. There were more staff than customers at the bar, but I am sure they figured more folks would be coming in.

General Impressions "A cast of thousands! A cast of thousands!" That's what the guy near me at the bar said to the bartender as she found a way to leave him, to get back to work. He spoke a lot. Told stories about his family and friends. Cast of thousands, he said. Not here at Joey's at this moment. There were a couple folks at the tables eating early and then solo men sitting by themselves and each of them got the attention of one of the bartenders and then spun tails and complaints to them. Maybe its different later on in the day, but at this Magic Hour, the bar felt like the place where older men can confess their sins and feel connected to the world by talking at female bartenders. "Forgive me bartender, but it has been six days since my last barstool confessional." And then the bartender-priestesses would give absolution, or at least shots of Absolut.

One of the men asked the woman who served me, who might be one of the owners, where Joey was. "Its Thursday," she said, "He's home having a guy's night." I thought that was what bars were for. What do I know?

Amount of Time in the Joint 15 minutes

Will I come back No. Nice enough looking place. Friendly staff. Affordable drink. Just didn't have a feel for it. Blame the art on the wall, I guess.

Stop #84 - Mai Tai

The Bar Mai Tai - this is the second restaurant bar I have been to named after a potent cocktail (Sake Bomb the other) and I didn't care for either. Is that a sign that I should avoid any bar named after drinks. Do you want to go to the Pina Colada Lounge, Dante? No thanks.

The Address 69 Green Street

The Day and the Time Friday at 8:30

The price 5.86 or something like that. Tax is silly.

Did they ask me if I wanted a lime She just put it in

What was the type of gin It was a well gin

What was the gin and tonic like It was harsh. Like a little lighter fluid snuck in. Hey, there's nothing wrong with lighter fluid cocktails I suppose, just don't come too close with a lit match is all.

The Joint On the door going in, there was a sign saying all that entails proper dress code. To sum it up, don't dress like a gang member. It is never a hopeful indicator when there is a sign posted saying, don't be this way. It kind of means, that many of their would be clientele are THAT way exactly.

It is a cold, generic restaurant with soft lighting, a long bar and a few people around. There was about 10 people at the bar. One was a solo older guy drinking what seemed to be two drinks at once, and the rest were young people in groups having Mai Tais, scorpion bowls and other fruity concoctions. The bartender was decent, though a little slow. Some groups were at the tables eating, but mostly the action, if we can call it that, was at the bar. Perhaps it heated up with more properly dressed people later in the evening. That was possible of course.

General Impressions I feel for the bartender stuck with the talkative patron. Next to me was the older guy I mentioned. When he talked, you could tell, this was not his first drink or his third. "I haven't had any thing to drink since New Years. I was taking a break until this weekend to watch the Super Bowl. But I have to stay sharp, I have to ref a game in a few weeks, and I want to be perfect." He went on. I think the bartender asked how he was doing, and this is how it went. And then it went on to how he thought the Patriots were going to do in the Super Bowl against the Seahawks. He went into a very detailed, very slurred response on the previous game and why the Pats were going to dominate. The bartender started shifting her weight, putting her hands on her hips, looking at the other drinkers at the bar to see if anyone needed anything to get her away. But she stayed, trying to interject and not being allowed by the drunken sports monologuist. This went on and she kept on putting her "I'm listening to you face" and then there was a pause, she said, "You bet, you're right" or something to that effect. He stared at his newest drink and she went off to the other side of the bar. Rescued by the momentary silence.

The place, outside of this guy, seemed to be a young folks hang out, drink sweet drink and shout out loud kind of place. It lacked any energy when I was there. Ready to leave.

Amount of Time in the Joint 15 minutes

Will I come back No

Stop #85 - Takara Sushi and Japanese Steak House

The Bar Takara Sushi and Japanese Steak House

> **The Address** 10 Kelly Square
>
> **The Day and the Time** Friday around 8:45
>
> **The price** 7.50
>
> **Did they ask me if I wanted a lime** They just put it in
>
> **What was the type of gin** Well, or whatever they had
>
> **What was the gin and tonic like** It was bland but okay. Nothing

fantastic, but still acceptable.

The Joint This has a cool feel. It is a cramped slightly confused place that feels like a Chinatown joint. I liked the low ceilings, the pictures of customers taped to the wall by the front door. I liked the four hibachi grill tables and the regular tables thrown up front. It was on the fair side of clean, but only by an inch or two. This has been around for a while, but I haven't been in before. One person said to me, "I don't know how they're still in business."

It was a Friday night and there were people there. Three of the hibachi tables had people around them, but no hibachi. They were all just having sushi and entrees. It was a weird way to eat, with all of the customers having a small counter like area for all their food and drinks around the cold metal hibachi table. The other tables up front were mostly filled as well as a few couples at the bar, which was both sushi and booze bar, everyone's favorite kind. People were drinking Mai Tais and something Scorpion Bowl-ish. The crowd was young and getting ready to go to clubs. There was a group of ladies dressed in sparkly little tops, that were not appropriate for the outside temperature, but looking goooooood has nothing to do with keeping warm, I suppose. I know, I am an old fuddy duddy, I see those clothes and I want to have them change into big bulky sweaters and nice cozy mittens.

It was busy but not packed and yet the staff was moving around like it was all hands on deck. They were moving around like a hot mess. No one seemed to have just one job, staff was flying about like things were in chaos mode. Like electrons flying about, ramping up for critical mass.

General Impressions I sat down at the bar and someone asked what I wanted and I said I would like a gin and tonic and he said, "I get someone who understand." He went and got the sushi chef and I repeated my request and he said "Gin and tonic water?" I nodded and I got my drink. Two people to get my drink. I drank it and then a third young man asked me if I was all set and because I never got a bill or anything I said, "I just want to pay for my gin and tonic" He nodded and went off. Five minutes later he reappeared with another gin and tonic. This is all lack of common language, but it does speak to the hot mess-ness of the place. If I had one person taking care of me, perhaps I would have gotten out easily. I said, I just wanted to pay and got up to the cash register and paid for my drink and I was pretty chagrined and gave a hell of a tip. But that's the problem with the place, they had no system to take care of a customer. Hell, I saw it at the tables, two or three staff were interacting with each table. There was a lot of repetition going around. There was a lot of repetition going on. See? Even here.

Amount of Time in the Joint 20 minutes, mostly waiting for my bill which turned out to be another drink.

Will I come back The place felt fun and comfortable but the disorder got to me. Maybe if the food was awesome, I could deal with the chaos. But it was weird that they didn't have even one hibachi going and they were just using it for large groups eating. So, the answer is no.

2019 Update *Hey look at that, the white middle aged guy was upset that a non-English speaker couldn't get his order right. It's interesting looking back at these five year old dispatches and seeing my own flaws. With that said, the place was a big slab of run around crazy. They closed a year or so later. There is a Vietnamese restaurant there now.*

Stop #86 - Brew City

The Bar Brew City

> **The Address** 104 Shrewsbury Street
>
> **The Day and the Time** Sunday at 2:30 on Super Bowl Sunday
>
> **The price** 5.62, without tax it was five and a quarter.
>
> **Did they ask me if I wanted a lime** She did.
>
> **What was the type of gin** It was well. I could tell by that cloying syrupy taste that it was my old nemesis, Gibson's Gin. What does that say about this tour that I now can identify rot gut booze at twenty paces? It is a dubious skill, at best.
>
> **What was the gin and tonic like** Like all Gibson gin and tonics, it was work, baby. It was work.
>
> **The Joint** This has been around on Shrewsbury Street for a while and I have been to eat here twice quite some time ago. I thought it was okay, and I remember the fries being good, but I never felt the need to return. On going in this time, I am struck once again about how weird their front door is. Its not on Shrewsbury street. Its in the back parking lot. It always feels odd when that happens. I want to go in from the street, but no, walk to the parking lot little Dante.

There is a nice sized dining area and they also have a separate bar area that was probably designed when you could still smoke in bars. This is nice in that it feels like a bar first and a restaurant second. The bar area has exposed brick and large area to drink, as well as tables. There were a few folk there, getting ready for the Super Bowl. People were talking sports and local politics, but it was not a loud place. Folks were eating, Beers were drawn. Things were moving along. The bartender was good and attentive. Always a nice thing

> **General Impressions** Its a sports bar. It was good. It was alright. I liked it. I felt comfortable being there, but that's about it. I was not excited about it. It was a good middle of the road place, but it didn't do much than make it a good place to have a beer and leave. There is

nothing wrong with it, from my time there. It didn't wow me. Later that day, someone asked me about the tour and I said, "I went to Brew City. Its very sports bar. I liked it." And then I shrugged.

Amount of Time in the Joint 15 minutes

Will I come back Maybe. If friends want to go, I will go.

Stop #87 - Volturno

The Bar Volturno

    The Address 72 Shrewsbury Street

    The Day and the Time Sunday at 2:50 on Super Bowl Sunday

    The price 8.52

    Did they ask me if I wanted a lime No, he just put it in

    What was the type of gin Well

    What was the gin and tonic like It was good, a little on the flavor deprived column, but a fine refreshing drink.

The Joint A large high ceilinged Buick dealership has been split in two. One side is Sweet. The other side is this place. It is big and airy. The rectangular bar is in the middle. It is clean and almost too big for a pizza joint. But this is fine dining pizza, which is a funny thing to write. There were a few eating at the bar and a few lingering at the tables. There were TVs in the bar area, but they were unobtrusive, you have to be in the bar to see them, which is a lovely concession for those who want to eat but not have TVs in their eyeline. While I was there, a couple hipsters came to the bar to get dirty martinis and debate over which pizza to have.

General Impressions I was having a drink at another bar, waiting for the next snowstorm to show up and was in a conversation with Bartender Brian's Brother (that's a lot of Bs) and I mentioned that I was recently at Volturno and BBB said he hates that place. He hates all those artisanal pizza places. He just want a good old Greek style, thick, greasy pizza. He can't stand how the pizza at these hoity toity places gets cold right away. And who comes up with all these crazy toppings? Just a pizza that's good and greasy. Is that so much to ask?

On the quiet times, it's interesting to watch the waiters all gather by the bar to talk, to kibbitz, to complain. They were just clustered by the end of the bar like no one else was there, and I guess at this time of day, after a busy lunch service, 10 or so folks eating and drinking can be considered no one. This afternoon's conversation seemed to be about martial arts training and one waiter was showing off his moves. The clustering of wait staff: I know this happens in many restaurants, but I am beginning to dislike it more an more. This hanging out, chilling in front of the dirty public. It just adds to the us against them mentality between servers and customers.

How do you judge a place on down time, especially because the bar area seems to be made for waiting for a table and for single people having a meal and not for a bar sense. The bartender asked me if I was going to watch the Super Bowl. Which is a pretty funny question because we are in New England. It is like asking someone if they have skin. He was attempting a friendly little repartee, I know. No harm. But he was happiest when he said his shift was over in an hour. Good for him.

Amount of Time in the Joint 15 minutes

Will I come back Maybe. The pizza might be good. This is not a bar to hang out in, but as a restaurant, why not?

2019 Update I should state that this was the part of the tour affected by the weather. We had a hell of a winter in New England. I think there was something like one hundred inches of snow in Worcester. This slowed me down. I couldn't find street parking and so I didn't try as many places.

Stop #88 - O'Connor's

The Bar O'Connor's

The Address 1160 West Boylston Street

The Day and the Time Tuesday at 12:30 (I picked this place, because it was one of the few places I could park at, what with the snow taking all the spaces)

The price 5.99

Did they ask me if I wanted a lime She did ask

What was the type of gin It was well

What was the gin and tonic like It was a good drink. It was refreshing. When people say, I like a gin and tonic in summer because its so refreshing, this is the kind of high ball they were talking about. Of course, those hypothetical people were probably drunk when they said it, so truly, what do they know. A nice drink.

The Joint Ah, O'Connor's The big behemoth of Irish Food and Drink in Central Mass. I need to give a caveat. I have been here several times over the years, I mean, how could I not. And for the most part, I have not enjoyed it. I think the food is good, though sometimes its not, so spotty at best. But one thing I have never enjoyed is the service. It is slow, inconsistent and sometimes they are surly, and not a fun surly. When my wife, who mostly likes it, wants to go, she knows to go with friends and not me. There are too many options in the world to have to go back to a place you don't like too much, so I don't. Also, we have friends who love the place, but have had bad experiences there recently. And its so popular, you can wait a long time to go in and feel packed and crowded.

It is a huge gigantic place. It must have started small and just added rooms and rooms. It is covered in gallic memorabilia, but it feels authentic and heartfelt from the staff and not kitschy. It feels right all around, except for its large rabbit warren size. Its the Watership Down of Irish joints. The bar area is lovely with dark wood and a huge bar. When I went in on this, one of the many snowy days, there were about 15 people there, but the size swallowed them and it felt like no one was there but me. A few people were at the bar, eating and drinking solo. A group of teachers, off for a snow day, were at a table, talking loud about issues at their school. One of the teachers brought her two kids, but they were at their own table, ignoring their food and playing on their tablets. Even with this slow day feel, I did witness a guy at the bar get a nice looking burger, he took a bite and brought the bartender over and spoke to her. She said sorry, took the burger back to the kitchen and returned with it in a few minutes with her apologies. So even on slow times I saw some service issues.

General Impressions But no service issues getting beer and drink. They do that fine. This was a good efficient bar and she did it well. I drank my good drink and stared off thinking thoughts, perhaps on the Troubles, perhaps on where I was going to put the snow I was shoveling from my drive way later in the day. I had my elbows up on the bar, and they felt good there. This felt like a good bar to lose time in thought. I liked how it had people there, but it was quiet and accepting. I liked it on this, the off hours. Where you can be with yourself or a friend and just drink nice and slow. This is not the case on the busy times,, or when getting food. But in an off hour time and the need only for a drink, I couldn't have been happier.

Amount of Time in the Joint 15 minutes

Will I come back Yes, for the bar on weird hours of the day. Not when its busy and not for the restaurant. But its a hell of an Irish bar when you see it that way.

Stop #89 - Shangri La

The Bar Shangri La

    The Address 50 Front Street

    The Day and the Time Wednesday at 8"20

    The price 5

    Did they ask me if I wanted a lime No and I did not get one

    What was the type of gin It was well. The Well of Sorrow. The Well of Anger. The Well of Bad Taste.

    What was the gin and tonic like It is like that old joke that was in a Woody Allen film. Two old ladies were at a restaurant eating the same meal. One of them said, "This meal is awful. Its disgusting, I wouldn't serve this to my enemies. It is just plain bad." And the second woman said, "Yes, and such small portions." That's how I felt about this mostly icey glass of supposed gin and tonic. It was really not a good drink, and then it was suddenly done.

    The Joint This used to be several large Irish bars and has been empty for several years. It is great that it's being used. There is no parking around, so I don't know how it will do, but it's a large good looking place (still feels like an upscale Irish Restaurant, but that really isn't such a bad thing). The bar is on one side of the room and there are plenty of TVs but only one keno screen. It was odd, during my stay there, a guy came over to where I was at the middle of the bar and gave the bartender his Keno slips and then went back to the table at the corner that was close to the Keno screen. He came back often to get more keno, like a migratory bird. Like a gambling addicted swallow returning to Capistrano.

    For a Wednesday with much snow outside, there was a good amount of people. The bar had about 15 or so people eating, drinking, watching keno. There were three large circular tables filled with college age Asian customers. My guess is that there were from one of the nearby schools. They were all enjoying the food and the company. I have eaten here at Shangri La when it was at its old location and I liked the food. It was good decent Chinese food and a friend has told me the sushi is excellent. The place gets a lot of business lunch traffic, which is nice to hear, because a place downtown is hard on a guy who has to park his car.

General Impressions Throughout my time drinking here, I realized I was singing to myself. The whole time I was singing under my breath. No wonder no one wanted to sit near me. I had to listen to my own crooning to realize I was singing the Kinks's song Shangri La. One of my favorites. You should go here and sing this song to your dish of lo mein. Practice Practice Practice.

As a place to gather, its alright. There was a nice selection of people at the bar, different ethnicities and ages. It was all over the place and there is not a lot of joints that do that, so it went up in my estimation. The drink was lousy, but at least it was five bucks for the honor. And the food, from what I hear is still good.

Amount of Time in the Joint 15 minutes

Will I come back I can say probably yes. I have liked their food. But parking downtown,..sheesh. It is not my favorite Asian restaurant bar on the tour, that would be Ken Chin's, which is crazy. But this one is alright. Now sing it with me, "Now that you found your paradise/This is your Kingdom to command/You can go outside and polish your car/ Or sit by the fire, in you Shangri la."

Stop #90 - The Citizen

The Bar The Citizen

The Address 1 Exchange Street

The Day and the Time 8:45 on Wednesday

The price 8

Did they ask me if I wanted a lime He didn't and I didn't get one. This shocked the hell out of me. And I know, I shouldn't be shocked by anything. For such a place to not even ask and not give you one. Call the Press. Call the Police. Call Ms Manners.

What was the type of gin It was their basic gin, I didn't catch what it was, but it was a very decent one.

What was the gin and tonic like A very nice drink. I liked it. I could tell they used Fevre Tree Tonic Water. It does make a difference. I would have liked a lime, but that's just me being a philistine I suppose.

The Joint I ate here once with my wife and a few friends and never came back because, though the food was good, the service was terrible. I mean the waiter started snapping at us when we asked if we were going to get our food (food was coming out in dribs and drabs and we just wanted to make sure all the dribs came with the drabs) So I never returned. My wife did go again, and said the service was still kind of lousy. Can someone explain to me how bad service is accepted? I don't get it.

But this was different for I am on my tour-quest. This was me just going to the bar. Which should be fine, and for the most part it was. Though I was the invisible man once again and getting the bartender's attention was tough. This is slightly understandable because when I went to sit, I took a seat at the bar that was partially obscured. There were beer taps between me and the bartender's gaze. But I was hoping he would see me. It took him five minutes to notice me. He apologized and got me my drink. There were other people around, mostly business people out for dinner and a few dates. The place is nice but relatively non-descript.

General Impressions It was interesting to notice the business people couples. They were here for work and drinking and eating and trying to get along. This is the kind of person who would go here, and for that, its seems perfect. Complicated comfort food and high end drinks. Its a nice place to be where people order Negronis. The dates were interesting too. One couple were at the bar chatting and smiling and then the guy got a call on his cell and went to the door to have a long conversation. The woman of the couple just did things onto her phone, texting or facebooking, she would break out into smiles while staring at the small screen of her phone, occasionally taking a bite of her food. This is how we go on dates now.

My invisible status continued when after a while I had finished my, very good, drink and waited to pay and leave. The bartender still could not see me well so I suppose was out of sight. The restaurant manager saw me there and pointed me out to the bartender who then came over and took my money. Swell of him. (A brief break from the snark to say I thought the bartender was very friendly, just could not or would not see me)

Amount of Time in the Joint 20 minutes

Will I come back Nice enough drink. Nice enough high end atmosphere. Enough. No.

2019 Update *It closed last December. I am pretty sure nothing has taken its place.*

Stop #91 - The G Bar

The Bar The G Bar

The Address 62 Green Street

The Day and the Time Wednesday 8:30

The price 5

Did they ask me if I wanted a lime He didn't and I didn't get one

What was the type of gin Well

What was the gin and tonic like Abhorrent. Okay, that was mean. Let's just call it sub-par

The Joint A strange confused place. It has the front of a sports/ Irish Bar- long bar and tight area with tables. But in the back was a place for dancing, for boogying, for getting down with yu bad self. And to make sure that you had the realization that this was a dancing joint, there was a disco ball emitting many colored lights across the walls and the patrons. There were strings of lights around the place blaring opposition to a joint that felt like a sports bar, a bar to watch the game in. And the bartender, who felt like the owner, truly wanted a sports bar. On the TV was the NFL Network's rebroadcast of the Pats - Ravens play-off game. So what was this place. Pretty empty is what it was. Four at the bar and three at a table.

General Impressions The bartender (owner?) finished with getting me my drink (he was attentive and speedy, no problems there) and went to our side of the bar (the paying customer side) and sat with a buddy. He said he wished that the NFL was still going on. He talked about the Super Bowl, where the Pats won, dontcha know. He said there was a lot of people in then. And thank god the Pats won because all those people would have left right away if they had lost. With them winning all the folks stayed till close. They just kept on buying drinks and celebrating. And then the bartender (owner?) said "I wish we had a night like that every month. That would be great." I am not a businessman, but let me say that hoping for a monthly Super Bowl win to generate liquor sales is a bad business plan. Get a crowd and then do better with a good sporting event. Not the other way around. It does not bode well for them. But what do I know? I am the idiot who pledged to have a gin and tonic in every bar in the second largest city in New England, my judgement should not be considered valid.

Amount of Time in the Joint 10 minutes

Will I come back No

2019 Update *It should not be a surprise that this place closed. I am sorry about it. People start a bar as part of a large dream. They want to have the bar they always wanted to exist. But running a bar is a tough go. It starts out as a losing proposition. This location is now Buck's, which is a whisky and burger bar.*

Stop #92 - The Lucky Dog Music Hall

The Bar The Lucky Dog Music Hall

> **The Address** 89 Green Street
>
> **The Day and the Time** Wednesday at ninish
>
> **The price** 5
>
> **Did they ask me if I wanted a lime** He didn't and I didn't get one. But that was alright.
>
> **What was the type of gin** Well
>
> **What was the gin and tonic like** It was in a plastic cup. It was ice from a bin. It was gin from a bottle. It had tonic that came from bottling plants deep inside Middle Earth. It was all those things and more.
>
> **General Impressions** Once again, I was the only one there. This shouldn't have been too surprising, a couple weeks ago I went here to try a gin and tonic and it was a ten dollar cover charge because bands were playing. I gave a pass. So I came up with a policy of no big cover charge for this tour. I am sorry, I ain't made of money. I mean I am not getting top shelf booze here, I'm a well drink kind of guy. But I still want to get to all the bars on this tour that I can, so I wanted to try to get those cover charge joints on quiet moments. I checked out the Lucky Dog's website where they said that on Wednesdays people come and play dominos. Okay, no cover and dominos? Sign me up!

But all I saw was the bartender watching South Park. He was Al. He was personable. He was bored. I was it for custom (poor guy). He told me that the owner usually works Wednesdays and would bring his friends over to play dominos. But the owner is on vacation so its just Al and no dominos. We chatted. He got pizza delivered, he even offered me a slice. He works the weekend and working at a music club is tough. Some nights are awesome, some are just the band and their girlfriends. It is a crapshoot. Some nights are great, packed.

The Joint This is a rock club. It has pictures of Betty Page in the bathroom, it is the image of roadhouse glory in the middle of Worm Town. This is a place that's about the people listening to the band. When its empty, it's just dancing in the skeleton. It's a good place. I've been here before to see some bands. Hell, I saw the Bindlestaff Family Circus here and that was a hell of a show. The kind of show you don't forget.

Amount of Time in the Joint 20 minutes

Will I come back Why not. For a drink, I don't think so. But a good band shows up, or a friend playing bass in trio, why not. This is a fun place to see bands, but its a little sad when its empty.

2019 Update They were sold to another person who wanted to keep it a music club. It became the Cove and it survived for several years. But the landlord upped the rent to something nutty and now it is a shell. The landlord is hoping for something big when the Ball Park comes in. Everyone is hoping for something big.

Stop #93 - Primo's Extension

The Bar Primo's Extension - Ladies and Gentlemen, we have a winner. We have no need to continue with the rally. The winner is in. The worst name for a bar in Worcester.

This is a complicated tale to tell. I have actually been here before for the tour when it was the bar for Center Bar and Grill and then it was sold to the Primo's and the bar was called the District. The restaurant part is Primo's, which used to be one of my favorite restaurants on Shrewsbury Street. I loved their risotto. Now, I debated putting it on the list of bars to go to. Thinking it might be the same as it had been.So I crossed it off the list. And then, a few weeks ago they changed the name to Primo's Extension. Primo's Extension? Thank you Gods of Blogging! I wanted something easy to rag on, and thou provided in abundance to your supplicant Dante.

One bartender friend said, when he heard of the new name, "They're not even trying." I think that's incorrect. I think they are trying. Trying hard. Trying long. Trying for that extra inch. Trying like an ad in a 1970's men's magazine, where the need for extension appeared to be tantamount. Come to Primo's, we can take care of any inadequacy, at the Extension.

Or perhaps I am being too naughty. Maybe it's an extension like you didn't finish your final exam and you con the prof to give you an extension. Or an extension from the banks. There is so much this Green Street place can be, and more!!!

Okay. I'm done. And I'm slightly sorry. But how could I resist? It's called Primo's Extension for god's sake.

The Address oh wow, I still have the rest of my review to do. The address is 106 Green Street

The Day and the Time Friday at 9:15

The price 5

Did they ask me if I wanted a lime He asked, do you want a lime, a lemon, or both. And then I realized that it was the same bartender from when I came seven months ago when it was the Center. Then he gave me a lime and lemon, which I called The Donnie and Marie, a little bit country, a little bit rock n roll.

What was the type of gin Rot gut well

What was the gin and tonic like It was bad, but not bad bad. Just not particularly memorable.

The Joint It was a non descript bar. Nothing to recall about it. There were three loud girls at the bar. One was wearing a tiny sombrero (call Vogue, the next trend has been unearthed) and one very drunk guy who talked to the bartender for the length of my stay. They talked about DUIs (aways a nice bar conversation) and bartenders who sucked who are still working. I didn't know how I felt about listening in on such talk. Who am I kidding? I live for this mishigoss.

General Impressions It was dead. I was happy to leave. I spoke highly of the bar when I was there the last time, when it was Center, but this time just felt sad. But, I did see several dishes passing by to the dining area and they smelled amazing. Primo's still got it, for the food part.

Amount of Time in the Joint 15 Minutes

Will I come back Not to the Extension. But I do want to go to Primo's, the ristorante. It smelled good and they were great back in Shrewsbury Street days.

2019 Update They didn't last long. What came in it's place was the Hangover Pub. That is a popular gastropub that features bacon in almost every dish.

Stop #94 - Industry

The Bar Industry

    The Address 109 Water Street

    The Day and the Time Friday at 9:45 (still too early it appears for the party to be partying)

    The price Six dollars.

    Did they ask me if I wanted a lime No and I didn't get one

    What was the type of gin Well

    What was the gin and tonic like Surprisingly acceptable. It had a sweet taste to it that reminded me of the times me and my college roommate Tom would drink Booth's gin and Sprite. Not that this Industry drink had Sprite in it, but there was a feeling of soft drink about it. I don't know why. But it was an easy enjoyable libation, no matter what the ingredients were.

    The Joint What you expect from a city dance club. There was a very long and very narrow joint. Two areas. The front for drinking and chatting. The back, for drinking and dancing. The only problem with this, there was no one present but the staff and me.

    General Impressions What the hell? It's like a Twilight Zone episode. Or a 50s SciFi movie called the Last Drinker on Earth. Wherever I go, whenever I go. I am the only person there who wants to buy a drink. I wandered around, looking for Rod Serling who would no doubt pop up behind a wall and say, "For your edification we present a tourist drinker who thinks by going to every bar in the city he lives in he is being interesting and funny, but he will be greeted by empty bars and dancerless clubs. He thinks he's having a gin and tonic in every bar in Worcester, but in fact he is having a plastic cup full of loneliness in the bar district of the Twilight Zone."

    Okay, in all seriousness. I know it was before ten, but just barely before. And still, no one about.

    Amount of Time in the Joint 10 minutes

Will I come back In some ways, its better I came when it was empty. I don't like dance clubs with blaring music. It's not the community I search for. So maybe I was given the best possible outcome. But I don't know if I came too early or if no one came at all. There are people who want to dance and drink and hook up. This place looked like it could be alright. But man, almost 10 o'clock and tumbleweeds. To answer the next question. No. I will not be returning.

2019 Update *What's the expiration date on dance clubs? Two years? Five? Six years? This lasted for a bit and then closed up shop. The location stays a place for night clubs though. Until this year, it was the address to District Nightclub. Now, it is becoming Vibrations Nightclub.*

Stop #95 - Tatnuck Grille

The Bar Tatnuck Grille

    The Address 638 Chandler Street

    The Day and the Time Friday at Four

    The price 5.89

    Did they ask me if I wanted a lime She just put it in.

    What was the type of gin She asked what I wanted, "Bombay, Bombay Sapphire. Tanqueray." I said no. Just the basic. She didn't look at me as she headed to the gin bottle of shame.

    What was the gin and tonic like It was a pretty weak drink, which was okay. Not a great drink, due to the lack of flavor, but it wasn't terrible.

    The Joint It's a restaurant on one of its sides and a long bar on the other. The bar is bright and people are there for Keno. Its a real Keno place. About ten people were there, drinking a little, but very intent on looking at the Keno screen. Some of them talked amongst themselves, some of them were silent in their hope and contemplation. The decor was bland. If you like the company and the food, then that's what might recommend the place. It had a very neighborhood type of feel. Not a dive bar, but a place where people living by Tatnuck Square can have affordable food and beer.

    General Impressions The bartender was a comedian type of bartender. I haven't seen too many of them, but they are memorable. These are the types of folk working behind the stick who feel that people are here for the show that is their personality. They are always on. In the ten minutes I was there, she happily berated several regulars, played air guitar, complimented a regular and got drinks. She was working hard for the money. So hard for the it honey. She is working hard for the money, I should hope that home somebody treats her right.

The first thing I noticed about the bartender-floor show was how she complimented a woman at the bar as being so funny. Just so funny. I was thinking, now we have to say, no, you're the funny one. The woman who was told she was so funny got the appellation by saying her losing at Keno was her voluntary tax for Charlie Baker. She and the bartender did a little air guitar to the Kinks song playing on the radio, the great All Day and All Night guitar solo. An older gentleman returned from smoking and the bartender gave him some guff. He turned to me and said, "This is what I have to put up with here. She always is like that with me." And I thought, and you love it buddy. It was a nice friendly enough place and I was ready to move on.

Amount of Time in the Joint 10 minutes

Will I come back I don't think so. Nothing wrong with it. But its not that enticing to me. I like how the regulars can sit and josh about or be quiet, that the bar is long enough for all kinds. But still, I don't think I need to return.

2019 Update: *They are no longer in business. They are now an Irish bar, apparently called Scruffy Murphys.*

Stop #96 - Viva Bene

The Bar Viva Bene

The Address 144 Commercial Street

The Day and the Time Sunday at 7:30

The price I can't recall. Which is weird, because my memory is not that bad, but there was something about this place that just robbed me of thought. It was a drain of a joint and it did it to my powers of recall (damn you Viva Bene! Damn you!)

Did they ask me if I wanted a lime I didn't get one. Oh wait, I think I paid eight bucks for the drink, I think that was the price point, because I have a memory of thinking, "Eight bucks and no lime." So let's pretend that I am a steadfast reporter and I know that it was eight bucks (I'm not quite sure, but I am steadfast)

What was the type of gin I think after some difficulty I got Tanqueray because they were out of well gin. It took the bartender a bit to realize that the bottle was empty so had to set up a fresh one.

What was the gin and tonic like It was fine. If when I state fine I mean I thought it was a placeholder drink. A drink of no consequence with the hope something better might appear on the horizon.

The Joint It is a long mainstay of downtown, a venerable Italian joint that has weathered the vagaries of time and every time I have walked by it, it has been completely empty. This is true, this is the fourth time I have walked by the place thinking I would go in and have a gin and tonic. The first three times, there was no customers in the place. I am not exaggerating, no one was there. And this wasn't Monday at three in the afternoon, two of them was me walking by on a Friday around eight or so, and yet, still no one there. I wasn't up for the sadness of it. I didn't want to be so alone in such a large place. This time, I earlier had a conversation with a friend who hates the place. He hates the food, hates the service and hate hate hates it and was not surprised that it was empty, so I figured, this is the next stop whether people are present or not.

This time there were people. But for a reason. They were having a concert starting in about forty minutes, it was the Worcester appearance of that great band of the 70s, The New Riders of the Purple Sage. Yeah, I don't know a damned thing about them. Not one bit. Wait, let me go to wikipedia and see if I know them. Be right back.

Well that was an illuminating two minutes. So Jerry Garcia was in the band in the beginning. Well he isn't any more. I'm pretty sure.

But with all my ignorance, and I certainly do have that in abundance, people were out for the evening. There was about 40 or so older people present who had paid 35 dollars to see them, so what do I know. I think I, in my forties, was one of the youngest person there. Let me just say one thing, they made everyone (not me, I talked them into letting me in for a drink without paying) wear one of those plastic bracelets that you see the kids wear when going to a club. I must say that I think it's ridiculous they made a bunch of people in their fifties and sixties wear these impossible to take off ID bracelets. Were they worried there was going to be a lot of people sneaking in to see New Riders of the Purple Sage for free? Was this a true security concern? .

General Impressions Despite the influx of people there that I had never seen before, it still felt lonely. It still felt sad. Maybe if the food was great. Maybe if they had awesome forgotten bands playing every night it would be great. I watched one of the bartenders struggle with a beer tap that was sudsing up and seeing her frustration with the equipment and the establishment and I knew to leave.

Amount of Time in the Joint 10 minutes

Will I come back No. I don't know how it is still in business, but good for them. I know that I left a half filled joint feeling like it was some barren outpost of a long forgotten Worcester. Remember when Viva Bene was great and vital? Remember when we listened to New Riders of the Purple Sage? Those were lovely times indeed.

2019 Update *They were empty by the end of the year. The space is still empty.*

Stop #97 - Pho Dakao

The Bar: Pho Dakao

    The Address 593 Park Avenue

    The Day and the Time Wednesday at 4:15

    The price 6.50

Did they ask me if I wanted a lime, No. She looked at the bar fruit and said to me, "I'm going to cut up some fresh lime for you. The lime here looks pretty sad." I agreed and thanked her. No one wants sad limes. But that might not be fair to the lime slice. They might not be sad, they might have clinical depression. There is no reason to make fun of a slice of citrus with a mental issue. I think we should start a fund. We can have a telethon. Please give for Happy Limes and Quinine!!! (which should be the tagline for this blog)

    What was the type of gin House gin, as she said.

    What was the gin and tonic like It was forgettable. There was nothing wrong with it. It was a serviceable drink that did its job, edged off a long day at work

    The Joint This is a good Vietnamese restaurant that I have eaten at before. I really enjoy it. The bar was on the left side of the restaurant. A typical horseshoe bar, but with fake bamboo around it as an almost partition to make you realize that it is the bar area and not the restaurant, and that it is the kind of place that believes in fake bamboo, to be fed to fake panda bears I suppose.

For the time of day, the restaurant was starting to pick up. People were eating and having a nice time. I was by myself in the bar area though. So by myself that there was no one to man the bar. A waitress noticed my solitary status and came over to offer me respite, or at least a drink. She made my drink. Looked up what the price would be for such a concoction and then went back to the lively restaurant part. I was alone to drink and watch ESPN on the TV and to be stared at like a museum piece.

General Impressions My solitude, without any other drinkers or even a bartender was fine. It was a good sturdy bar, the place to have a good sturdy drink after work. After a long day filled with frustration, people have always gone to bars to drink it out. It might be one of those universal constants they talk about. Sometimes at these after work sojourns, they want to talk about it and be loud with other patrons, sometimes they want to have appetizers to go with the anesthesia. But then there is the guy at the bar who sits with the drink square in front of him and you know that that is his only function. To drink and sit and not to speak. Maybe it's these restaurant bars that are best suited for the quiet after work drink. The alone in public libation. The I will have just have one here and then off and back to my life type of cocktail. Maybe later it will get busy and raucous, so drink quickly, exit resolutely, and leave a good enough tip that will allow you to do this near silent ritual at this restaurant bar again.

Amount of Time in the Joint 10 minutes

Will I come back Yes, but not for the bar. The food smelled amazing, and I know from the past that it tastes great as well. Don't let my maudlin typing dissuade you. Its a good joint, and the bar, for what it is, was fine. We have a bunch of good Vietnamese restaurants in town, this is my wife's favorite. So there.

Stop #98 - Greendale's Pub

The Bar: Greendale's Pub

The Address 404 West Boylston Street

The Day and the Time Wednesday at 8:45

The price 5.50

Did they ask me if I wanted a lime No I didn't get one

What was the type of gin Well

What was the gin and tonic like It was a bland drink with a little bit of a kick. Nothing out of the ordinary anyway you look at it.

The Joint It is a big room. A bar on one side with tables on the other. I guess you can get food here but I did see a few folks bring subs in to eat. A pool table was a center of attention. I saw one guy bring in his own pool cue. Does that really mean anything? Can you learn anything about the player by the fact they schlep their own stick along? The main attraction was the large stage area where older men played blues. It was their Wednesday blues jam open mic thing. I don't know how it worked, because while I was there, it was the same band playing the whole time. But guys were signing up. All the musicians and the folks that brought in instruments were guys. The music was not too loud, and it was decent for Wednesday at a blues jam. There were women there, just not playing music.

Everyone was a regular. Almost everyone coming in was greeted with familiarity if not a big shout and a hug. It was the place these people come on Wednesdays. One couple brought a large stack of Girl Scout Cookies, and other regulars picked up their orders. A few of them opened up the boxes and tucked in. By nine fifteen or so, I think we had 30 or so people in the house, which is nice.

The place is not immaculate. It is real run down. But do you want immaculate in a place like this? The ages of the patrons skewed older. I was one of the youngest people in their and I am in my mid forties. (when did that happen?) Someone told me that all the folks that hung out in Gilrein's in the eighties have found refuge here at this joint (on Wednesdays).

General Impressions This was more fun than I care to admit. The friendly atmosphere, the worn but lively blues covers, the serviceable drink. This is what you want some time. I got a kick watching the older woman in the tank top, the dyed spiked hair, and the unfortunate tattoos dancing in front of the band, rocking out with her bad remembered self. Sometimes a guy would be dragged up to dance with her, but really, she seemed satisfied dancing solo.

Amount of Time in the Joint 20 minutes.

Will I come back Yeah. I can see it. I have been here before to see a friend play in a pick-up band a while back and had just as good a time. So yeah, not often I don't think, but I can see it happening.

Stop #99 - The Raven

The Bar: The Raven

    The Address 258 Pleasant Street

    The Day and the Time Wednesday at 9:52

    The price 5

    Did they ask me if I wanted a lime He did ask and I got a thin slice to accompany my libation.

    What was the type of gin It was well

    What was the gin and tonic like Not a bad drink. Once again, the old Gin and Tonics Across Worcester Axiom - If the place is good, the drink will improve.

    The Joint This is not a place with a lot of buzz in regard to no one mentioning it in the litany of rock clubs in Worcester, and that's wrong. Sure, it's in the worst part of Pleasant Street, but the joint is wonderfully deceptive. The outside makes it look like a run down house. Hell, you have to go into a side door, and as you enter, you get a huge large clean rock club. Hey presto, it appeared out of nowhere!

The place is big. And it has a hell of a stage and from what I have been told by multiple people, an amazing sound system. The bartender-owner told me that they can have 100 people in and it doesn't feel packed. That's a good sized joint. It's big enough for a couple pool tables and dart boards and a side bar and and....

This was open mic night and it was supposed to start a half hour before I got there, so of course it hadn't started yet. But that's open mics. They occur in a wormhole of broken clocks and discarded guitar picks. A large, older guy with a big beard was roadying the sound system from the stage. Playing guitars in different spots of the stage. He looked like one of the Hell's Angels from the film Gimme Shelter 30 years late (but much nicer).

There were about ten adorable people in faux punk gear waiting for the music, soaking in the scene. They were young and clean and dressed to be punk rock kids. You just want to take them home in your pocket.

Also at the bar were local faux tough boys from the neighborhood playing pool. One of them tried to act gangsta and impress the college punk girl at the bar. It was awkward. There is a strange dichotomy about the music kids and the local tuffs playing pool. I could imagine issues occurring, that they would all break into syncopated rumble dance routines like they were the Jets and the Sharks. I have been assured by friends who have been there, that though this weird divide between locals to Pleasant Street and the kids coming for the music is there, the place is big enough for it to be amicable. I didn't see any music, but I liked the strong rock club feel. Bartender Brian said that it reminds him of the clubs he ran into in LA. It felt a little like the Whiskey on the Sunset Strip. That's high praise indeed. For me, it reminded me of the Living Room in Providence, though the Raven is bigger and cleaner.

General Impressions I came in older than most there, though the friendly bartender was about my age, which was nice. He was one of the owners of the place and he grilled me on why I showed up and what I think of the place. I lied a little, or a lot, but we had a mutual acquaintance and chatted about him and about music. He was welcoming to everyone. He made the place even a little better.

Amount of Time in the Joint 20 minutes

Will I come back I can't imagine I won't. I really enjoyed my time there. It was the better version of all those clubs I went into in my twenties when my friends's bands were playing to almost empty houses. It's in a bad stretch of town, but I liked it a lot.

Stop #100 - Jillian's

The Bar: Jillian's

    The Address 315 Grove Street

    The Day and the Time Friday at 8pm

    The price 6

    Did they ask me if I wanted a lime She just put it in, yah!!! Go her!

    What was the type of gin She asked if I want Tanqueray and I shook my head and said "Just the basic please." Maybe the Ice Age that was to come was done out of spite that I was a Well Drink kind of plebeian. It was well. I don't know how it was, though I think it tasted of the dreaded Gilbert's gin.

    What was the gin and tonic like It was a pint glass of ice. A lot of ice. I have had ice filled gin and tonics on this tour before, but this was the iciest. (Song of the Blog- You're as Cold as Ice by Foreigner. Go ahead, sing along). I do understand that the bar owner wants to have the best amount of profit margin and one way is to give a small amount of product and putting gin in a ice filled pint glass is one way. This was a pint glass, but she filled it past the bridge with ice before pouring. There was a jagged dome of ice over the lip of the glass. Some of the ice was over an inch past the top. I thought she was going to shake off some of the excess ice, but no, she began to pour. But she didn't have to do it for long. A little gin, a little tonic and boy howdy you have a drink. Actually you have a glass of ice. Even after the liquid was put in there was still a good sized cornea of ice over the top of the glass. I know this is the usual tactic at McDonald's, but there the soft drink is under three bucks and you can close the lid, not on this one.

    A couple sips and the drink was over. It was not good gin, but I still wanted something for my six bucks. Let me put it this way, At Cisero's, for 3.25, I had a gin and tonic in a plastic Dixie cup and I do not think I am wrong when I state I had more drink in the plastic cup than I did in the pint glass at Jillian's. I guess this is how they get your money without paying a cover. For six bucks, you get to enter the vaunted halls of pool table land and you get a complimentary cup of ice. A bah-gain.

The Joint I haven't been here in a long time and my memory is that it was a big place with pool tables and games and video games. I recall a nice balance of pleasant distractions. Now, it is still big but it feels mostly pool tables. There are a few other games and a couple air hockey tables, but it feels like a cool kid pool hall now. Couples playing pool. Its a fake pool hall. All the cool factors of pool halls are not present, but you have pool tables and you can order large glasses of ice. Lots of young folk in black looking hip. There is something nice about a drinking place that also has things to do. Playing pool or darts. A band was setting up, so they did use the huge space well. It was clean and well lit enough.

General Impressions As I sat at the bar, playing a video trivia game, I got to hear another server and bartender conversation. The kind of conversation that does not take into consideration that paying customers are nearby. She said, "Yeah, so I went over to his house and yeah I stayed over. No. I didn't sleep with him. He tried, but I wasn't into it, not that. But you know its nice to know that I could if I wanted it. If I really need it. Nice to have the option." And then she went off to a table to do some work I suppose. Hi, Dante of Worcester here, don't mind me. Sorry I am here at your bar interrupting your discussion. I almost expected them to get annoyed at me for my presence in the midst of their bitch session.

While playing the video trivia game I got a high score and got to put my name on the top ten players. For my name I put down "Weakassdrink" but the computer would not allow that so if you go to Jillian's you will see that my name being Bad Name. (I guess that's their default for naughty words) But Bad Name is pretty good.

Amount of Time in the Joint 15 minutes

Will I come back On this experience I will say no, but I can see coming here if friends want to gather. I would not recommend it, but I wouldn't be adverse on going if asked.

2019 Update They closed. The building was still there the last I looked. I got to say, I don't miss the place.

Stop #101 - The Hotel Vernon

The Bar: The Hotel Vernon

    The Address 16 Kelley Square

    The Day and the Time Thursday at 8:45

    The price 4

    Did they ask me if I wanted a lime No and I didn't get one

    What was the type of gin Well

    What was the gin and tonic like It was a lousy drink that I ignored for a while. Was I expecting brilliance in a glass? I do not think so. At this place you get drinks not for flavor but for strength and fortitude.

    The Joint Ah Dive Bar, thou has been discovered. You can't get any more perfect than this unclean gem.It is the bar of a welfare hotel. It doesn't get more dockside gritty than this. There are tales of its life as a speakeasy, but what people really know is that you can get dollar drafts (in mostly clean glasses). It is three rooms, the front room where the bar is. It has ugly dirty paintings of pirates that are just fantastic. There is a back room where the pool table is and then the ship room where bands and what not happen. That's a good place to hangout, I have always liked that space, but it was closed this evening.

Two female bartenders made sure the cheap drinks were flowing. One was bubbly and flirty. One was a little brooding. I liked the yin/yang of it. These two handled the crowd well. I do remember being here once when a pretty young bartender was working and a guy was being uber creepy to her, telling her how pretty she was and how nice she was over and over. You could watch her get paler and paler as the hour passed. That bartender left the employ of the Vernon soon after.

While I was there, a very tall man slowly came and set up in a corner speakers and set it up to his laptop. He was the DJ (he is what he plays). There is not a lot for DJs to do lately. He didn't smile, just tap away at his computer. I was there to hear Pet Shop Boys doing West End Girls and then Black Sabbath came on with War Pigs. People ignored the music. This would be the place to hear Sinatra, but that's just me. I mean, War Pigs is a fine song.

General Impressions : The bar was mostly occupied. People came and went, depending on their schedule and their budget. Some moved about with spry step, some slower, with hunches and shuffled feet. One young woman took out a cane to get to a side table to play chess with an insistent man who wanted to play chess and had asked several women if they were up for a game. She was willing and moved with some deliberation. The place had a feel of a hidden picture. It looks like a normal run down bar, but concentrate and look harder and strange delights appear, as if almost by magic.

The guy I was sitting next to seemed like a normal chap, in a well worn jacket. He was quiet and focused on his draft of Gansett. One of the bartenders came over and asked him if he wanted another and then, suddenly, he devolved into a non-speaking nether creature. he might have mumbled an assent and then picked up from under his stool, a plastic bag and began to scurry through it, like Gollum searching for his precious. The guy mumbled a secret language to himself as he searched the bag and searched. The bartender waited and then crossed her arms and began to get bored as the guy still scurried into the bag. He finally re-emerged with a crumpled single. He handed it to her. She grabbed the bill and poured him another. I looked at him again with different eyes. When he got his beer he quieted down and began to slowly sip at the glass.

The place feels like a genuine dive bar but with training wheels attached. Its beginners level drinking hovel. It felt like a place you can hang out in Dive Bar splendor and still feel safe. Relatively. I did mention the guy asking all the female patrons to play chess with him. This might be a fun place for men, but women might have a tougher time.

Amount of Time in the Joint 30 minutes

Will I come back Sure. Its a fun joint. I used to come in a lot. Not recently. There are times when it is filled with young hipsters acting cool and correct, but this time felt like a run down joint to get a drink and that's a fine enough thing to be.

Stop #102 - The Red Lantern

The Bar: The Red Lantern

The Address 235 Shrewsbury Street

The Day and the Time Sunday at 6:30. Easter Sunday and people were coming out from their family obligations and getting a drink or two.

The price 5.50

Did they ask me if I wanted a lime No, she put it in.

What was the type of gin Well

What was the gin and tonic like It was harsh, but fine considering.

The Joint Someone who knows of this tour I am on asked me where I have been lately and I said, "The Red Lantern." She stepped back, shocked. "That's a strip club." "No, it's a Chinese restaurant." After a few minutes, we figured she was thinking of the Lamplighter, which is not on the list of the tour, in case you're wondering.

But that's the kind of place it is, nice but easily forgotten and misidentified as something else. This is a good sized Chinese Joint that is clean and decent looking. I don't know anyone who has eaten here, so I can't say much about that. On this Easter evening, people were coming in, happy to be out. A gaggle of regulars were playing Keno. And there it is, not a strip club, but you are still tipping a dollar at a time to the Keno balls shimmying its groove thang on the video screen (know, that's a lousy analogy but its the best I got, so I'm keeping it.).

Two women were seated near me, catching up, but most were drinking and playing Keno. The bar is on one side of the restaurant, and it had one Keno screen, though I can't see why they don't have more.

General Impressions Here's the story I heard. One of the Keno regulars was telling another regular why the bartender (a usually lovely woman, full of infinite jest and all that) was in a sour mood. The woman said that some drunk came in and ordered a bunch of dishes, like Garlic Shrimp and other expensive things and then five minutes later changed their mind, canceled the order and split. The regular said that because the bartender put the order into the kitchen, she's on the hook for it. "The night just started and she's already forty bucks back, no wonder she's not happy."

It's nice to have a place where people like to come and feel welcome, if only that could happen without the need to Keno.

Amount of Time in the Joint 10 minutes.

Will I come back Not a bad place, but no.

2019 Update They closed last year. They were in business for fifteen years, which seems like a good run for a joint resting in the middle of a long restaurant row.

Stop #103 - Kenichi

The Bar: Kenichi

    The Address 270 Shrewsbury Street

    The Day and the Time Sunday at 7

    The price 5.35

    Did they ask me if I wanted a lime He did and I got one.

    What was the type of gin It was the dregs of society

    What was the gin and tonic like It was a gin and tonic. Something you get through on the way to something you like

The Joint: It is a small Sushi place on Shrewsbury Street. The food smelled alright, the bar was busy for an off time. Filled with regulars. Most were drinking and watching a Fast and Furious movie on the TV.

General Impressions Let me just say that I cannot understand the purpose of the Asian Restaurant bar. It is the hangout of people, but I don't know how it works. In Red Lantern, they are there, I think for Keno. This, I don't know. They were all regulars at the bar, here on Easter Sunday, ten people were gathered and were drinking and talking. There was three people near me and they were the show. A couple and their female friend. It struck me that the girl in the relationship was much more into the guy than the guy was. She was leaning on him, pecking his cheek, being three sheets to the wind cute, and he was glowering, being stoic about it.

They talked about getting a good price on tickets to see Kid Rock. There was a debate between whether the tickets were 20 bucks or 40.A ridiculous conversation, because Kid Rock is worth any price. One of the girls asked what a friend's contact number was and the other replied, "508 I'm a drunk" which I don't believe is an actual number. Kid Rock showed up again in the conversation, I think it was in someone's Match.com profile, being a lover of Kid Rock. Am

I missing something? Did he become popular again or did I stumble into a wormhole and wind up at a bar situated comfortably in 1997?

Then, as we were all having a fine time fueled by Rap/Rock nostalgia, a guy down the bar looked at his phone and then said, "Pablo." The guy near me who was part of the couple looked at someone calling his name. The guy with the phone said, "Jerry is coming in, he will be here in a couple minutes." The guy and the girl in the couple looked at each other, they both sat straighter. True to the word of a text message on a phone, a guy came in and someone said, Hi Jerry. Jerry went over to Pablo and they said hello, but nothing was happy about the handshake. Jerry went down the end of the bar and got a beer. The happy banter was over, the tension had arrived. The tension of regulars. The problems of people all wanting to go to the same bar even though no one wants to cast eyes upon the other. Short story instructors can have a week's worth of writing prompts based on this moment. Me, i was just trying to have my drink, which I saw was almost empty and so I left, feeling more relaxed the further I got from whatever it was I was sitting next to.

Amount of Time in the Joint 20 Minutes.

Will I Come Back No

Stop #104 - Armsby Abbey

The Bar: Armsby Abbey

> **The Address** 144 Main Street
>
> **The Day and the Time** Friday at 4
>
> **The price** 8
>
> **Did they ask me if I wanted a lime** She did and I got one

What was the type of gin I didn't see, something above the bottom rung I believe.

What was the gin and tonic like It was decent. A little harsh on the back of the mouth, but alright. I know this gets tedious, but when we get to the eight dollar or more range of Gin and Tonics, I really want a damned fine drink. And I might have enjoyed this one at 4 bucks, or 5, but at 8, I think my taste buds gets snootier and more unnecessarily discerning.

The Joint A very popular place. It was getting packed at four, that's saying something. People were having a lot of designer beers and food on strange plate like surfaces. The Place has an old pub feel with chalkboard listings explaining the intricate details of the beers on tap and folks were cool and hip and staring at their smartphones. There were a lot of large beards and black jeans. The wait staff was efficient and moved at a pace. One could only imagine when the true rush occurred. The bar was decent and I was comfortable there.

Full Disclosure Section of our Proceedings: I don't like the Armsby Abbey. I have been there a few times half a decade ago and did not enjoy myself any of the three or four times my friends and I went. The food, the service or the general demeanor of the place. I saw rude bartenders, annoyed waitresses who you had to rustle up to get your food or check, and food that was so extreme in seasoning it was almost uneatable. People love the place, and that's fine, I just am not one of them. That's how businesses and tastes work.

But what really set it for me is that I was having a conversation a couple years back with a bearded tattooed individual at another bar and the topic of the Armsby came up and I said I didn't care for the place. He got upset with me, and started to interrogate me (truly interrogate me) on why I would think such factious ideas. He wouldn't let me be done. He kept on asking details, he needed details. So I gave him my reasons for not caring for a bar and he kept on explaining to me why I was wrong in my thinking (which is always a great way to make a friend).

He explained I didn't understand what I was saying. I was wrong, The Armsby was great. The bartenders weren't rude, they were just professional. The waitress wasn't unhelpful, just busy, don't I understand the difference? The young man, by saying that was implying that I was a philistine with no sense of taste and that I must change my ways in this Microbrew Inquisition or be labeled a heretic and only be allowed to get boneless buffalo wings and Budweisers at the Chili's location of his choosing. Alright. This guy wasn't an owner of Armsby, though he shamelessly name dropped the owners' names, in explaining why their decisions were sacred word brought down from Restaurant Heaven. But it was the fervency that annoyed me. This proselytizing was unpleasant and if this is the way the lovers of the place act, then I wanted nothing to do with the Armsby.

But here I am on my silly little project of going to every bar in Worcester and to have a gin and tonic. I am nearing the end and still I have been putting off going here. But I figured, get it over with, and it might be a great time and.....

General Impressions ...it wasn't bad. I thought it was a decent, busy joint. The oncoming crush would get rid of the ability to have a relaxed and leisurely visit but it wasn't bad. The one weird thing I noticed was with the wait staff and bartenders was the lack of smiles. One was half heartedly smiling, but you could almost tell that she was trying to remember not to. The others I saw had it down, not exactly frowning in their work, but at no time would their mouths twitch up. Is this a mandate, to be serious and stoic at all time, because that's why we go to bars, for the abject stoicism of the activity. Bartender Brian was not surprised about this when i told him, he said this place and Legal Seafood, you will never see smiling, they are just too busy. Well, where's the joy in that?

Amount of Time in the Joint 20 minutes

Will I come back No. I was relieved it was an okay time (good though unsmiling service and a serviceable drink), but there are so many wonderful places in town, why bother with a place where you have had bad service or poor food? It's great to try every place and to give a joint a second chance, but with this one popular location, I will probably beg out of invitations.

Stop #105 - Mezcal Cafe

The Bar: Mezcal Cafe

    The Address 30 Major Taylor Turnpike

    The Day and the Time Friday at 4:30

    The price Six dollars

Did they ask me if I wanted a lime He just put it in..

What was the type of gin He asked me what I wanted. I told him that I would have the basic and he went through a few thoughts and poured me one with Boodles which he then went on saying that to his mind, it is better than Bombay or Tanqueray, so there.

What was the gin and tonic like It was a nice drink, nothing bad to say about it. It was well proportioned and had taste, can't be anything but pleased here.

The Joint This is a big industrial sprawl of a restaurant. It doesn't have the warmest feel, due to the cold design, but it's a hell of a place nonetheless. I mean, they have a wall with paintings of luchadores, how can you not like a wall of luchadore paintings? The bar is big rectangle and the bartenders have to work hard to navigate it. It was not busy when I was there, but still people were at the bar for a drink and an appetizer and folks were coming in for dinner and what nots. The bartender said that this was the slowest it had been all day and he was sure that that was not going to last.

Just to be honest, i know the bartender, he's a casual friend, though unaware of this tour. We spoke of friends and things that were happening. Another acquaintance of mine who works here, ran over and gave me a drive by hug. This is a Gin and Tonic Across Worcester first. The first surprise hug of the tour. Neither of them, I think, knew of my nefarious intentions, so bwa-ha-ha, to you all. I was a booze tourist wolf in tipsy sheep's clothing.

General Impressions I have eaten here and like it. The bar is good as well. Its' a loud boisterous after work place. The place focuses on tequila drinks, but the high ballI had was good. There is something to be said about the large loud, after work joint. Nothing wrong about a good one, and this was good.

Amount of Time in the Joint 15 minutes

Will I come back Absolutely. Maybe not for the bar, but for the food, no doubt. I like the place and I was happy that the gin and tonic that was not eight bucks and it was good. (I mean that's why you all read this blog, right? To find out about gin and tonics? Correct?)

Stop #106 - Smitty's Tavern

The Bar: Smitty's Tavern

    The Address 611 West Boylston Street

    The Day and the Time Saturday at 2:30 in the afternoon

    The price 5 bucks

    Did they ask me if I wanted a lime She did and I got it

    What was the type of gin It was their well, which was Boodles.

    What was the gin and tonic like It was good, a little too much gin, making me taste the alcohol more than the other flavors.

    The Joint Its two room separated by a couple steps. There is free over-salted popcorn (which I partook and adored), there is a horseshoe shaped bar, there is a sense of wear and age and there is the worst parking for a bar in Worcester. Hands down, I would rather park right in front of the Hotel Vernon and risk my car and my life on waking around Kelly Square then trying to vertical park right off of West Boylston Street. Getting out of there gave me a heart attack. There has got to be a better way to arrange parking than what they have.

The bar was barish. It had its Keno regulars and its residents talking about all the fun they had there the night before and what they were doing for the rest of the day. One of them wasn't drinking, though his wife tried to get him to, because as he said, once he starts drinking, he can't stop and he has things to do that day. (Buddy, there are church basements for that issue) Everyone was nice and friendly. The bartender was attentive. There was a good local vibe going on that was not exclusionary.

The bartender swiped her hand on the bar and mumbled to herself, the two regulars closest looked at her and she said, "We got little ants everywhere recently. They're all over the place. They'll be gone in a few days, but right now they're annoying." The guys she was talking to smiled and nodded, but I found myself staring at my highball glass intently, seeing if I could spot any foreign movement. My issue with this is not that they had spring ants, but that she was talking about it to the patrons. Let it be unspoken. Just your little secret.

General Impressions It's a bar. A while back, someone in the comments of this blog, mentioned this place as one of the great bars of Worcester. I am happy for anyone to read this, and happy for those who love a bar to state it loudly and proud. But I will respectfully disagree. It wasn't bad, but it wasn't spectacular. A neighborhood bar. Nothing wrong with that. Actually, a lot to be said for such a distinction.

The bartender had a baseball cap that was in camo colors. A regular came in and complimented her on it and she said, "Yeah, it says Keno on it. I got two of them. The Keno rep came in earlier and gave them to us. You want the other?" She gave the guy the other Keno camouflage cap and he put it on his head quickly like he had won something. This brings up a lot of questions. Does Keno need to push their wares so much? Don't they already have a set and addicted clientele to begin with? And why camouflage? Does Keno need to go stealth on us? Keno will blend into the surroundings and sneak up on you like a state sanctioned gambling commando and shoot you in the face. Or something like that.

Amount of Time in the Joint 15 minutes

Will I come back No. Neighborhood bar not my own. Also, horrible parking.

Stop #107 - Evo

The Bar: Evo

The Address 234 Chandler Street

The Day and the Time Saturday at 9:30 in the evening

The price 7.23 (aghhhhh! Just give me a real price)

Did they ask me if I wanted a lime She did

What was the type of gin From what I saw of the bottle, I believe it was Gordon's. A fair though not outstanding libation.

What was the gin and tonic like. It was light and fine. Nothing spectacular, but certainly not an insult to the good name of Gin and Tonic.

The Joint This is a hoity restaurant that I have never cared for. They do high end health food derived dishes and I have never enjoyed it too much. My wife used to really like it, but the last few times she went, the food was not as good as she had had in the past. She had me bring home their version of a Hawaiian style pizza and it was pretty lousy.

It is a snazzy looking place that is clean and tres presentable. If only the food was the same. Anyway, I came near closing so it was not super busy. The bar is small and is some kind of metal. I am not versed enough in bar design to tell you more. The bartender was helpful and polite. There was a couple finishing a huge glass of wine debating whether they want to go to the movie after all or just go home. This went on for almost the entire time I was there. I was tempted to take out a quarter from my pocket and have them flip for it. For those who want to know, I believe they skipped the flick, but that could have changed when they got to the parking lot.

General Impressions Feh. It was a bar in the back of a restaurant. Not a lot of personality. It is just there. Nothing bad about it as a bar, but it's just an appendage to a restaurant, not an entity onto itself.

Amount of Time in the Joint 15 minutes

Will I come back No

2019 Update The restaurant closed and reopened as Bootlegger's Prohibition Pub. I went there once. It had a nice sized bar and the place was lame. Sorry, it was. That was closed and became a Grab and Go food section of the Living Earth Market.

Stop #108 - Victory Bar and Cigar

The Bar: Victory Bar and Cigar

The Address 56 Shrewsbury Street

The Day and the Time Sunday at 2pm. This was in the middle of a long weekend and the sun was out and people were gamboling along Shrewsbury Street. A lovely day to sneak into a dark cigar bar where sunlight is not allowed.

The price 7.25 (I believe, I was given a bunch of change and I think that's what it came to)

Did they ask me if I wanted a lime She just put it in.

What was the type of gin It was well

What was the gin and tonic like It was fine. I enjoyed it. It was a little weak, but that's alright. You don't need a hammer of a drink on such a nice day.

The Joint When I came in there were a few people at the bar. A few were watching the NHL Playoffs on TV, a couple was at the corner of the bar playing cards. I don't know why, but I have a definite thing for people playing cards in bars. Or reading a book. Or both. I like that sense of calm, or relaxation, that allows you to crack open a volume or shuffle a deck. It was in the middle of the day and the place was dark. Dark in the daytime, as David Byrne would say. Two guys who worked there were cleaning the walls and the ceilings with rags, one proudly said they were getting ready for their big 11th anniversary party. He was jubilant, which is surprising to see in a cigar bar at Sunday at two, blame it on the beautiful day. It is small, but has a back room and big leather seats and dark wood that is well kept. It feels like a men's club from the fifties, which is pretty much what they were aiming for.

General Impressions The place reeks of cigarette and cigar smoke. There ain't no amount of cleaning or filtering will hide the fact that this is a joint for smoking. Drinking, sure, but I got such a strong ingrained tobacco odor. This can't be a complaint, because its a cigar bar. The two guys were cleaning and cleaning, but I would think that it will be slightly in vain.

It looks like an old club and it feels like an old club. It plays the part well. If I was a smoker, I could see myself hanging out, watching sports, talking with man friends about all the man things I might want to discuss in a manly tone of voice (is ballet an acceptable topic of conversation? Just checking. How about the intricacies of macrame?). The bartender and the employees were happy and helpful.

Amount of Time in the Joint 15 minutes

Will I come back I don't think so. The non-smoker part of me precludes that. But out of the three cigar bars I have hit on the tour, this is the one I would like to go back to.

Stop #109 - The Green Hill Golf Course Club House (The Grill on the Hill)

The Bar: The Green Hill Golf Course Club House - the receipt I got when I paid for the drink said that its called on the Grill on the Hill. Grill on the Hill, doesn't that sound like the kind of bar Dr. Seuss would come up with?

The Address 1929 Skyline Drive

The Day and the Time A lovely Sunday at 2:20 in the afternoon

The price 5 bucks

Did they ask me if I wanted a lime She did and then I got it

What was the type of gin Well

What was the gin and tonic like There was nothing special about the drink, nothing at all other than the part that it was a nice day for a drink and I liked being at a golf course drinking without having to schlep clubs and swing at the itty ball.

The Joint This is the club house for the local public golf. I never had this on my list of bars to go to, but I was driving on this lovely Sunday and saw someone put a bag of clubs in their trunk and I thought, isn't their booze at the golf course? I didn't know, but I was willing to find out, for you, my hoard of gin and tonicers. The worst that would happen would be I went up, saw nothing like a bar and then split. It has happened before. I went and did find a club house restaurant. It had thin old carpeting and old wood furniture, like you would expect. The bar was a corner and was pretty small, but the bartender was friendly and attentive. She told me that because they were just opening up for the season, they only had paninis and some appetizers, the main menu was starting the next week.

General Impressions It's nice to have a day this year when you can play golf. I spoke to the woman behind the bar and she said that they only opened up the weekend before. I asked if this is the latest they ever opened and she seemed to think there was one year a while back that was this late. But it was a beautiful day, the day before Patriots Day and the bar was kind of empty, people were outside playing golf, who wanted to be inside drinking? Well.....me. But's more a calling than a desire. There were four guys, finished with their round, sitting and shooting the shit. They were trying to figure out the best time to play again together and comparing which their favorite courses were in the area. They were having beer and one was having one of the sandwiches that were available. On the TV was bowling and myself and everyone else was drawn to it like moth to the ten pin flames. It was after a few minutes when the bartender said, "Wait, what time is it? The Sox game is on. Does everyone want the Sox and not this?" She got no serious response and then the Red Sox was turned on.

At a nearby table, three women were having food and wine. They were all friendly and chatty like they hadn't seen each other in a while. I spent some time pondering them, wondering if they were golfers themselves, just done with the links or were they wives of golfers, thrown together with friends like ports in the storm. I hoped I was wrong, that they were golfers, but they weren't dressed for golf, but what do I know about Links Sartorial Splendor? Some folk were outside. It was a good relaxed way to be.

Amount of Time in the Joint 20 minutes

Will I come back I'm not a golfer, so I don't think I will hang out here. I also am not a golf groupie, wanting to sit next to local legends who hit birdies everytime. I know, no one does that, but this is just me going on. So I will say no, but I do have to say that I have been to clubhouses before and this was a friendly one. I don't think anyone would be upset with the service or the view.

Stop #110 - The Flying Rhino

The Bar: The Flying Rhino

    The Address: 278 Shrewsbury Street

    Day and Time: Sunday at three-ish

    The Gin and Tonic Story (The Gin and Tonic Story, doesn't that sound like a lost Preston Sturgess film?): Dear Readers, I did get a gin and tonic from Flying Rhino, but it was two weeks ago and nothing has stuck from my time there about the gin and tonic. There is nothing that I recall. I remember that it was just okay. I don't remember how much it was, maybe six or seven bucks. I don't remember the lime situation. Usually, I have a strong memory of those things due to my Super Gin and Tonic Abilities that I have honed since I was a child, but this time, its all gone. You will see, it just didn't work for me, so I apologize for not being too precise on this one - Red Faced Dante.

    The Joint The place was busy, and has a inviting funky feel to it. I must say that with all that, it was looking like it could deal with a little freshening up. New paint, new something. Nothing wrong with it, just felt a wee bit (and I do mean a wee bit) tired. All and all, a nice enough place. Busy, that's nice too.

    General Impressions: I ate at Flying Rhino in the past twice. Both times, the food was poor. I learned my lesson. I have not been there in 14 years. It is saying something that there is a restaurant that has lasted 14 plus years, that's a great accomplishment and there must be something very appealing about it. I don't know what it is. The bar was busy for Sunday at 3, which is great. The outside tables were filled, people were laughing and eating and drinking. Yes, there must be something appealing about the joint, but none of it rubbed off on me. I got my drink and the bartender was professional but not friendly, which is fine for a busy afternoon. There was no seats at the bar so I stood and drank. I got no interesting details that I wanted to impart here. I got no positive points I wanted to mention. What I got was a drink at a busy restaurant bar. I don't know why I am so ambivalent about it, but there you go. Maybe its because earlier that day I hit Victory Bar and Cigar, then Wormtown Brewing and then to the Golf Course Club House and had a nice experience in all of them, that maybe I was tired or tight or whatever, the Flying Rhino is just didn't sing to me. All I know is that after two minutes I drank my high ball quickly because I just was not excited about being there. There is nothing scientific or anthropological about it, I just didn't dig it. I can't say that any survivor of the restaurant is bad, there are many people who love it, i just wanted to be somewhere, anywhere, else. I am sure that is me and not the bar. Blame it on the final leg of the tour.

Time Spent at the Joint: 10 minutes or maybe less

Will I Come Back: No

Stop #111 - Via

The Bar: Via

The Address 89 Shrewsbury Street

The Day and the Time Sunday at 5pm.

The price 7

Did they ask me if I wanted a lime He put it in.

What was the type of gin It was well for them, which was Tanqueray

What was the gin and tonic like Judging from the gin and tonics I have had at other places where they used Tanqueray, not all things are equal. This was better than most. Not too much gin where you can taste things and the tonic was fresh. This is becoming a thing I notice, if the tonic is old or flat, you can have top shelf gin and it will still taste like swill. All this to say, this was good.

The Joint A behemoth of a place with people already there and eating. The set up for the place, to get to the bar is weird and not fun. You have to go round the back and then traverse through dining rooms to make it, at last, to the Oasis of the bar. It is big and accommodates a lot of people, but the set up of rooms and flow seemed to be created by a four year old with an incomplete set of tinker toys. Once I made it to the bar, all was right in the world. A large comfortable, clean bar.

General Impressions This is fine dining as seen as assembly line. It is pleasant but not too personal. This is a restaurant that has a bar and those sitting at the bar were eating and then having a drink. The bartender was good. The people next to me were post college and loudly discussing one of their party's possible move to California. They were telling her what she should do, always a great way to keep friends. They also were complaining about an old boyfriend of hers, they called him The Asshole. There is something kind of amazing about having such a loud personal conversation in public as if no one else is around. Perhaps that's why they pay the prices of the drinks and food, so they can be personal and talk privately for all to see and hear.

Amount of Time in the Joint 15 minutes

Will I come back I don't think so. The food looked and smelled good, the place was striving for elegance and achieved it, the bar was what you would want it to be, but I prefer my Italian restaurants to be small and quaint, and my bars to have just a tad more personality. Seems like a fine place, just not for me.

Stop #112 - Mambo Drink Hookah Lounge

The Bar: Mambo Drink Hookah Lounge

The Address 105 Water Street

The Day and the Time Cinco de Mayo at nine thirty.

The price 7

Did they ask me if I wanted a lime No, he seemed to have a hard time finding the gin. I was the first one in, though they had opened thirty minutes before and the bar was not set up and then came the long process of getting the gin and tonic. From ordering to receiving the drink in an empty bar was five minutes

What was the type of gin Well

What was the gin and tonic like Pretty lousy. It was a drink, and that's something, there was a moment when I thought I wasn't going to get any kind of a drink.

The Joint I have a no cover charge rule on this tour, but that does not mean I don't want to go to those places, it just means that I will try to go when they don't have a cover, on off days. This is the second time I have done that (the first was at the Lucky Dog) and with the same results: I was the only one in the joint. I thought I had planned this out because I saw a flyer for Mambo saying they would be open for Cinco de Mayo (a Tuesday) and there would be no cover. The doors opened (says the flyer) at nine. I got there at nine thirty. Only one there save the staff of five. They were only just setting up the bar when I got there. So they didn't expect anyone this early. I do wonder how the crowd would be on a Tuesday, I don't know. If anyone was to show, I am sure it was going to be closer to eleven then my ridiculous nine thirty.

What I saw was a long thin room that had flashing disco lights and laser doo hickeys and they were pumping a smoke machine to give it a clubby from the nineties feel. There were tables and chairs and large swaths where the invisible people can boogey down (I just like typing the term boogey down). They had large plasma TVs showing the visual to a SexySexySexy music video (they look sillier without the sound on). It looked like a perfectly acceptable and dare I say, good place for night clubbing activities. Just add people.

The one thing that is odd is its Hooka Bar designation. I didn't see any hookas on my once over of the joint. I didn't see any tobacco menu or anything similar to what I found at Electric Haze and the Shisha room. I wonder if Mambo has the designation so that people can smoke, I don't know, but it certainly was more a regular nightclub to my eye than a hooka emporium (not that I am complaining, I'm just stating). Everything there is geared for Spanish speakers, and that's wonderful we have a location for a part of Worcester community that might not be taken care of in other places.

General Impressions: Let me just say right now, I know the goal is to go to every bar in Worcester for my gin and tonic fix, but I am just rubbish at night clubs. I am middle aged, married with kids, and I never did like going to dance clubs when I was young and single. I have a job that starts early in the morning. I can't start the tour at eleven at night or later so that I can truly see what's what with a joint. If this tour is to see the cultures of bars and drinking establishments in this City, than I suck at it, because I just can't stay up that late. And this problem is not just night clubs, I estimate that in 10% of the bars I have been to on this tour, I have been the only one there. That's not the fault of the bar, per se, just on when I can make it to a bar. But you know, the bar is open for business, so it really is no blame on me when the joint is empty either. All I'm saying is that I will not have a good sense of night club culture from this tour. I have two more night clubs that are still on my list, wish me luck that I will see something. I suck at night clubs, but I did get a gin and tonic, so mission accomplished.

Amount of Time in the Joint 15 minutes, most waiting for the drink.

Will I come back No. I hope they get customers, but I know its not my place

2019 Update They closed. There was some violence associated with the place, but I don't know if that was why it closed. It is now the site of a country music bar.

Stop #113 - The Wexford House

The Bar: The Wexford House

The Address 503 Shrewsbury Street.

The Day and the Time Sunday at six on Mother's Day

The price Eight bucks for the tall Gin and Tonic. I don't know what I was thinking getting the large. I would have been just fine with a small. Especially because it wasn't that good.

Did they ask me if I wanted a lime He just put it in

What was the type of gin Tanqueray

What was the gin and tonic like It was harsh. There was something wrong with it. There was bitterness that didn't seem right. I think it was bad tonic. I don't know, but it was not an enjoyable drink.

The Joint A basic meat and potato place is very comforting, where you can get a turkey dinner special or a basic steak dinner, where the place is brightly lit and generic. Where the carpet is clean but worn. This is the place where your grandparents go to. This is the place you take your grandparents to and hope they pick up the check. There was Keno screens in the bar and in the dining rooms. There was large parties being accommodated for Mother's Day. It felt bland,which I think was intended. I noticed the fact that the food was served on modern white rectangular plates because it was the only thing that seemed out of place from a restaurant from 1992.

General Impressions I had a drink in a place that serves affordable meals. People working that day were friendly. The drink came quickly. At the bar, people were holding on to their leftovers. One guy was just there because this is where he usually is. Its a place. Its been here a long time.

Amount of Time in the Joint 10 minutes

Will I come back No. Though I can imagine taking an aunt here if I am in a bind on where to go.

Stop #114 - Bocado

The Bar: Bocado

> **The Address** 82 Winter Street
>
> **The Day and the Time** Sunday at seven on Mother's Day
>
> **The price** 7
>
> **Did they ask me if I wanted a lime** He asked and put it in with skill and grace.
>
> **What was the type of gin** Bombay
>
> **What was the gin and tonic like** I haven't talked about it, but the glass that they used was good looking and felt good in the hand. Maybe because most of the glasses are basic and utilitarian. This glass was nice (This section of Gin and Tonics Across Worcester is sponsored by Crate and Barrel) The drink was very good. I had Bombay gin once before in this tour, and this seemed to be the better of the two drinks. It was a very nice drink..
>
> **The Joint** I still think of this as the place that used to be SPQR, an Italian coffee and drinks place that lasted just a tiny bit a decade ago. It's been Bocado for some time and it's a nice, good looking restaurant. The bar is small and it's more for eating and waiting for friends then as a bar. I liked how it still felt like a bar.
>
> **General Impressions** I can imagine having a drink here waiting for a friend or for having a few appetizers. At the bar were a couple folk from other Niche restaurants having drinks, talking familiar with the staff. The bartender was good, he knew his game. It was a pleasant time having a drink, which is not something I always feel when at a restaurant bar. In a lot of instances, I feel like I am putting in time before I can leave, that there is something odd about me just having a drink and no food. Here, I didn't have that problem.
>
> **Amount of Time in the Joint** 15 minutes
>
> **Will I come back** Sure. I like the restaurant, I like the area. The bar was good.

Stop #115 - The Urban

The Bar: The Urban

    The Address 225 Shrewsbury Street

    The Day and the Time Thursday 8:40

    The price 8

    Did they ask me if I wanted a lime Yes

    What was the type of gin Tanqueray

    What was the gin and tonic like Eh. Just eh. Well, I really felt uncomfortable during my seven or so minutes there, so I didn't enjoy the drink.

The Joint For years, this was Coral Seafood, a perennial of Worcester. Now the owner's kids have taken over and made it a charcuterie. The insides are nice and feel like a hip joint (more in a second on that) but on the outside, they have done nothing. Nothing. They have not taken down the Coral Seafood sign. Instead they put a big plastic banner and hung it over the Coral Seafood signage, which you can see peeking out. That's an okay stop measure, but this plastic sign has been out there since the end of December, so five months. I'm sorry, but you want to be a serious business, change the damn sign.

The place has a nice design and warm colors. I liked it. Behind the bar was a huge projection screen where they were playing, without sound, On the Waterfront. I liked that a lot, I thought it was cool. All you need is people to make it good and I know I always hit the wrong times, but I don't think Thursday at 8:45 is a time to roll up the sidewalks. Really.

General Impressions While there, I had one of the weirder conversations during this whole gin and tonic thing. Before I went in, I decided it was time to check the place out because I saw through a window people sitting at tables drinking and chatting. When I walked in I realized that what I saw was not the Urban but the window to the coffee house right next door. That place was busy, this place, it was not. There was a bartender and a woman at the bar, who was a waitress who had finished her shift. There were two other people wandering around as well, who from time to time perched like birds at the bar.

The girl at the bar, the waitress, looked at me and started asking me questions in a monotone, that could have been from exhaustion or a sense of existential annoyance. She asked me questions in a lackadaisical manner, but still you could tell she wanted answers. Why did you come here?" This is always a strange question. Shouldn't you be happy for customers, not questioning? I said I was in the area and decided to have a drink (my standard non answer). She asked me what I was drinking. She asked me if I liked gin and tonics, even though I told her I drank them. She asked me if I like beer. What beer do I like. All in a weird bland tone. A medicated interrogation. This was going on for a couple minutes. Then she asked, "Where were you before you came in?" I am not quite sure, but I took this as the oddest of questions. I paused and then said, "What?" She asked the question again, and I paused and said, "I just walked in for a drink."

She stopped the grilling and then the two others at the place went back to the bar and apologized to the bartender (their friend) for what happened before, for all the chaos and they hope she won't get in trouble from her boss. The bartender shrugged and said she didn't care. What the hell did I miss?

I spoke to Bartender Brian afterwards and we thought that the off duty waitress's strange behavior could be three things. She could have been hitting on me in the most horrible way possible. She could have figured me out as Dante of Worcester, which we both thought was not too likely. The one we thought most likely was that she just hates waiting tables there and hates the place and was asking these questions because she couldn't understand why anyone would want to come to this place that's totally empty at 8:45 on a Thursday.

Amount of Time in the Joint 10 minutes, if that, the waitress at the bar kind of freaked me out. I don't know why exactly, just that I was looking forward to getting away from her and her robot voice questions.

Will I come back No. Come for the cool atmosphere. Come for the sad emptiness. Come for the lame banner that almost hides the fact that the Urban Kitchen is just a plastic throw over from years of Coral Seafood. Come for the uncomfortable questions from the off duty staff, which is always fun. Yes, do come. No.

2019 Update It was closed soon after that. It was sold to be the site for the British Beer Company, a chain restaurant. That didn't last too long either. It is now the site for a small local chain of Mexican restaurants.

Stop #116 - Mi Reyna

The Bar: Mi Reyna

    The Address 394 Belmont Street

    The Day and the Time Saturday 8:30

    The price 8 dollars

    Did they ask me if I wanted a lime He did and he did.

    What was the type of gin It was a nice high end one that tasted good but I didn't write down the brand so the truth is lost to history

.

    What was the gin and tonic like It was quite good, though it could have stood a little bit more gin, the young man gave me a shot glass measurement of gin. I shouldn't complain all too much because I'm the one who goes on about drinks that have an over abundance of booze. So who am I to kvetch about a carefully proportioned glass?

    The Story: My friend told me about this place with glee, knowing I want to get to the end of my list of bars to visit, and can't seem to get there. This used to be a D'Angelo's sandwich shop and it looks like it. I went in and there was a foursome eating what they call Latin American Tapas. There were people at the bar, but it turned out that they were folk related to the restaurant. The first impression of the place could have been better, You walk in to see the industrial kitchen. If I could make a suggestion. Put up a curtain. Or love beads. Everybody digs love bead curtains in Latin American Tapas joints. It got better from there.

    The main room has a small bar that worked nicely. The best part is though they had a TV by all the nicely appointed liquor bottles, the set was not on. This was great. I must say, I want to see less TVs and more talking or drinking or both. I have been to 120 bars for this tour at this writing and I can count on one hand how many bars didn't have a TV on during my visits. I guess people want TV, but my time at this place was good without it. I talked. I drank. I was aware of my surroundings. (Wow, end of sermon, please).

At the bar was the daughter of the waitress and a girl who was building the website for the restaurant. The group at the table were finishing up, and all seemed happy. The young guy behind the bar (late teens or early twenties) seemed nervous at my order. Told me a couple times that the guy who does the bar all the time, who is awesome at making drinks, was away at his daughter's graduation and he was recruited for this weekend only to be behind the stick (He didn't say behind the stick, I seem to be the only person to still use that term for bartender anymore, but dammit, I'm trying to bring it back). The young guy asked what gin I wanted, I said I was in his hands. He hesitated, picked a gin and made a drink. "Here it is," he said, "If it's not right, let me know and I can fix it." Oh crap, I was charmed. This adorably lost kid, with such a shayna punim, just wanted to do right by the customers, no matter how many or few of them he had. I liked this place. Don't ask me why, I just liked it.

But this was not an easy place just to have a drink and split. I felt very conspicuous. So I decided to break my rule and have food. I couldn't justify not. A nice group of people, not a lot of people at the place. I wanted to do right by it. The food choices were unique and the menu listed what part of Central and South America it originated. I picked a shrimp ceviche which came from Mexico. It had marinated shrimp, coconut and raisins. This was like nothing I have had before. It felt authentic and it was delicious. Maybe a little sweet for my tastes, but I really enjoyed it and would have liked to try more dishes. And it worked well with my gin and tonic, so it had that going for it.

I kibbitzed with the waitress, the bartender and the others attached to the place. I asked the bartender kid if this was his first gin and tonic he ever made and he admitted that it was. "Was it okay?" he asked worried. I said it was great and "It's a hard one to mess up, it has four ingredients: gin, tonic, ice and a lime. You got all four. You did well." He smiled with such naches. I must have liked the joint, I'm bringing out all my yiddish phrases.

Will I come back Yes. I want to try a bunch of dishes. If the main bartender is there, I might try a tequila drink. I want to share this with my friends. I want to share this with you. I liked it, it's different and good. I usually don't go out on a limb for this tour, but please, give this small place a try.

2019 Update With my impassioned plea, you know this place didn't last a year. I don't think it lasted six months. It was in a lousy location and it was different. We say we want authentic cuisine, but we really don't. I think this might be one of my favorite stops on the tour. And while I was there, eating and drinking and having a nice time, I knew it was not meant to be.

Stop #117 - Meze

The Bar: Meze

The Address 156 Shrewsbury Street

The Day and the Time Saturday getting around 8:30 on Memorial Day weekend

The price 8

Did they ask me if I wanted a lime He did

What was the type of gin Tanqueray

What was the gin and tonic like It tasted off. I don't know why, but there was an aftertaste. I have had worse, believe me, but it was a little incorrect about it.

The Joint Everyone wants to make small dishes and call it tapas. And with that you have to have a bar, must have bar. This one was very modern and full of lights and clean lines. A good bar area that has its own ambience and space different from the rest of restaurant, which is a nice thing.

General Impressions No one was at the bar. The two bartenders talked to me apologetically about the lack of people. They blamed it on the Memorial Day weekend. They told me they normally have an hour plus wait for a table and the bar is moving and hopping until two. This was not the case now and they tried to explain it all to me. I don't doubt the bartenders who tell me, "I don't get it, its usually so crowded this time of night." But boy do I hear that a lot. Thou protesting too much, baby?

The TVs had music videos on, they said it was European MTV playing. They also had Greek TV on too, they told me that was important. That's cool. Keep your audience happy. I like how they know who their customers are and try to create something for them.

Amount of Time in the Joint 10 minutes

Will I come back No. Nothing wrong with it, and of course I didn't get a good look from it being empty at the bar, but for me there are so many choices, I just don't need to return. Nice staff and clean place, worth looking at if you are so minded.

Stop #118 - Grille 57

The Bar: Grille 57

    The Address 57 Highland Street

    The Day and the Time Wednesday 7:50

    The price 8

    Did they ask me if I wanted a lime She did. Let me just say she seemed a pissed off bartender. Even if I wanted another drink from her, I don't think I would have.

    What was the type of gin Well

    What was the gin and tonic like It was a light thing, but decent. Nothing bad.

    The Joint Welcome to the weirdness. You thought the weirdness was gone, but no, the weirdness still lives in Worcester in the parking lot to a confused restaurant that serves pub like food and then on the weekend turns into a Euro Dance club. It morphs like Bruce Banner into another creature they call the Kapri Lounge. I didn't check that out, because as you know, I suck at getting to nightclubs. I recall this place when it was Bravo Cafe, which I liked sort of. The pizza was tasty and it was always empty which suited my mood when I decided to go. Now it has a new name, actually two new names, and the insides are exactly the same as they were 15 years ago. It has old tables and a weird glass Lego like wall in the middle. The bar is a reverse scallop. And did I mention the surly bartender? But that's not the weirdness. The weirdness was the singing and drumming and the show like thing that was happening in the parking lot.

    General Impressions In the parking lot on this lovely evening of comfortable weather, they put out tables in the front parking lot and roped it off so that an SUV can't park on the guy eating his pasta and drinking his insanely huge stein of beer. In the corner was a white haired gentleman, sitting on a bar stool, with a microphone in one hand, while looking at the computer in front of him. He was singing to a karaoke backing track. The backing track and his vocals were coming through a speaker next to him. On one side of him was a guy playing drums. The songs were Sinatra and Bennet and that ilk. So let me explain this, there is a guy crooning Sinatra tunes in a parking lot with a drummer and a karaoke track. The drummer would stop from time to time to talk to his girlfriend or have a selfie taken, but that's okay, because you don't really need a drummer when you have all the instrumental tracks on a computer file. The crooner had a decent voice and was singing "Fly Me to the Moon." I stood in the parking lot with mouth agape. What the hell was this? He was singing Volare now for all his worth. And there were people coming for the show. About ten or more with beers and food brought out to them while he puttered with the computer to get the right version of Fly Me to the Moon going. I guess he has several he can choose from, and I bet you it's hard to chose because, dammit, they're all good.

Folks were into it. The owners and the singer were talking about moving it inside because it might start to rain, the singer was disappointed. The rain did not come, but the oddness poured down over all. There are things people like and its wonderful we have places that supply those needs and wants. You want a guy singing standards with a pre-recorded backing track and a live drum thrown in for good measure? We can make that happen. They all seemed to be satisfied. In a few days this place will be a Euro Dance Club. Then it will be a restaurant. Then it will be a Crooner's Corner in the Parking Lot. I am waiting for the time it morphs into a giant robot that can protect us from space monsters.

Amount of Time in the Joint 20 minutes

Will I come back No

2019 Update *How that place lasted as long as it did is a mystery. It is now in the process of opening as a video game bar. Let's see how that works. I will probably give it a try.*

Stop #119 - Baba Sushi

The Bar: Baba Sushi

>**The Address** 309 Park Ave
>
>**The Day and the Time** Wednesday 8:30
>
>**The price** 9
>
>**Did they ask me if I wanted a lime** Yes she did
>
>**What was the type of gin** Tanqueray
>
>**What was the gin and tonic like** It was decent. Nothing special but it was a well poured drink, no complaints I could find.

The Joint A small handsome, dare I say intimate, restaurant with a small bar. There were people still eating, three guys got a huge sushi tray. Insane. A couple was at the bar having the last cocktail of the night. For a small place winding down they had a hell of a lot of staff. I counted 8 people working. On a Wednesday. All were dressed in black and looking quite chic. This is not a mom and pop sushi joint, this is serious diner me bucko.

General Impressions I can imagine bringing someone here to impress. Being that I have no one to impress, I just thought it was a tad ritzy for me, and one of the higher prices for a drink as well. But people were there having a pleasant time and the service was good and the place was fancy but still comfortable. I didn't question my attire while being there, so that's a good recommendation.

Amount of Time in the Joint 10 minutes

Will I come back Maybe. Not for a drink but maybe for a nice meal, but there are already sushi joints I like, so I don't know.

Stop #120 - Mahoney's

The Bar: Mahoney's

    The Address 413 Park Avenue

    The Day and the Time Wednesday at 8:50

    The price 5

    Did they ask me if I wanted a lime She asked and I got.

    What was the type of gin Well

    What was the gin and tonic like Flavorless, nothing special. It was a five dollar neighborhood bar special.

    The Joint Someone who reads this blog praised Mahoney's in a comment. I love people having favorites and sharing them. It is a good sports?Irish bar with space for an elevated area for darts and table in the middle of the room and a clean demeanor. It has sports playing and keno going and really really really loud metal playing (damn I am getting old and persnickety) There were 25 or so people and it was not packed at all. The ages ranged from young to middle age and that's nice. The staff were young. A good amount of staff on a Wednesday, about four people working. A lot of folk were out smoking. There was the Wednesday Dart League going and people were alternating between golf course quiet to rowdy shouting.

    General Impressions This is a bah. The bartender was a young woman in a low cut t-shirt. It felt like this was the uniform for the female staff. She was efficient, giving out drinks. While I was there for a few minutes, a lull occurred in the drinks demand and she leaned back and stood impassive, blank. She picked at a cuticle, she stood like a blackboard wiped of information. This statue pose and neutral expression went on for two or three minutes and then three guys came in. She saw them and like a switch put on the smile and an eye twinkle, rolled her shoulders back and went back to work in being the happy attractive bartender making me think of the line by T.S. Elliot, "There will be time, there will be time/To prepare a face to meet the faces that you meet." That's right, here at Mahoney's in Worcester, we have the Lovesong of J. Alfred Prufrock with Cleavage.

A bah is a good thing. It was a social place and the drinks were not too pricey. It was a drinker's place, you could tell by the little plastic cups they filled with shots. I am sure there has been someone shouting Wooooooo here recently. Energetic and mostly young, this could be a place people might want to try.

I would have left this stop on the tour happier and more content if not for something right at the end. The dart match was won by the Mahoney's team. They shouted and applauded and the losing team left to go outside. As they left, one of the Mahoney's people (a guy drinking with the staff, so he might be a friend or an employee, I don't know) looked at the retreating losing team and shouted at them "Pussies!" Yeah. Lovely. That just took a nice enjoyable bar moment and made it unpleasant. Making me think of a few more lines from Elliot. "We have lingered in the chambers of the sea/ With seagirls wreathed with seaweed red and brown/Till human voices wake us and we drown." Yes, this is the crap floating through my head while I do this tour.

Amount of Time in the Joint 15 minutes

Will I come back I liked it, it was very bar. But the attitude I saw at the end, the neighborhood bar not my own feel makes me say that I will pass on this one. You might want to try it, but I am good with going this one time.

__2019 Update__ It was sold and became Brewskis. I must say, that is a terrible name. It is up there. When are they going to open the bar, "Black Out Drunk?" Anyway, the bar has changed once more. It is now being mutated into a sports bar.

Stop #121 - Kai Sushi Bar and Grill

The Bar: Kai Sushi Bar and Grill

The Address 68 Stafford Street

The Day and the Time Thursday at 1pm

The price 6.95

Did they ask me if I wanted a lime She did

What was the type of gin Tanqueray

What was the gin and tonic like It was alright. Light and good. Not a bad a drink.

The Joint This is a strip mall sushi joint. The outside looks uninteresting. The interior is small, clean and has a nice look. There were only a few people in at that time. Three people at the bar, eating and drinking, and four women at a table talking as loud as if they were at a convention. The bartender was attentive and good. Solid with all that.

General Impressions: I had a day of no work and decided to go to a Lunch place. I heard an interview on NPR with Adam Gopnick (New Yorker writer) about how the Lunch as an entity is gone. That old line "Let's do lunch." is never heard anymore. That there was an industry supporting business lunches. Those high end New York lunch places are all closing or are gone. He said that the problem is that businesses like their workers to eat in the building or at their desk, so Lunch as a thing is no more. It was interesting but I felt that it might have to do with just New York lunch scene.

I was interested to see if I could find a place that had businesses lunches going on. No luck. 111 Chop House doesn't have lunch. And Ceres was empty so I didn't want to try it (actually, this is the fourth time I have looked into Ceres and found it empty, what's the deal with that joint?). On other parts of the tour, I have seen business lunches occurring like at Mezcal, but for the most part, people are getting a sandwich and moving on.

I was about to call the tour off for the day and try another time when I drove by Webster Square and noticed this place for the first time. I was annoyed because with me finding new places to go to, I will never be done with this tour, but happy that I can try someplace. I went in and it was drowsy, but nice. The only business conversation I heard was two young women at the bar complaining about their lousy second shift jobs. One was trying to get the other drunk, to cheer her up. That's nice and neighborly. I don't know why she could be upset. She had a nice dish of sushi and a large glass holding mixed drink goodness.

I had a drink. In a quiet place that seemed alright. So there.

Amount of Time in the Joint 10 minutes

Will I come back Lots of sushi bars to choose from in town, this one looked alright, but I don't think I need to make a plan to go.

Stop #122 111 Chophouse

The Bar: 111 Chophouse

>**The Address** 111 Shrewsbury Street

>**The Day and the Time** Wednesday at 8:15

>**The price** 7.50

>**Did they ask me if I wanted a lime** He put in and it was nice glass.

>**What was the type of gin** I don't know what it was but it was decent one.

>**What was the gin and tonic like** A well poured drink. I enjoyed sipping at it. It had flavor and it worked for me.

>**The Joint** If you imagine a high end steak house, this would be that thing in your head. Dark wood, large ceilings, Early 20th Century French Posters, photos of jazz musicians on the wall. The people working were in white shirts and wearing the garb of the traditional American steakhouse. The place was busy for Wednesday. A lot of the people had convention Expo badges still on. This is an expense account joint, and don't you forget it. The bar was large. Three quarters of a square. Two bartenders were working. One bartender was really on it and was very good, the other one.....

>**General Impressions:** ....the other bartender had a Cat who Swallowed the Canary smile. Someone at the bar knew him and asked him about the bartender's personal life. The bartender cracked jokes and talked to his acquaintance. And talked. And talked. The other bartender, who was very tall, started giving the other one, the talking shorter one, looks. After five minutes the tall bartender put his hand on the short bartender's shoulder. The shorter bartender kept on talking and joking, not working, while the tall one was bustling to all parts of the bar. Finally the tall bartender flicked a bottle cap at the other one. The other felt it, look down, said goodbye to his friend and then went back to pouring drinks. (I must say I was

surprised to see anything other than professionalism and precision at this place. I ain't talking about the bottle cap flick, but how the shorter one ignored everyone to jaw with a buddy. That's a thing to see on a second rung sports bar.)

With that aside, the place was fancy and surprisingly, not forbidding. I felt smarter and cooler just hanging out there having my drink.

Amount of Time in the Joint 20 minutes

Will I come back You know, maybe. I can see situations where I want to sit down in a comfortable place for a drink and a conversation. This could work. I am not a steakhouse guy, so I don't think the restaurant will be my place. But I liked this old school Chicago Steakhouse ambiance. They created it to be enticing and I am that sucker who it works on.

Stop #123 - Piccolo

The Bar: Piccolo

The Address 157 Shrewsbury Street

The Day and the Time Wednesday at 8:30, I think. I didn't have a watch.

The price Seven dollars. It's a Shrewsbury Street Bargain!

Did they ask me if I wanted a lime No. She intuited the need for such a thing. As a matter of fact, she took another lime and squeezed the juice into it.

What was the type of gin I was given a choice between Tanqueray or Bombay Sapphire. I chose the Tanqueray.

What was the gin and tonic like It was good. I liked it. But it's the axiom of this tour: you like the bar, the drink tastes great. So there.

The Joint I decided to pop in when I saw a large rowdy group of young people drinking and kibitzing in the outside tables. They seemed to be having a great time, so I figured I should check out the small bar inside. I was going to not go to this place for the tour, because I didn't think it would show me anything other than another bar at another restaurant.

Their were 7 people at the bar eating and drinking. Everyone seemed to be a regular. Two bartenders were friendly and made it comfortable. The decor was Italian Restaurant, by way of an old bank that it used to be and aspects of that are incorporated, but then it turned a corner and wound up in oddville. They had, above the bar, framed photographic portraits of the cast of the 1970s feel-good flick One Flew Over the Cuckoo's Nest. That's right, photo portraits of Jack Nicholson, Danny DeVito, Christopher Lloyd. Pictures of Actors playing Crazy People. What the hell is this about? I don't know, but it's that kind of odd idiosyncratic tic that makes a joint its own thing. Come for the friendly service, stay for the glowering visage of Jack Nicholson leering down at you.

General Impressions I was talking to my friend Epicurean Eric about my problem with the tour at this point. I have about 20 or so places on the tour and I want to be done, but every time I finish a bar on the list, I discover another bar I never knew existed so I put that on the list. Eric thought I was crazy and said I should close the list and just not put anything else on it. I agree with him, but then I wouldn't have gone to Piccolo and I would have missed one of the more pleasant bar visits I have had in awhile. There wasn't anything in particular that makes me say this. It just was that if felt like a great neighborhood bar, and it is an excellent restaurant. It has regulars and a wide range of ages coming to drink and eat. They were friendly and professional. I have heard the food is great and the bar was good. The bar is small, but in this case, it made it more intimate.

Amount of Time in the Joint 25 minutes (long for me, but what can I say. I lingered)

Will I come back Yeah. It was a nice time.

Stop #124 - The Boynton

The Bar: The Boynton

    The Address 117 Highland Street

    The Day and the Time Wednesday 8:20

    The price 6.50

    Did they ask me if I wanted a lime She just put it in

    What was the type of gin What house gin they had, Bartender Brian (who was with me) tried to figure out which cheap brand it was. He couldn't see that far but whatever it was, it was not a good one.

    What was the gin and tonic like It was sweet and syrupy. Not a good drink but it was alright for it what it was.

    The Joint This is such a popular place. It is usually filled with college students but at this time there was WPI students and people who were older. Who were these people? What were they doing here? All these important questions, none to be answered.

It was crowded at the bar, I couldn't get a seat and most of the tables were filled. It's a big place and that's saying a lot that it was rocking on a Wednesday. With all that said, it took me 7 minutes standing at the bar looking like the guy at the train station 45 minutes after the last departure left. When Bartender Brian showed, she noticed us and gave us drinks. Bartender Brian was unimpressed with her as a fellow tender of bar. "You and I are only getting a drink, we are the type of customer you don't want sitting at your busy bar. She should have given us menus right away and seen what we want to order. That's where the money is." Single drink visitors just fill up the valuable real estate. Look at me, I'm the alcohol equivalent of a squatter. She also had some difficulty finding the gin. She looked new. Brian pointed out an older bartender and complemented how that guy was moving and serving and how aware he was of what was going on.

The place is loud and big and for whatever reason I have never liked it. Maybe it's all the loud conversation about school and thesis presentations, maybe its because the food used to be good but now the portions are smaller and the choices are dicier to navigate. I don't know, but it's not my place.

Actually, I do recall one time my wife and went there on a Sunday at noon for lunch and we asked for a seat and they said they could sit us but we might need to wait for a waitress. We waited for 15 minutes in a table by the bar. At the bar was a guy already drunk swearing so much i felt we were in a Mamet play. We waited for another five minutes and then just left without being served. Maybe that's the thing that made me not like it.

General Impressions: I was talking to my friend Epicurean Eric about how i never liked the Boynton and he seemed abashed about it. "If you never liked it Dante, why didn't you say something about it all the times I had you meet me there?" That was a good question, and I said, "Well I don't hate it, and if you like it that much to suggest it of course I will come. I was coming for the company, not the food or service." And that's the way I feel. People like the place. Eric likes their french fries. It is busy and crowded and people have a great time. On the tour, Bartender Brian (who also doesn't like it) and myself just stood there looking grumpy at the place. This is the thing about bars, one thing can make you love or loath a place. It might be a small thing that is no longer remembered, but you harbor that emotion, that feeling everytime you go there. You might like a joint and defend it even after it has gone downhill, or still despise a place that is really quite nice and the beer selection has improved.

For me, it might be the loud maw of a crowd that is constantly at the Boynton pressing down at all times. I like to sit and talk and drink at a place. I don't want an empty bar, but I want one where I will be seen and served and seated and other things starting with the letter s.

Amount of Time in the Joint 25 minutes.

Will I come back Given my druthers, I would say no. But I know friends will pick this as the lowest common denominator joint (people really like it here) and I will smile and attend. So let's call it a Yes Under Protest. This was fun going out on the tour with Brian and we hit two more bars that evening, so stayed tuned.

Stop #125 - The Sole Proprietor

The Bar: The Sole Proprietor

    The Address 118 Highland Street

    The Day and the Time Wednesday 8:55

    The price five fifty (which was amazing to me)

    Did they ask me if I wanted a lime He just put it in

    What was the type of gin Well, but decent well. Their well is made from fine stock I suppose.

    What was the gin and tonic like A good drink, one where I could sense the tonic, which is usually the forgotten element of a good gin and tonic. It can be flat or too little or just a lousy type, but this one was noticeable and did well with the gin.

    The Joint It is a handsome, well appointed seafood restaurant with a good sized bar. The bar was not big enough because at nine on a Wednesday, Bartender Brian and I could not get a seat. It was packed. The bartenders were fast and serious. This was one of those "no smiling" joints, not because the staff don't have a song in their heart, but that they are too damned busy and professional.

Brian mentioned that someone at the bar was listening in on our conversation and so I quickly added more vulgarity to my conversation and changed the topic to gun running and other delightful pastimes. Brian just rolled his eyes and drank his beer. There is nothing wrong with eavesdropping at a bar, I mean, that is where half of the topics of this blog came from, from good old fashioned listening in.

The hostess was working damned hard, she set up a table and cleaned it for a party waiting for a seat, but not fast enough. When she returned to seat the party, they said they waited long enough and left the restaurant.

General Impressions: This is a high end joint and the people at the bar were eating and drinking fine cocktails and were enjoying themselves in the way you can in an expensive crowded eatery. Brian and I gossiped about friends and people he works with at the old saloon. One of the conversations we had is worth mentioning. I went on my rant wanting more bars with no televisions and Brian shook his head in an authoritative fashion and said, "Bartending, I love televisions, and I love cell phones. Cell phones have been the best thing for me." I stared agape at him and he continued, "It keeps them there. Before cell phones, people would have a beer and get bored or lonely and then go home or move on. Now with cell phones, they are attached to whomever or whatever. A cell phone is good for another two or three drinks. People linger with a good game on the TV and they really linger with Words with Friends or Facebook updates. It might make people more anti-social, but they are more anti-social in public with drinks in front of them."

I understood what he was saying, but for all of that, I was enjoying talking to a friend in a bar more than anything the TV or social media can give me. This is a good place for that. It's a nice backdrop and facade for conversation. Also, if you are by yourself and want a good meal, I think this would be a good place to sit at the bar with a book or a smartphone and just be.

Amount of Time in the Joint 30 minutes

Will I come back I can see it. I have eaten here a while back and it was terrific. The bar feels like a bar, though crowded in the middle of the week, crazy, but its a nice place to settle. Brian and I went to one more bar that evening, keep your eyes on this blog!!!

Stop #126 - Sahara

The Bar: Sahara

The Address 143 Highland Street

The Day and the Time It was Wednesday around ten PM. This was the third bar that Bartender Brian and I hit on our tour within a tour of Highland Street drinking establishments.

The price 8 bucks, but there was a reason for that. I made choices. He asked if I wanted a short or tall, and because I was still being social with Bartender Brian with me, I went tall. And then I had a choice of well gin or Tanqueray, with Tanqueray being a buck more. I said the hell with it and paid the extra buck. Call me kooky.

Did they ask me if I wanted a lime He did

What was the type of gin It was Tanqueray.

What was the gin and tonic like You know, this tour is becoming a big old advertising for Tanqueray, or so it appears. Because Tanqueray is the safe affordable gin. Let's hear it for a gin that tastes of juniper and spices and not of some alchemical experiment gone buggy. It was a fine glass. I paid a little more for it, but after two drinks already of questionable merit, this extra expenditure was warranted. (Look what happens when I go a week without writing one of these posts, my vocabulary leans to the show offery. sorry.).

The Joint You know, after 16 years in the Worcester area, I have never been in here. Just never found the need and no friends invited me there. What a nice space. It had large ceilings and it was bright and airy. The bar was in the back and it was long and accommodating. It could have done with a few more wiping downs, but still a good surface to lean towards. Brian told me this used to be a clothing store way back. I just liked being in there. The bar had people and the bartender was damned friendly.

General Impressions We were there for a while. Brian went for a few more drinks and I switched to Diet Coke (I was driving) and the bartender said that it might get quiet for a while but many times around ten or eleven they get people leaving the Boynton or Sole Proprietor. This is the second or third stop, and I can't see why not. A lot of times bars in restaurants are after thoughts, just something to have to provide liquor for the diners. This had a bar feel and happy I was about it.

Bartender Brian noticed two women who used to go to his bar, but he hadn't seen in a while. He bought them a round and chatted with them. He was pleasant and told them to stop by his bar sometime they feel so inclined. After they left he told me he fears that they had a not great experience at his joint, and he hoped to bring them back, they were nice customers. He was happy they seemed to find a good place here at Sahara, but one can go to both places. This was a nice piece of alcohol outreach.

Amount of Time in the Joint About an hour or so. It was a nice time talking to Brian and the bartender and the others at the bar who came and went.

Will I come back Here is the amazing thing about this tour, if you asked me what bar was going to be my favorite of the three Highland Street joints we hit that night (Sahara, Boynton, Sole) I would never had said that Sahara was the most enjoyable bar, but there you go. It was a nice time and I do want to go again. Not by myself, this is a bar to go with a friend.

Stop #127 - Chuan Shabu

The Bar: Chuan Shabu

> **The Address** 301 Park Avenue
>
> **The Day and the Time** Thursday at 7pm
>
> **The price** Nine bucks (one of the pricier ones)
>
> **Did they ask me if I wanted a lime** She put it in
>
> **What was the type of gin** She gave me some choices and I think

I picked a high end Tanqueray. I smiled and nodded and just agreed to what she said, like every good improv actor is trained to do.

What was the gin and tonic like It was a good solid drink, strong, but good.

The Joint This is an interesting place. It is a restaurant that focuses on hot pot cuisine where people put raw food into hot broth and then eat the results. Its a very participatory way to eat and this evening had four or so tables of people having a good time. This was not sedate eating and it seemed that the people at the table were having a good time.

The joint is clean and ultra modern in a mid twentieth century kind of way. The bar was handsome with lighted shelved for the drinks. The lights slowly changed colors. It was neat for my limited stay there but I could imagine that it could drive a fella to madness after a while. "The bar was green and then it was blue and then it was red. It was just what the squirrels told me would happen! The squirrels always know!"

General Impressions The bar had three other people there. One off duty fireman looking mopey. The bartender knew him and tried to joke with him about his job and other things and he just stared at her with icey fervor. Another couple were drinking and eating and talking and talking. It seemed like a light night. This bar had a cool sophistication as does the rest of the place. I don't know if it will find its audience, I hope it does because its different. Its a clean, fun bar, but as it was, with more bar space than patrons, it also felt sad and lonely.

Amount of Time in the Joint 10 minutes

Will I come back Maybe for trying the shabu hot pot, that seems fine, and the place does strike me as a nice looking place, nicer than most, but as a bar, not for me. Like I said, I hope people who want this bar finds it.

Stop #128 - Maxwell's Silverman's

The Bar: Maxwell Silverman's

    The Address 25 Union Street

    The Day and the Time Friday 9:50

    The price 5.25

    Did they ask me if I wanted a lime She asked and I got

    What was the type of gin Paint thinner, I believe. whoah.

What was the gin and tonic like I remember that I was so excited about a good affordable gin and tonic after a large battalion of eight dollar drinks. I found myself a table to lean on to watch the madness of the dance floor and took a generous sip and I almost gagged. I had a bad science experiment in my mouth and there was no potted plant to spit it into. What the hell was I was drinking?

The Joint This is a giant old school dinner place that looks good and presentable for its age. They have a bunch of things from the tool and die factory that was there previously and that kind of thing works for me. There was a small dance floor to the side and that was why we are all here. This is where disco lives, for people over fifty (or so). They dress up and dance and drink and then sit with panting shoulders. There were some very old people up there going at it, and that was cool. The wait staff looked resigned, wondering why the hell they were picking up after this group (not a lot of smiles in the employees). I saw one woman who looked younger than the man she was with then I saw her speak, or try to. Her plastic surgery made it difficult to move her facial muscles. Or was that the botox. She had a lot of work done, let us just keep it at that.

It was funny to notice that some of the dancing rituals were just like I remembered in high school. There were still groups of women dancing and men coming in looking on at them from the corners, drinking their punch (I mean beers). The popular girls flitted around chatted with people in each of the groups. Of course these popular groups were grandmothers, but who's to say they still aren't passing notes in class and meeting up with the cute guy by the boiler room, I mean the bar that makes boilermakers?

I was still kind of early and people were coming in and the dance floor was filling up. People were having a fine time to the great Abba songs of the 70s.

General Impressions My friends told me I had to make it here to see, as they call Jurassic Dance and I am glad I did. But as much as I feel the desire to mock and make fun, who's to say you won't see me there in fifteen or twenty years? Of course I don't see disco. I see in 25 years going to the Punk Rock Night at the Rec Center where codgers put on our leathers and mosh pit move, careful not to knock over anyone's dialysis machines. The Ramones, the B52s, the Talking Heads. Every band our grandkids roll their eyes at. We will drink one old fashioned cocktail and wonder why the young wait staff are snickering at us, don't they know this is Rock and Roll? This is youth. This is a good night out. Yeah. I can see that, so who am I to say anything about this place. People in their fifties and higher need a joint to let loose, why not this place?

Amount of Time in the Joint 20 minutes

Will I come back No. Happy there is the place, but it's not somewhere I need to be. I wish the staff was happier.

Stop #129 - Nuovo

The Bar: Nuovo

    The Address 92 Shrewsbury Street

    The Day and the Time Friday at eight or so

    The price 8.50. This was an eight dollar drink with tax making it a drag. Damn the man!

    Did they ask me if I wanted a lime I think he put it in. This is one of those snooze fest joints that make it hard for me to recall all these pertinent details.

    What was the type of gin It was Tanqueray.

    What was the gin and tonic like Fine. It was okay. I liked it. I was bored with the joint.

    The Joint Piano Bar with Lounge Music Stylings Warning! You want a well dressed kid tinkling the ivories singing neutered versions of the songs of the seventies and eighties? This is the place for you. I don't know who else this is for. It is an Italian place but the decor was bland and non descript. The place was only half full on a Friday. The people at the tables were sitting waiting for food, like they were waiting for the bus to arrive. It was not a joyous room. The bartender was nice and professional. He made a quick efficient drink. The place is clean, but just bland.

    General Impressions This was one of those, "The Bar is Empty and I Should Come Back When There are People Are There Joints" and I did that about four times. This time, I jumped in and sat at the empty bar. The place just was. Nothing wrong with it. I hope the food was killer, because nothing else about the place screamed personality.

    At the bar I am at now, I spent several minutes butchering the name of this restaurant when I stated this was the latest dispatch from the tour. I couldn't figure out how to say Nuovo. One woman at the bar was able to pronounce it satisfactory, but who knows if she was right. I will call the place Mikey. Might as well be Mikey.

Amount of Time in the Joint 10 minutes

Will I come back No

Stop #130 - Ceres

The Bar: Ceres

The Address 363 Plantation Street, in the Beechwood Hotel

The Day and the Time Friday at 8:45

The price 8.56

Did they ask me if I wanted a lime She just put it in

What was the type of gin Tanqueray

What was the gin and tonic like It was fine.

The Joint I have stopped in four times and every time there was no one at the bar. This time I just went and eventually three others joined me at the bar. It is an ultra modern restaurant and the bar is a strange thing that reminds me of the Milk Bar from the movie A Clockwork Orange. It is circular and it has lights in it. The bar glows a soft white light. There is no easy way for the bartender to get out of the bar and she has to do a strange variation of Limbo to remove herself.

General Impressions The three people at the bar were acting friendly and familiar with the bartender. They had been here a lot over the last few days. I thought it was a wedding or a convention. But it wasn't. There friend was in the hospital across the street. He was having seizures. They were waiting for word either way from the doctor. They were at the bar complaining about the wait, the uncertainty. They had been here a lot over the last few days. They compared notes on how they reacted to all the texts and calls from friends who couldn't make it to Worcester to vigil at the hospital bed and the bar stool. They began to feel numb more from the replies they were obligated to give then waiting to hear whether their friend was going to make it. They drank and asked the bartender how she was doing this nice quiet evening. Another bartender came in and one of the drinkers asked him about his motorcycle. They went out to look at it. Something to do. Something solid you can rely upon, something with a good suspension. They had been here a lot over the last few days.

Amount of Time in the Joint 20 minutes

Will I come back Everyone was nice and everything seemed alright, but I can say that I would prefer a warmer place. A friendlier esthetic for me, thanks. For those who need a bar near the hospital, this seems like a decent place to be.

2019 Update Ceres was not the first high end restaurant in this location and it is not the last. Currently, it is a restaurant called Sonoma.

Stop #131 - Kyoto Bar and Grill

The Bar: Kyoto Bar and Grill

    The Address 535 Lincoln Street

    The Day and the Time Wednesday at 9:10

    The price 6.96 (I would have paid the extra four cents just so I didn't have to fuss with the pennies. Sheesh. Really? Just take the pennies. Please)

    Did they ask me if I wanted a lime He didn't. But still, when the drink came, there was a lime.

    What was the type of gin I saw him pick up the bottle and I gasped quietly. It was Gilberts. The enemy of this blog. Gilberts. The evil empire of bad gin. Hello old friend. I see you have made yourself at home at this hibachi joint. Well, so be it.

    What was the gin and tonic like It was a drink. Not a good drink, but when you have poor ingredients, what can you expect. It was a nice enough place, so the drinking of it was not at all arduous. It just wasn't a good drink.

    The Joint This is a local sushi and hibachi joint that is surrounded by chain restaurants. I didn't even have it on my list, I figured for something that rubs shoulders with Ruby Tuesdays and Texas Roadhouse, that it must be a chain joint. It's a good looking, typical hibachi place. I got there late so none of the tables were filled. It had an oval bar and it was presentable. Okay, I am near the end of the tour and this feels like a lot of other hibachi-sushi joints I have been to. There is nothing wrong with it, but the staff need to be dressed as clowns for me to notice anything unique about it.

    General Impressions At the bar at this off hour, there were three couples drinking and talking at the bar (and me, I was the outlier, the eavesdropper in the ointment. Is this the kind of place where young people go for dates in the middle of the week? Do they crave pseudo Asian drinks to help lubricate a first date? On listening as much as I could, I did notice that on these three instances of coupled people, the women were doing all the talking. Can I learn something from this observation? Absolutely not. Just thought I would share something I noticed. One of the couples were loud and swearing. Another was dropping a lot of Dr Who comments and pop culture lingua franca. The last couple were just talking. People they know, things that happened to them recently. I don't know if these were established couples or if we had a passel of first dates. I was more odd man out than I usually was, which is saying some.

Amount of Time in the Joint 15 minutes

Will I come back No. Nothing off or unpleasant. It was just a place with a bar.

Stop #132 - Stakes

The Bar: Stakes

> **The Address** 1281 Pleasant Street
>
> **The Day and the Time** Thursday at 8
>
> **The price** 5.50
>
> **Did they ask me if I wanted a lime** He asked and I got
>
> **What was the type of gin** It was a well gin.
>
> **What was the gin and tonic like** Ah, what you need to do to be a completist. There are a lot of fair to middling gin and tonics out there and I seem to be getting my fair share of them. It was a little flat and the poor gin didn't help.
>
> **The Joint** I guess you can get a sense of deja vu when you go into enough neighborhood bars. There is the long bar on the back wall. I've seen that. There is the pool table. The dart board. The KENO screen. I've seen that too. There is the worn nondescript carpet. The serviceable chairs and stools. "Baby, I've been here before. I know this room. I've walked this floor." Oh my god, I've stumbled into a Leonard Cohen song!
>
> The place was fine. It had three people drinking and talking and watching the slow decline of the Red Sox, as it always is. It felt empty.
>
> **General Impressions** The older woman came in and said, "Where is everybody. It's empty. Where are all the folk." The bartender said, "It's Thursday. We get people for Karaoke on Friday and Darts on Wednesday. You know that." She got her bottle of white wine that she then put half into a glass and talked to a regular. Even paid for his next beer. She talked loudly about how great it is when people are here. She likes the Karaoke. She's a big one for the Karaoke. She went on talking until she faded into the background buzz like the TV and the jukebox.

The bartender was friendly and confirmed that it is a lazy place except for Wednesday darts and for that crazy Japanese singing craze that happens on every other Friday.

There is nothing wrong with the place, but I have to wonder how a bar like this stays afloat. That's one of the things I don't get. how to get people to come and stay. Maybe it's a little too much like every other bar, I don't know. It was alright enough.

Amount of Time in the Joint 15 minutes

Will I come back No.

Stop #133 - The Ranch

The Bar: The Ranch

The Address 70 James Street

The Day and the Time Thursday at Nine. During the week, the ten dollar cover charge ceases at nine and then I can enter. Gin and Tonics Across Worcester has a no cover charge policy. It doesn't mean I will give up on the place, it just means I will show up at odd times like Thursday at Nine.

The price Six fifty

Did they ask me if I wanted a lime She asked and I got it.

What was the type of gin It was well gin

What was the gin and tonic like Not too great, but this is a place that seems to sell a lot more bottles of water than beer or drinks, so you can't expect mixological greatness in the joint.

The Joint This is a very large space that is located in a huge, immense building and could fit in other clubs and businesses but seems underused and it comes across as shabby. The building, not the bar. You do have to walk down one of the hallways to get to the Ranch. Sorry, You have to mosey down a hallway to get the Ranch. There. Better.

The Ranch is big, the bar not as big as you might think, but as I said earlier, people seem to be there more for the dancing than the drinking. And even at nine on a thursday there were about 30 or 40 people on the dance floor doing the line dance thing. I come from a world of bad high school dances where the boys leaned against the gym risers and tried to not feel awkward. I then graduated to mosh pits and general dancing destruction, so this line step rule based dancing is foreign to me. But that doesn't mean that it is wrong or bad, just different.

The bartender was friendly, but seemed happier when friends would come by the bar so they could chat and plan their days off together. Near the large dance floor was a grouping of tables and people were gathered there mostly when not feeling the need to go out and heel toe heel toe kick and turn and heel toe (I mean shake their groove thing).The place was brightly lit. Near the front, an employee was putting cups of water in a pattern on a table, preparing for drinking game shenanigans to start later no doubt.

General Impressions You could tell the regulars, they had cowboy boots. No matter what they were wearing, they had cowboy boots to finish the ensemble.

Recently, someone was complaining that there was not enough places in town for him to go to. Places he liked. So thought he didn't like Maxwell Silverman's and the scene, he wanted to dance and that was the place he wound up at. The Ranch fills a need, a niche. One cannot complain that there isn't a place to country line dance in Worcester. Those who want to will go here. And judging from the friendly familiar conversations, they certainly do go here and have created friendships based on this place. If this is not your thing, don't go here. but if you do and don't mind the ten dollar cover on the weekends and before nine PM during the week, then have at it.

There were younger people there who knew the dances and sang along to the songs. There were also older folk out for an evening trying to figure out which foot kicks and at which point. I like that there is a place that makes people happy to be out. I of course was singing Talking Heads tunes to myself while working at my poor drink.

Amount of Time in the Joint 20 minutes

Will I come back No. And I knew that going in. But its a fine enough place. There is a sense of self selecting community going on here. Want a country music based community to be a part of? Go to the Ranch. It's decent. Me? I am not looking for such a place, so will boogy down into the sunset while no one shouts out after me, "Shane! Come back Shane!"

Stop #134 - The Wonder Bar

The Bar: The Wonder Bar

The Address 121 Shrewsbury Street

The Day and the Time Saturday at 10:10

The price 6 dollars

Did they ask me if I wanted a lime she asked and then gave it to me

What was the type of gin It was a vile well drink, you know, my favorite kind

What was the gin and tonic like It was alright, the bartender (or the person acting as bartender) seemed a little off her game, she didn't have a good flow on finding the drink and ringing it up. This does affect the drink experience. It's all a show. If you are shaky making the silly thing, then it won't be a great time having it.

The Joint There is a nice feeling in realizing that this great Worcester mainstay is back. It was gone for about two years or so. It was sad when it shuttered. Another owner has it and he did a lot of repair and cleaning in it. I miss the dark cramped of the old Wonder Bar, but hey, its open. The bar is now twice as long and the place is scrubbed and bright. I don't know how the pizza is, I hope it is good, because it didn't have much of a personality. Nothing bad really, but there was something about that old wreck of a Wonder Bar. This is a nice presentable pizza restaurant.

General Impressions And now....

Dante of Worcester's Guide on How to Make a Casual Walk-In Drinker Unwelcome. This is great to know if you just finished a long rush of diners and now it is the ungodly hour of ten o'clock (ten o'clock? is anyone even awake at that time?) and you want to go home or maybe stay at the bar and eat and chat with friends, not help anyone else out, doesn't this guy know that you should not enter a restaurant bar when the staff is mentally done?

The best way to make him feel unwelcome is before you greet them (why greet them, they shouldn't be here, they should be sitting in a Barbary Coast bar stool with a trap door dropping them into a cell) you should look them straight in the eye and say, "The Kitchen's closed. You can't get pizza anymore tonight."

That's the way to do it. Don't say hello. Don't ask them what they want and then let them know what's available. Don't do any of those things. Just tell them of all the things they will not be able to have and give them the hint that this is a good time for them to leave and find a Dunkin Donuts to bother. Now it is true the bar is still open, but come on...... Really. This place is a pizza joint. Sure it says Bar in the name of the place, but that's just part of a pun, right?

A smart guy will make for the door, but this one doesn't and asks if he can get a drink if that's alright. Dammit. You're screwed. You put on a smile and get him his drink. A gin and tonic? That's a lame drink. Make sure you take your time pouring it for him. Make him know that this is a hassle. Stop in the making of it to talk to your friends who are working with you and are lucky to not be bothered with a customer. Who is this guy anyway?

Once he gets it and pays, ignore him. Talk to your friends. Give them drinks quickly. Don't ask him if he wants anything else, because really, he shouldn't even want to be here. The real customers were the ones who came during the rush and waited and sat and tipped and left. People drinking at the bar are just loiterers. If you ignore him long enough he will get the hint and leave. And thank goodness, he does. And only a dollar tip? Fucking cheapskate!

Amount of Time in the Joint 10 minutes
Will I come back No

Stop #135 - Basil and Spice Thai Cuisine

The Bar: Basil and Spice Thai Cuisine

The Address 299 Shrewsbury Street

The Day and the Time Wednesday at 12:45 in the afternoon

The price 8.45. Damn. One of the higher priced gin and tonics. Top ten. And you know the forty five cents was the tax. Really? Charge me 8.50 or better yet, charge me eight bucks. What has this tour come to that I am wanting people to charge me 8 bucks for a two ingredient cocktail?

Did they ask me if I wanted a lime She didn't but she cut up two slices and put them in.

What was the type of gin The bar did not have a huge amount of bottles and it seemed like there was no well for the basic bottle. She pointed at the three bottles of gin they had and I picked Tanqueray because that seems to be the high end basic gin I have come across.

What was the gin and tonic like, I watched her measure out the amount of gin and I cringed, but who are we to comment. The interesting thing I noticed was that she poured the gin and then put the ice in. Kind of different or at least I have not been aware of this before. She gave me the drink and I must say, in praise of measuring out the gin, this was a good, well balanced drink. I thoroughly enjoyed it. I tasted the Tanqueray, I got the tonic, which was not flat. The freshly sliced lime also helped. I really liked this cocktail.

The Joint For years, this hidden away Shrewsbury street local was an Indian place. It is behind Funky Murphy's. You have to be looking for it and you know, I think it might be worth the quest. The interior was airy and clean. The tables were well presented and it was nice to see that for a new place, they did have diners. It didn't go overboard on Asian decorations, which to me is a good thing because it allows the food to be the focal point. The bar was small but fine for a restaurant. I was the only one at the bar, but that ain't a surprise for me.

General Impressions: This was a nice restaurant to come into for a drink. It was welcoming and comfortable. The staff was nice. The food, from what I saw, looked awesome and it smelled enticing. The TV had the coverage of the endless deflate gate, but you could ignore that with aplomb. I wanted to stay and get some food. Which to me, is high praise for restaurant bars. They did have a cocktail menu with several offerings featuring lychee fruit. Of course they had the Mai Tai, but everyone has the Mai Tai.

Amount of Time in the Joint 15 minutes

Will I come back Maybe not for just drinking, but it could be a nice alternative to Funky Murphy's next door. But this is a big yes, I want to try the food.

Stop #136 - Rocky's

The Bar: Rocky's - this was the location where Grey Hound Pub was. This is now owned by a guy who used to be a state representative but resigned, which stopped the investigation against him (which is nice for him) now he is a publican and who doesn't want to go from politician to booze slinger?

The Address 139 Water Street

The Day and the Time Friday at nine

The price 5.50

Did they ask me if I wanted a lime She just put it in, how nice, how politic.

What was the type of gin It was a vile well gin that was distilled on the banks of Chernobyl.

What was the gin and tonic like It was bad. But what I am to expect. I should be more positive about my prospects, I should give it some Beacon Hill spin, so instead I will say that this gin and tonic has potential, it has will to improve, it is a striver, and who can ask for more than that? (actually, I can ask for more than that, but who am I, just a tourist really.)

The Joint It is an improvement over the Grey Hound Pub decor. It doesn't feel like some football fiend's man cave slash parent's garage. The place is open and the wall was taken out to have alfresco dining. It had sports on because everything in Worcester must consider themselves a sports bar. Let me just go on the record here and say that I believe if you are projecting at ear bleeding levels the Rod Stewart dittie "Forever Young" you are not a sports bar, you are something else.

There was a score of people there, all older, except for a few at the bar who seemed to be related to the owner and they were grumpy looking. The older crowd all seemed to know each other.

General Impressions I was a true outsider here and it was obvious I was not part of the usual group of cronies, I mean friends, and I stuck out so much to the point that the owner came over and introduced himself to me and said he was the owner and shook my hand while searching the environs for any baby to kiss. I must tell you, I have never had the owner of a bar introduce themselves to me when I came in during this whole tour. It was odd and made me want to split fast.

The crowd were all friends and some seemed bored. The music blared disco and the bartender turned down the volume but the owner spoke to her and the volume went back up to Spinal Tap This One Goes to Eleven levels. No one was dancing and the owner went over to his buddies at the tables and spoke to them and entreated and they all went up to dance, sort of. This act reminded me of nothing but that scene in Jaws where the Mayor of Amity noticed that no one was swimming on the Fourth of July so he went to his constituents and got them to reluctantly enter the possibly shark plagued water. That's what this looked like. Instead of an ominous John Williams score, we had the very loud stylings of ABBA (its hard to decide which is more frightening).

Amount of Time in the Joint 15 minutes

Will I come back My vote goes to No.

2019 Update *They are gone. Shocker.*

Stop #137 - Dino's Ristorante Italiano

The Bar: Dino's Ristorante Italiano

    The Address 13 Lord Street

    The Day and the Time Friday at 8:30

    The price 6.70 (I hate weird drink prices, I miss the age of cash when drinks were priced to be easily divided by the money you had in your wallet and not a random association of numbers that mean nothing because you put everything on a credit card)

    Did they ask me if I wanted a lime He just put it in

    What was the type of gin It was well

    What was the gin and tonic like It was light watery. It was alright, nothing special.

    The Joint This is one of the perennial places of Worcester. It's on a dead end road off a Plantation. It has been around since the Mesozoic Era. The place is big, though the bottom floor was not opened this evening. A couple were having their food at the bar, and an older guy, who works there was also at the bar intently watching the Sox game. The decor is large chunky furniture. They have an old mural of the Italian coast on the wall. The food I saw looked good, and the portions were ample. Some people at the tables were well dressed and others were shorts and tees. The place feels like the Italian joint you go to because your great aunt likes it, though she will be annoyed the portions aren't as good as they used to be.

    General Impressions Why do couples eat at the bar instead of a table? In the case of my barmates, it was because the guy in the relationship wanted to keep on watching the baseball game. So it's win-win, she gets a nice pasta and seafood dish and he gets to watch a rare win by his team. I guess that's one reason to have a bar in a restaurant. The older man who worked at the place, sitting at the bar, and another older employee talked about the lousy Sox team. They were annoyed that the team was doing well, because it was messing up their Rotisserie league. The bar did not have a lot of liquor, it seemed that the patrons drank wine and beer. The bar was an eight seater and it was fun to sit and watch all the people eat their meals. It's not the worst place to watch a game, but this is a place where you here for the food, not for the bar elan.

Amount of Time in the Joint 15 minutes

Will I come back I don't think so. Maybe if I need a middle of the road Italian joint, I have heard conflicting opinions on the food. The nostalgia factor of a real old school Italian place is fun, but there are so many other options in town. Nothing is around the place, its a real destination eating place, but it's a destination you might not want.

Stop #138 - Chioda's Trattoria

The Bar: Chioda's Trattoria

The Address 631 Franklin Street

The Day and the Time 8 o'clock on a Thursday

The price 6

Did they ask me if I wanted a lime She did ask

What was the type of gin House Gin

What was the gin and tonic like A bad cheap gin and tonic, the kind of gin and tonic that you drink a sweet wheat beer afterwards just to get rid of the aftertaste

The Joint This is an odd place. When I say odd, I mean the snark, she is a coming. It is in nowhere. There is nothing around it. Just broken industry buildings and this place. They have ten dollar Italian meals on Wednesday and Thursday, a nice butt in chair action, but there was only four people eating. There were more staff than diners. Maybe they get a lot of early birds, who's to say. The staff spent their down time complaining about their other jobs, the jobs that pay. The dining area was middle of the road and mostly presentable looking. Then i went to the bar....and all bets were off. Let's talk about the bar.

General Impressions The bar. The heart beat to any drinking establishment. The plank of wood that you lean upon and rest the glass on and see what's happening near you. The plank of wood that calls you home.

Then there is the bar at Chioda's.

Dear bartending staff at the under attended Italian Joint in the Middle of the Industrial Apocalypse,

Hi. Dante of Worcester here. Can you do me a favor? Can you wipe down your bar? I mean its sticky and messy and filled with the vestiges of last year's mixed drinks. There is a place in your bar that is worn down past the stain and is actually concaved. What the hell was resting there? And why do you not fix it? Sand it down, re-stain and keep the goddam thing clean. Now we know why I was the only person at the bar, because everyone else wanting a drink forgot their hazmat suits.

I did learn a valuable thing about myself at Chiodas, I learned that I am a bar leaner. I lean my forearms on the bar where I am drinking. I leaned in and found it sticky and pulled back and then didn't know what to do with my arms. I was so uncomfortable not being able to lean. Well for that, thank you disgustingly unclean bar, you made me know myself a tad bit better.

Amount of Time in the Joint 6 minutes (flat)
Will I come back Uhhhhhhhhhhhhhhhhhh. No.
2019 Update Chioda's is no longer there.

Stop #139 - Muse

The Bar: Muse

    The Address 536 Main Street

    The Day and the Time Saturday at Nine

    The price 8

    Did they ask me if I wanted a lime He did and he put it in with great elan.

What was the type of gin I don't know, but it was a good one. Its one of those places that take pride in not having rot gut booze, even for their well options. Of course, sometimes a fella just wants a good shot of rot gut to make the day complete, so take this as you will.

What was the gin and tonic like I really liked it. It had balance, it had bright notes, it had a lot of things you would read in a fusty Wine Spectator review. I drank slow because it was an enjoyable glass. Speaking of a glass, the drink was served in a classic High Ball glass, very nice. For a place that was opened for two days, this was one of the five best gin and tonics I have had on this tour.

The Joint This was the soft opening weekend for the former Red Barron - Jak's Pub. Let me just say that I want a good fun bar in downtown. I wrote a lot of praise (perhaps too much praise) for Jak's because I just want some options for downtown. I want a bar, even a dive. I want a little life. This hit home hard while I walked down Main Street to the new bar Muse. I walked past the building that still says that it is Rehab - Irish Times. I walked past other gone black store fronts that were bars and night clubs. Now empty, forgotten. It was a damned depressing walk to a new Hail Mary bar to have alcohol (a well known depressant).

The bar smelt of new paint. Nothing was on the walls. The place no longer has a big pool table to kill the space, like Jak's did, so an improvement already. A few people were there, all seemed to know the owner, who was at a table working on the Muse website. He made my drink and then ceded the floor to his bartender who seemed confused with the next beer order. The bar had that annoying type of beer dispenser where it doesn't say what the beer is on the tap and the bartender has to know the placement perfectly. It's a thing, Armsby has that thing. I don't know, I don't mind the taps saying the beer names, call me a philistine. The beers and the liquors are good and interesting, including Bully Boy liquors and other things I think I might have recognized. All of these seemed good.

General Impressions I spoke with the owner as he attended to me and the other customers, and he was enthusiastic about creating a cocktail bar, and a true cocktail bar. He then told me he didn't want to have a TV in the place, and my heart melted. I know my bartender friends love TVs for keeping people in the seats, but there is a part of me who wants a pure bar where you are there for the stool and the glass of booze in front of you. You might have a conversation but you might just want a drink. I had a good drink here. The owner told me he was going to hang local artists work on the walls, and I think that's great too. This is a kind of bar we need. We need cocktail lounges that want to give you a warm, comfortable place to have a good drink. Its close to the Hanover, and I will tell you, you should go here before and after you see a show there. I like what I saw on this soft opening and I want it to plant a seed downtown. Here I am going hard on the sell, but this is important. The dead streets crave something living, and Muse is a good step to that.

Amount of Time in the Joint 20 minutes

Will I come back Yes. You should too. Give it a try. Please.

Stop #140 - El Rincon Spanish Bar

The Bar: El Rincon Spanish Bar

> **The Address** 187 Washington Street
>
> **The Day and the Time** Saturday 9:30
>
> **The price** 7
>
> **Because I was in there for only five minutes, I will only write five sentences about my visit.**

1.The joint has a reputation for cops being called there and Bartender Brian did not want me to go alone, but I couldn't find anyone to go with, so he timed me and only gave me ten minutes before he would get people to check on me, but I didn't need such a long time. because in the world of Gin and Tonic Tour Drinking, ten minutes is an eternity.

2.A gentleman at the door politely asked me if he could frisk me and of course I agreed, because I am an agreeable person and I certainly don't want people to take the wrong idea about me and he laid hands on me in a fast professional manner and finding that I was not packing anything I was allowed in.

3.Once again I arrived too early and it was mostly empty, though the place was clean and presentable and the music was loud and really good and I wanted to dance but that's not what I do and there was no one to dance with, but it was a nice looking nightclub and I am sure the weaponless patrons will have a good time when they show up.

4.I ordered my gin and tonic and got it and drank it and realized that it was a bland thing, though with some punch and I was done very quickly, thinking that maybe I should stay and listen to the music and see who shows up and what draws people to a nightclub such as this and it was actually an alright place to sit and be, but my drink was done and I left with a nod.

5.I got back to the bar where I started and Bartender Brian asked if I left yet for Rincon and I said that I was already done and he laughed and asked how it was and I said there are a lot scarier, and dirtier places to have a drink and part of me was pleased they were checking for weapons but of course it goes without saying that that is the only time I am going to El Rincon Spanish Bar and I was happy I tried it out, albeit briefly.

Stop #141 - Foodworks Chinese Restaurant

The Bar: Foodworks Chinese Restaurant

The Address Southwest Commons, 50 SW Cutoff (Route 20 and Route 122)

The Day and Time: This was Friday at eightish

The Price: Six dollars

Did they ask me if I wanted a lime: I think so. This was an unhappy production. The harried looking woman asked me my order and if I wanted a lime. She disappeared and the man working with her showed up and brusquely said, "Is this yours? This drink? Is this yours?" I said yes and oh how happy I was to be given such dulcet service.

What was the type of gin: Gin distilled from sulfur and sadness (well gin as seen in this kind of place)

What was the gin and tonic like: Like the place itself, it was mean and unpleasant. You know that belief that dog owners look and act like the dogs they picked, the same is true for bars - the attitude of the bar can be found in the cocktails they serve. A great place will have great cocktails despite the ingredients. And lousy places will have lousy drinks, even if they were pouring from the top shelf, but of course, those places never serve from the top shelf.

Wait, stop, you are being very mean here Dante, what's the deal?: Yeah, well in this 140 plus tour of bars of Worcester, I have been to places I didn't like, or places that were downright scary, and many places I knew immediately I would never go back to, but I have never left a bar thinking, I really hate this bar. Well, here it is friends.

I hated my ten minutes at Foodworks.

I hated how mean and unhappy the bartenders were. I hated how brightly lit it was and that you could see all the unhappiness in the place. It was clean and presentable, but it was clean and bright like a three am airport lounge and who doesn't hate those? I hated watching the guy drag his six year old daughter up to the bar area from their table with the Chinese food getting cold, so he could play more Keno. I hated the drunk next to me who hit me friendly like, but still unwelcome, and when I told him to not hit me, he got pissed off and so I moved my seat and he followed me so he could mock me some more and tell me he could really hit me if he wanted. I hated how the bartenders and the crowd of Keno castaways just ignored what was going on or noticed it and didn't give a shit. I hated the long pull on the straw I made to finish my drink and split. I was happy to be out of there, and that might be the only thing I didn't hate, the escape.

So Dante, aren't you going to do your typical write up now? No. The place ain't worth it.

DAVID MACPHERSON

Stop #142 - Mare E Monti

The Bar: Mare E Monti

    The Address 19 Wall Street

    The Day and the Time Friday at 8:25

    The price 6.50

    Did they ask me if I wanted a lime She did, with professionalism and grace.

    What was the type of gin well

    What was the gin and tonic like A nice simple drink. Nothing wrong with it.

    The Joint: I had not gone here because I was under the impression that this was a BYOB joint. But driving by on my way to Vincent's, I saw a bar through the door. I parked and went in. The lobby could fit a lot of people waiting for tables and the bar had about eight or ten stools. This was a classic Italian joint where people drank in the lobby waiting to get into the dining room. There were quite a few people waiting, but it was not a hardship it seemed. The bartenders were fast and friendly and there was space in the room, which was nice.

    General Impressions Amid the bustle and anticipation of the couples and families and first dates, waiting for their tables, there were two people sitting at the bar by themselves. Both stared ahead or at their phones until their food arrived and then the focus could be on that, One was a woman, the other a man, both in their late thirties or early forties. Were they stood up? Were they stuck in Worcester for business? Did they just want a nice meal and no hassle of rustling up a dining companion? As I stood in the lobby area, sipping my drink, I imagined that they would look up from their pasta dishes and see each other. Recognize something familiar in each other's solitary dining and move to sit next to one another without saying a word. I could imagine the plates touching. Smiles exchanged, loneliness in a public setting for once defeated. Yeah. I think a lot while drinking my gin and tonics. Maybe they were happy eating alone, maybe my daydreams were as half baked as most of my ideas. Stop thinking, Dante, and finish that drink.

Amount of Time in the Joint 20 minutes

Will I come back I can see going there for dinner. It looked good. A nice location. Why not?

Stop #143 - Vincent's

The Bar: Vincent's

> **The Address** 49 Suffolk Street
>
> **The Day and the Time** Friday at 8:45
>
> **The price** 7
>
> **Did they ask me if I wanted a lime** No i just got it.
>
> **What was the type of gin** Well
>
> **What was the gin and tonic like** It was good. But it follows the

rule. Like the place. Like the drink.

The Joint This is a hard one to write, because for a long time, this was my bar. This was the bar I would go to. If I was to meet someone, it would be "Meet me at Vincent's". Hell, part of the first date I had with my wife was at Vincent's. Coming in for this stop of the tour, it seemed impossible for me to look at this place objectively. It is filled with history and comfort.

There are the old 100 year old group photos. There are the taxidermy on the walls. There are the pulp paperback covers put into the bar surface. Around is a group of people ages from 20s to the 60s drinking and talking and watching the Red Sox blow it. A blues band sets up,they play loud. But there is escape to the back if the music is not your thing (They sounded pretty decent to me). The bartenders are moving and serving drinks like this is a bar where people want to get their booze.

All of this is true and I am sure I would have been charmed with it as I was 16 years ago when I first came here. It is a strange idiosyncratic joint and that is what makes it welcoming, it smacks of someone's particular tastes. If they are similar to yours, then you will feel good there. Now it's not for everyone, my dear friend Epicurean Eric did not care for it at all. But then there are places he loves that I don't like, like the Boynton. But that's why it's a wonderful thing to have such variety and choice. Don't want to go to Vincent's? Then you can go to Nick's or Muse or Armsby. Find the place you feel at home.

General Impressions I suppose one of the quests bargoers must go on is to find the bar - that bar that you will call your own. Is the place easy to get to? Is the asshole quotient low? Do they make the drinks you like? The thing about the quest and the questions is that you are going to spend an awful lot of time at this joint and its got to be right. The odd thing about this tour is that I always knew what my Bar was. I was never looking for a new bar to call my own. It is Nick's. It was closer to where I live and hits me as the more mature Vincent's and for me that's what I wanted. But being in in Vincent's is still a good time for me. I still like it. It's the old decorations and its retro feel but with a nice welcoming attitude.

Yeah, writing about the places you love and feel a part of your history is hard. Trust me. We all have the places we love, but that doesn't mean we can describe them well. I had a good time at Vincent's that evening. Like a lot of other evenings.

Amount of Time in the Joint 30 minutes

Will I come back Yes.

2019 Update For the last few weeks of writing the blog, I was mentioning the last stop on the tour was to be live at Nick's. I was to drink the last gin and tonic on the tour in front of an audience. About ten or so people showed. It was a lot of a fun.

Stop #144 - Nick's

The Bar: Nick's

    The Address 124 Millbury Street

    The Day and the Time Sunday at 7

    The price 8

    Did they ask me if I wanted a lime He did, that Bartender Brian, he is such a joker

    What was the type of gin I don't know. I don't care. Its gin and its tonic. Its a flavor sensation

    What was the gin and tonic like It was great. It was the best gin and tonic in the world because its the last one of 144 on the tour I just took around Worcester and to have it end in the bar I love best, the bar I call mine, it could not be any sweeter.

It's funny. So many times on this tour, I would come here and complain or at least kvetch about the bars I had just been to, so throughout this whole process, Nick's has been the olly olly oxen free homebase. I never had a gin and tonic when visiting however. Just beer and whisky, like any true drinker should. I left the gin and tonics for the tour (kept it at the office if you will.). You find a place where they accept you and the stool feels good underneath you and the jukebox is good and you even like it when it is absolutely silent, you have to respect that. Nick's is unique because of TCM playing old movies and the German paintings and the dark wood. It works for me. I like the bartenders. I like the pride they take in the drinks they pour. I like how after my first time at Nick's I knew that this was the place I was looking for.

The Story: For this last stop on the tour I invited people to join me. I had my drink on the stage, read a few pieces from the blog and answered questions. I had over 10 people join me for this, and it's great because going bar to bar got pretty lonely, The questions were fun and smart. They asked how excited my wife is for this being over (she's pretty stoked). One asked if I cared for gin and tonics at all by the end. The answer is that I am done with this drink. I have tapped that well. Another question was , have I returned to any of the bars I went to on the tour and actually, no, I went to Vintage Grill once more, but that was for the food and not for drinks (i liked it by the way). I was asked what was a surprise to me, and I mentioned Piccolos being a great surprise as a bar, but mostly I talked about how surprisingly welcoming almost all of the bars were: from Cisero's to Muse to scores more. I only had a handful of bad experiences, but even those places, I was welcome there. There was only one or two places I was truly not welcome (I'm looking at you Greyhound Pub, and I am not sorry that it is out of business). I was surprised by how after 18 months and 144 bars, I was still excited about the next place that I never knew existed. I am happy it is over. I am happy to be done. I am not going to continue the blog with another drink or food item. I am done. But I am happy to have done it.

But I would love someone else to discover Worcester by going to every (fill in the blank). Or if you live in another city, and you want to get to understand it, to feel connected to it, go to every bar, and get a gin and tonic.

I said all these things at Nick's last night, on stage, drinking a gin and tonic. I am so happy to have done it there. I love that place. I love that the doors are open foere r me to sit down and get a drink, any drink.

Yours,

Dante of Worcester (David Macpherson)

Afterword

And that was it.

Well, not quite. I brought the blog back two times over the next few years. Those efforts to get to the places I missed originally were never as good as the original tour. To be fair, it would have been better if I just stopped at the 144. None of those essays are included here. They can be found on the blog though.

And I would not be able to bring it back if I wanted to. Because, (he says with an embarrassed grin) I don't drink anymore. Drinking and acid reflux do not mix.

Even now, when new bars open in the city, I still get a thrill. A desire. I want to go in there and politely order a gin and tonic, like I have done many times before.

A lot of people should be thanked for aiding and abetting me in this ridiculous project: Heather, Sean, Bob, Jeff, Chip, Vincent, Nicole, Victor, Ted, among others.

About This Book

One cocktail. One Man. Every damned bar in town.

There are a lot of bars in the City of Worcester, Massachusetts. David Macpherson took it upon himself to go to every watering hole and have a drink. Which drink? Why a gin and tonic, of course. He wrote about each of the 144 bars he went to from 2014 to 2015.

There were good gin and tonics and then there was the time he got a gin and Coca-Cola. He found lovely people all around the city. He was also ignored and threatened. David was not reviewing the bars, he was taking a tour of the landscape of drinking and socializing.

Why do people go to bars? Why do people pick one bar to be their and ignore all the others? Bar by bar, drink by drink, David attempts to find out the answer to those questions and so much more. It is a funny, witty descent into drinking through the city.

About the Author

David has published over 20 eBooks. He has been a performance poet and still runs a weekly poetry reading at Nick's. He was a co-winner of the Jacob Knight Award for Poetry. You can reach him at 100pagedash.wordpress.com. You can email him at davemacp@aol.com.

www.ingramcontent.com/pod-product-compliance
Lightning Source LLC
Chambersburg PA
CBHW021139160726
47994CB00001B/17